# THE OFFSHORE NATION

## The Rise of Services Globalization

# THE OFFSHORE NATION

## The Rise of Services Globalization

ATUL VASHISTHA
AVINASH VASHISTHA
*Co-founders of the leading offshore advisory firm, neoIT*

**Tata McGraw-Hill Publishing Company Limited**
NEW DELHI

*McGraw-Hill Offices*
**New Delhi** New York St Louis San Francisco Auckland Bogotá Caracas Kuala Lumpur Lisbon London Madrid Mexico City Milan Montreal San Juan Santiago Singapore Sydney Tokyo Toronto

Information contained in this work has been obtained by Tata McGraw-Hill, from sources believed to be reliable. However, neither Tata McGraw-Hill nor its authors guarantee the accuracy or completeness of any information published herein, and neither Tata McGraw-Hill nor its authors shall be responsible for any errors, omissions, or damages arising out of use of this information. This work is published with the understanding that Tata McGraw-Hill and its authors are supplying information but are not attempting to render engineering or other professional services. If such services are required, the assistance of an appropriate professional should be sought.

**Tata McGraw-Hill**



ISBN 0-07-058327-7

Published by Tata McGraw-Hill Publishing Company Limited, 7 West Patel Nagar, New Delhi 110 008, Typeset by Devendra M Sharma, 5, 1st Cross, Gowdanapalya Main Road, Bangalore–560 061 and printed at SDR Printer, A- 28, West Jyoti Nagar, Loni Road, Shahdara, Delhi 110 094

Cover Design: Mesmerizers

Cover Printer: SDR

RQZCRRZBRAXZC

The McGraw·Hill Companies

***To our families and fellow colleagues in the globalization industry!***

# Praise for *The Offshore Nation*

"*The Offshore Nation* provides a balanced and insightful view of global sourcing and the various components that make it a successful strategy for organizations. This book is a must read for organizations charting their course in global sourcing."

**SUDIP BANERJEE**
*President, Enterprise Solutions Division, Wipro Technologies*

"*The Offshore Nation* is a comprehensive, thoughtful and fact filled guide for any company looking to tap the rapidly growing market for offshore outsourcing written by the leading firm in providing global IT and BPO services delivery advice."

**ED CASO**
*Managing Director and Senior IT Services Analyst*
*Wachovia Capital Markets, LLC*

"Atul and Avinash Vashistha have laid out the whys and hows of services globalization in a way that few others could. Their book, *The Offshore Nation*, delivers everything the savvy executive needs to both understand and take advantage of this new world without borders."

**MICHAEL F. CORBETT**
*Executive Director, The International Association of Outsourcing Professionals (IAOP) and author of The Outsourcing Revolution: Why It Makes Sense and How to Do It Right*

"A stunningly thorough rebuttal to Lou Dobbs, *The Offshore Nation: The Rise of Services Globalization* makes a compelling case for the globalization of services and provides a practical road-map for those with the foresight to seize the opportunity to establish competitive advantage in a global economy.

In a market that is over-served with experts preaching the mantra of globalization (reminiscent of Mr. Robinson's prescience concerning plastics), the Vashisthas have written a book that explains how to do it. I recommend *The Offshore Nation: The Rise of Services Globalization* to every company considering the use of offshoring to establish competitive advantage in a global economy."

**J. Ross Docksey**
*Partner, Sonnenschein Nath & Rosenthal LLP*

"In today's 'globalized' world, this book provides the complete guide to offshoring services".

**Andrew Holland**
*Research Head, DSP Merrill Lynch*

"*The Offshore Nation: The Rise of Services Globalization* is a timely and important work. It describes the confluence of a number of themes critical to business in the early 21st century. Those themes, globalization, outsourcing, the pace of technology, and the growth of a global services economy, combine to have a dramatic impact on corporate enterprises, country economies, and the career of individual workers around the world. This work provides real insight into how these forces relate and operate, and how workers, countries and companies can navigate to their advantage. It is essential reading for those not merely interested in what is happening, but by those who seek to take advantage of the forces affecting business today."

**Steve Huhn**
*Vice President, WW Strategic Outsourcing, HP Managed Services*

"*The Offshore Nation* is an easy to read, pragmatic guide on the offshoring phenomenon from one the world's renowned experts. It is a must-read for every executive determined to assure the future competitiveness of his or her enterprise.

Whether you are the CEO of a Fortune 100 company or running the corner store, understanding the impact of offshoring services is vital for the health of your business. The Vashisthas' lucid text illustrates how globalization, outsourcing and the aging demographics of western nations make offshoring services inevitable. The Vashisthas' show why business leaders and politicians must embrace offshoring rather than resist it."

**Andrew Kris**
*Chairman, Shared Services and BPO Association &*
*Founding Partner, Borderless Executive Search*

"For corporations committed to thriving, not just surviving, in our increasingly competitive global economy, *The Offshore Nation: The Rise of Services Globalization* is a must read. Corporate executives searching for ways to maintain and enhance their company's competitive position cannot afford to ignore offshoring. This book not only makes a compelling case for services globalization, but offers invaluable advice for corporate executives prepared to seize this opportunity."

**Daniel A. Masur**
*Partner, Mayer, Brown, Rowe & Maw LLP*

"The growing trend of globalization of services needs to be understood by everyone involved—businesses, customers, governments, citizens. This book provides a fundamental understanding of this important set of developments."

**Harris Miller**
*President, ITAA*

"Services globalization has allowed talent to be recruited, trained, and delivered across previously insurmountable time and distance barriers. This is a force that can equalize the opportunities and pace of development of individuals and regions across the globe. *The Offshore Nation* is an essential handbook for understanding the opportunities and pitfalls of services globalization—a must-read for business leaders who want to lead their organizations into the future."

**B.V. Naidu**
*Director, Software Technology Parks of India*

"Services globalization has without fail pervaded the board rooms of all top corporations and threatens to alter the face of how business is done. *The Offshore Nation* captures the spirit of this mega trend and forces you to appreciate the far-reaching and irreversible implications of this phenomenon. This is a must read for champions of industries and beginners alike to soak in and leverage one of the most significant revolutions of our times."

**ATUL NISHAR**
*Chairman, Hexaware Technologies*

"The pervasiveness of globalization is evident in the news, education, medicine, technology and even grieving, as the whole world responded to the Tsunami earlier this year. Services globalization is a logical extension and must be considered an essential part of corporate strategy. *The Offshore Nation: the Rise Of Services Globalization* is a well-timed book, and provides a framework on how to prepare your organization for the flawless execution of services globalization."

**DIJU RAHA**
*Chairman & CEO, Eximsoft International*
*Former Vice President of Nortel Networks*

"*The Offshore Nation* demonstrates the changes in how work is accomplished in supply chain, paper and IT-intensive industries in much the same way Henry Ford changed processes in car manufacturing."

**JERRY RAO**
*Chairman and CEO, Mphasis*
*Chairman, Nasscom*

"While offshoring of services is a strategic imperative for an ever-increasing range of companies, it also represents a significant initial investment (in both time and money). *The Offshore Nation: The Rise of Services Globalization* provides useful guidance for maximizing this investment, avoiding potentially expensive errors and getting it right the first time."

**ASHOK SOOTA**
*Chairman and Managing Director, Mindtree Consulting*

"Regardless of the size of your organization, if you want to compete in the 21st century, read this book!"

**TERRENCE TRAYVICK**
*President of Capital Markets Business, Fortune 250 Company*

"*The Offshore Nation* discusses globalization as more than a trend, but as an imperative that no responsible executive can ignore. The smarter ones will find ways to use globalization as one of their tools to leapfrog their competition. The smartest ones will also find ways to use globalization to delight and retain their customers."

**STEVE UNTERBERGER**
*HR Outsourcing Technology Leader, Hewitt Associates*

"*The Offshore Nation* offers a useful framework for how corporations and individuals should assess and embrace opportunities in the booming global services market. The Vashistha brothers, who helped usher in the 'services globalization' phenomenon, offer insights and best practices that savvy managers cannot afford to ignore."

**RUSTY WESTON**
*Founding Editor, Managing Offshore*

"*The Offshore Nation* provides a wealth of practical insight into the many facets and considerations in offshore outsourcing. It is a must read for managing today and preparing organizations for the future."

**BARRY WIEGLER**
*Founder and CEO, Sourcing Interests Group*

# Preface

Technology, communications, travel and attitude are all ingredients that fuel globalization. What began with automotive and steel has quickly accelerated to complex services such as software development and research. Globalization is not a passing trend; it is one of the key strategic imperatives for successful enterprises in this decade and beyond.

We have dedicated our careers to assisting companies, countries and people in leveraging services globalization, also often referred to as offshore outsourcing. Both the users and providers of these services are part of the offshore nation. We observed as the offshore nation evolved from one company leveraging a few resources offshore to nations vying to be the next destination for talent. Throughout this journey, we have seen a real need to help buyers and providers understand this new mega trend: services globalization.

While there are many recent books and market research studies that try to address this trend, we have not found one authoritative guide that helps organizations tie all of these pieces together. We have not found one guide that is both strategic and practical.

We handle globalization issues for major corporations every day. We see companies win and lose. We feel the pain that inexperience and lack of information can bring. And we celebrate when our clients finally reach the full potential of their services globalization strategies. Out of our experiences we have developed a step-by-step guide to help companies understand how to begin the services globalization journey, maximize return on investment and minimize the risks.

Our desire is to provide both strategic and tactical advice for leveraging the services globalization mega-trend. We want to help companies and individuals understand why services globalization constitutes an important part of the strategic plan of any successful firm. We want to demonstrate how to understand the diversity of the offshore markets, how to mitigate the risk of globalization, and how to leverage more than cost savings.

This book is intended for both C-level executives and practitioners—professionals who are making and implementing the services globalization decision. However, services globalization is a mega-trend that has the potential to impact everyone's life, both personally and professionally. It has the potential to enrich all lives. Therefore, we hope that academics, economists, politicians, consultants, investment bankers, lawyers, students-all-recognize that these topics are directly applicable to their future.

For all these reasons, we bring you *The Offshore Nation*.

Good Globalizing!

**Atul Vashistha**
**Avinash Vashistha**
**March 2005**

# Acknowledgements

This book was inspired by friends, leaders and countries that make globalization a reality. I would like to thank the many friends and business associates that contributed to the writing of this book.

Allisson Butler, the Marketing Director at neoIT, not only led this project but also provided content, criticism and support. This book would never have been written without Allisson's persistence and attention. Other contributors to this book and my research in outsourcing include many of my neoIT team members and industry colleagues, especially Eugene Kublanov, Usha Sekhar, Sabyasachi Satyaprasad, Ramaprasad Varanasi, G Suresh, Pradeep Mukherjee, Nishant Verma, Vinu Kartha, Brian Tumpowsky, Tarun Mehta, Mustafa Peracha, John Hartmann, Stephen Brown, Joe Vales and Ross Docksey. There were so many gracious contributors and I would like to thank you all for your numerous contributions.

Many thanks to the inspiration and support that my family provided, especially my wife, Jodie, and our delightful debater, Tia, our daughter. In our 11+ years together, Jodie has not only inspired me to SEI-CMM Level 7 performance (internal industry joke!), been my biggest fan but has also been my most constructive critic. Tia (our 6 year old) told me that not all people agree with me and so I need to listen to them too. I hope this book demonstrates that we did that. Enjoy the book!

**Atul Vashistha**

Services globalization at the heart of "The Offshore Nation" has been more than a decade long passion for me. Reflecting on this engaging journey, the road is paved with great learning, enlightenment and fun. I am sure there have been numerous persons unknown to me who have made my life easier. I would like to acknowledge and thank them. There are numerous known persons who deserve to be acknowledged and need to be thanked for making this journey so enjoyable.

I would like to thank the numerous people, institutions and practitioners who have been the inspiration and research partners behind this book. I would first like to thank Diju Raha—my mentor and the person who initiated me into this world of services globalization at a very early stage, supported me in this pioneering journey and showed me the shining star in the horizon. I would also like to thank my various colleagues at neoIT—Pankaj Sharma, Sabyasachi Satpathy, Allisson Butler and Nishant Verma—who have been major contributors in the research and writing of this book. Thanks to Vinu Kartha for being a great sounding board and his zeal for challenging my many hypotheses on globalization.

Many engagements and clients have provided the learning and experience that makes this book what it is today. In particular, I would like to salute my brave business associates who put their faith and traversed the pioneering path with me: Amelia Rowen, Kevin Baughan, Steve Unterberger, Kevin Campbell and Richard Jones. Many thanks to the service providers in India, China, Vietnam, Russia, Central and Eastern Europe and the Philippines who have been very supportive and engaged. I would like to thank Venetia Sangeetha, who persistently pushed to bring this book to you.

I owe a lot to my wife Garima who has been my soul mate both personally and professionally and a very supportive partner and mentor. If it was not for her seed of passion and her sharing of the vision for "Offshoring", this decade long journey may have traversed a different path. My three kids, Ankita, Abhay and Amisha, each born on a different continent, North America, Europe and Asia respectively, have each enriched and extended my experience in their own way. I am ever thankful to my parents for giving me my heritage, my passion for pursuit of excellence and the strength to aim for bigger goals. My family has foremost been very understanding and supportive of my professional endeavors including the never-ending time zones and travel.

**Avinash Vashistha**

# Contents

# Part 1

# The Rise of Offshore Outsourcing: Borderless Services

# Introduction

We have seen the benefits of global manufacturing in lower prices and increased buying power across the world. The economies of most developed nations are no longer manufacturing or agricultural economies but services economies. Services globalization is the next step in the evolution of global trade and capitalism. It is progress. It is efficiency. It is the race for competitive advantage. It is not just offshore outsourcing, but the wholesale elimination of borders as a means of restructuring the free flow of services. Indeed, many of the biggest players in offshore services are U.S. and European companies that have their own workers in their own facilities doing work on their own services in places like Manila, Shanghai, Budapest and Bangalore. Like manufacturing before it, companies are performing, buying, selling and transforming services at an incredibly quick global pace and breadth, both through outsourcing and insourcing.

This book is about what this mega trend is, how leaders need to rethink globalization, and how leading companies need to leverage this to create competitive advantage. Finally, this is also about how nations can evolve their economies to leverage their comparative advantage in the services arena. This is a strategy book first and then a best practices approach to global outsourcing. This is not a commentary on whether or not services globalization is good or bad for the economy. Rather, this is a strategic look at what role services globalization should play in your company, how to integrate it into your overall corporate strategy, and how to manage it on an enterprise-wide level. Along the way, we'll also provide some practical advice on issues such as how to build a globalization strategy, how to identify what functions and processes within your organization are mature enough to send offshore, how to pick the right business model for globalizing IT, back office and other services, which countries need to be part of this initiative, how to manage suppliers, and how to leverage services globalization throughout the enterprise.

If you are thinking about services globalization for your enterprise—and you should be—this is the book to read before you begin this journey. And if you are already in the midst of the process, this book will help you transform those engagements into a strategic part of your overall corporate identity, gain the maximum benefits from them, and reduce the short-term and long-term risks to your enterprise.

*Chapter* 1

# Futurizing Your Organization

The enterprise of the 21st century is searching for a way to define itself, a means by which to achieve stability, competitive advantage and a blueprint for the future. All such quests were manageable in the not–too–distant past. New methods of organization, new processes and new management techniques surfaced to help executives adapt to change and plan for it. Key books and top consulting firms led the way.

Unfortunately, all of these quests are now futile. Definition is meaningless, because innovation and the lack of definition is the only way to avoid obsolescence and stay competitive. Stability is impossible, because volatility is everywhere and will continue for the foreseeable future. And following any blueprint for the future is a recipe for disaster, because the future has never been so uncertain and so exciting.

So, what should an enterprise do to become and remain competitive? The answer is to be prepared. While that may sound like a page from a Boy Scouts manual, the fact is that futurizing your organization is all about being prepared, not only at an individual level but also at an organizational level.

*Preparation is not about trying to figure out what the future holds and structuring your organization accordingly. Preparation is about being prepared to flourish during rapid change!*

Preparation is not about trying to figure out what the future holds and structuring your organization accordingly. Preparation is about being prepared for anything! Having rain gear in case there's a downpour. Having calamine lotion in case there's poison oak. Knowing which side of the tree the moss grows on, in case you get lost. It is about being flexible. It is about having the right people, processes, products and services, and financial structure in place that allow you to:

- Adjust to new markets and new competitors as they surface and define themselves
- Adapt to rapidly changing political, business and economic climates, and shocks in the system
- Look closely at trends that are shaping your world and be prepared for them but also have the flexibility to adapt if the future turns out to be different from what you thought
- In short, being prepared means "Futurizing Your Organization" for a future that is undefined and rapidly changing but very exciting. A challenging task, to be sure. But one that is essential if firms are to remain competitive and become market leaders.

## COPING WITH VOLATILITY

The world is a more volatile place today than it was 10 years ago. Volatility is everywhere as you look at the geopolitics, terrorism, domestic politics, stock markets, economies, prices, consumer habits, interest rates and disruptive technologies. No matter how you slice it, volatility has increased. And it is not simply anecdotal—whether it is the standard deviation of stock market returns or the shifting pattern of global growth rates—volatility is indeed higher. This state has made corporate planning a nightmare, and it has increased the importance of effective risk management and cost management. Effective cost management is not about maintaining your cost structure at a level that supports your existing margins. It is about structuring your costs so they can also support shocks to your current model, whether you are dealing with a jump in oil prices, a sudden shift in consumer buying habits, the entrance of a new competitive business model, or a disruptive technology. Preparation for these shocks means streamlining costs across the board and maintaining flexibility to shift costs from one cost center to another, from one product line to another, from the fixed side of the T-chart to the variable side.

Preparation means managing your risks through diversification of revenue streams, supplier bases, and human resources, even management. It means hedging your cost and revenue structure against potential changes in geopolitics, currencies, economics, cultural clashes, market changes.

## INNOVATION IN EVERYTHING

Says Chris Anderson, the editor of *Wired* magazine in a January 2004 editorial, "Today, even innovative firms spend too much money maintaining products: fixing bugs and rolling out nearly identical 2.0 versions." Being competitive used to mean doing everything you possibly could to make your company more effective within its current structure and current markets. In the 80s, for example, it meant just-in-time inventory. More recently, it has meant real-time processes. These activities are still important, but they are not enough. To stay competitive, companies need to be able to throw out accepted ways of doing things and come up with completely new models—new products and services, new markets, new processes, new management techniques, new technologies, new suppliers, new sources of labor, new sources of intellectual capital, new ways of thinking about how to do business. Innovation in everything!

## THE ORGANIZATION OF THE FUTURE

Everything we knew about work and the workplace is changing rapidly, right before our eyes. The workers and companies that fail to recognize this will be left behind. The days of the career worker bee are over. Worker mobility is at an all-time-high, and is increasing. Flexible workplaces are here to stay—contingent work, contract work, work-at-home and telecommuting arrangements are more and more common. The search for talent no longer begins and ends within the company. Effective companies now stick to their core areas of expertise and outsource everything else. They bring in contract workers to fill positions and field tasks that require special talents and will not be required long-term. They make use of temporary labor not just to fill gaps but as a strategic tool that allows them to shift fixed labor costs to variable costs. They outsource products and services that just a few years ago would have been considered core.

"The boundary between bringing in contractors and sending out work that can be done by contractors overseas is really fuzzy," says Stephen Barley, professor of management science and engineering at Stanford and co-author of *Gurus, Hired Guns* and *Warm Bodies*, a book that looks at the use of contract workers in Silicon Valley.

In the new workplace described by top management consultants, and authors such as Daniel Pink in his book *Free Agent Nation*, and Tom Peters in his newest book, *Re-Imagine! Business in a Disruptive Age*, workers are realizing they can make more money and increase their quality of life by becoming free agents—working on a contract basis for whoever will pay more for their talents and services. They are reinventing themselves in the same way that companies are reinventing themselves—mastering their core capabilities, innovating when those capabilities begin to become obsolete. If companies want the best people, they have to adjust to these realities and go to where the talent is, in the same way that workers will have to adjust to competitive pressures from new pools of talent.

Says Peters: "I imagine a truly creative society: Each person moves from project to project, from gig to gig. Global Voluntary Communities of Interest, rather than corporations, provide the bedrock upon which we stand. The cubicle slave is dead; long live the free agent."

The challenge, then, for the corporation of today is one of self diagnosis—to identify the gap between where they are today and where they ought to be in order to be competitive, or even to survive.

> *The challenge, then, for the corporation of today is one of self diagnosis—to identify the gap between where they are today and where they ought to be to be competitive, or even to survive.*

## LOOK AHEAD AND BE PREPARED

Being prepared for any eventuality is paramount, and watching global trends and making adjustments for a changing landscape is important. Here are three trends that are sure to have a dramatic impact on your bottom line going forward: globalization, outsourcing of services, and the impending labor shortage in many developed nations such as the U.S. and Japan. Ignoring any of these would be tantamount to committing corporate suicide.

**The U.S. labor shortage** is expected to reach its peak between 2010 and 2015, when the maturing of baby boomers will push millions of workers into retirement age and as many as 15 million jobs will be left unfilled. Growth in the U.S. economy will reduce unemployment levels and push corporate staffing levels to the bursting point. Corporations, in a fight to remain competitive, will have to look beyond traditional labor markets—older, post-retirement-age workers, for example, will become a hot commodity; migrant workers will flood lower wage ranks, and it still won't be enough.

**Globalization** (more on this in Chapter 2), meanwhile, has swept the world, bringing all of us together into global communities of interest where goods, services, processes, people and knowledge jump from shore to shore almost without restriction. This is not just a U.S. phenomenon but has been adopted widely throughout the European Union (EU); and the restrictions that do exist are rapidly coming down. There's a memorable line in the movie *Jurassic Park* when modern-day dinosaurs have been designed not to breed—they're all female—but a chaos theoretician chimes in with, "Life finds a way." Sure enough, baby dinosaurs are born. It's the same with globalization. No matter how many restrictions we place upon it, globalization will find a way!

Take the manufacturing industry for example. Over the last two decades, manufacturing around the globe has gone through a significant transformation. Low labor cost countries quickly gained a large market share, but in the end lost to competitors that met both the low cost criteria with an abundant labor pool and exceeded quality metric standards. Free trade has boomed because suppliers and markets have demanded it. And over time, we saw the emergence of new supplier countries that became global leaders in manufacturing the most complex and IP related goods. We only have to look as far as China and Taiwan to see the benefits of this revolution. While Japan and other places dominated early, Taiwan and China have become leaders in higher value manufacturing, enabling smart manufacturing companies to pass the cost savings on to the customer. Now Malaysia and other nations are nipping at their heels. The global economy is full of better products that cost less, a direct result of where and how we manufacture and distribute goods.

**Outsourcing** is another trend that has and will continue to be unstoppable. America is no longer about the vertically integrated company that is all things to all people. It is about discovering what you are best at, and concentrating on developing those talents. Focus on your core expertise, and outsource everything that can be done cheaper and better by people and companies whose core capabilities are those products and services.

Says Bill Gates: "If we are not realistic about what we are good at, then there is a chance of going backwards in the face of further competition."

So how does globalization of services fit with all of this? In a way, it is the **natural progression and evolution of all the trends we have discussed in this chapter**. Globalization of services allows companies to better cope with volatility because it frees up resources—financial, human, facilities, etc.,—that can be moved and made better use of elsewhere within the firm. It also diversifies revenue and supplier streams across cultures, countries, currencies and time zones. It allows companies to be more innovative by bringing in new knowledge and capabilities, and new supplier models that can radically alter a company's cost structure and level of quality. It gives companies the flexibility and the resources to focus on their core capabilities, which is where innovative companies achieve their competitive advantages.

Globalization of services is another part of the organization of the future, where jobs are easily exportable and labor markets grow where there are talented people willing to work for lower wages. Offshore outsourcing helps companies prepare for whatever the future holds. But globalization of services isn't synonymous with offshore outsourcing. Indeed, more and more of the offshore operations that are being set up are captive centers in which the enterprise hires its own workers and builds its own center without relying on third-party suppliers. Ten years from now, when a labor shortage has companies scrambling to find talent, the pioneering companies that first established offshore bases will have the upper hand. Moreover, as globalization continues its unstoppable path, offshore outsourcing will no longer be called offshore outsourcing. It will simply be outsourcing, and it will be just one more way that globally competitive companies are interwoven among markets.

Globalization of services can drastically reduce the cost of business, and can be used as a weapon to gain a competitive posture for a foray into a new line of business, to improve customer service on an existing product line, to streamline the supply chain in order to beat a rival out of the door. If your 5-year or even 1-year business plan doesn't include globalization of services, throw it out and rewrite it or you'll be written off.

## THE NEED FOR SERVICES GLOBALIZATION

Over the last decade, successful companies like GE and Citicorp sought distant shores to build a strategic advantage through lower costs and higher service levels. Now these firms have over a decade of offshore experience. In many cases, services globalization began with companies that recognized the talent that existed for manning their own physical presence in many of the countries that are now market leaders in offshore services. Citicorp, for example, hired engineers to build software and perform various IT and BPO functions at its offices in Russia, Asia and Latin America, and it was a natural progression for those same people to extend their services to the corporate level.

Likewise, Y2K was a big boost for many offshore countries and their supplier firms, exposing them to numerous global buyers. Y2K was too big, too urgent and too global a problem for the developed world to handle on its own. What's more, it involved legacy systems, mostly mainframes, and there weren't enough engineers in the U.S. who were still familiar with them. The technology was already beyond that. Meanwhile, there were thousands of engineers in India, China, Russia and elsewhere who had worked on those systems all their careers, and were happy to lend their services. As a result, it brought offshore familiarity to many U.S. and other Western firms.

This exposure and experience has done more than improve the brand of these countries. It has built trust, loyalty and global brand recognition for many of the leading service providers. The resulting growth opportunities of the industry have led to the development of suppliers with critical mass and expertise. Large skilled labor pools, government non-interference, support and favorable tax schemes have fuelled the growth of suppliers as well.

## FROM A TRICKLE TO A FLOOD

Meanwhile, there were industries in the U.S. and other Western countries for which there simply was not enough labor force capable and willing to do the job. Healthcare, for example, was an early customer of offshore services. The demand for low-level data-entry personnel who spoke and read English fluently reached critical mass in the late 1980s and early 1990s. India and the Philippines naturally filled that void.

Then, when the tech boom came in the mid-1990s, the need for developers and programmers coincided with a high number of IT firms who counted foreign-born engineers among their founders. It was an obvious move for many of them to look to their native countries for talent.

While India has since cemented its ownership of the brand name for offshoring IT services, the claim for leadership in BPO (Business Process Outsourcing) is still up for grabs as low-wage markets like the Philippines, China and Russia compete with India

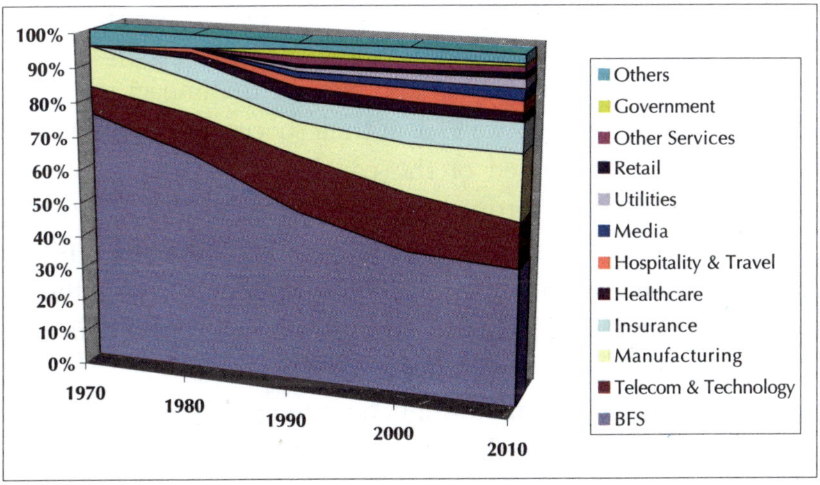


FIGURE 1.1

Timeline of leading industries using offshore services.

for market share. Buyers are diversifying the countries they source to and now look at their services sourcing as a portfolio of options (onshore, nearshore, offshore). The global sourcing portfolio approach is helping companies plan for the percentage mix of what is sourced to domestic and near-shore, versus offshore locations.

## FUTURIZING YOUR ORGANIZATION

Today's corporations are faced with the necessity of significantly reducing their cost of operations in response to decreasing profits due to weakening global economies. Outsourcing, and more importantly offshore outsourcing, certain business activities has developed into an attractive option as the global marketplace continues to expand. And while one point of emphasis should be cost, companies are also focusing on the greater value gained by process improvements, service level enhancements, scalability, flexibility and focus on what is core.

ChevronTexaco and P&G have established successful Shared Services Centers in the Philippines, while GE and Citicorp are doing significant back-office operations in India. These engagements are successful because of extraordinary preparation. Preparatory start-up and ramp-up plans were put in place and cautions exercised to not only manage internal impact but also manage the impact to clients and other stakeholders. As we look at their successful operations, we can be extremely reassured of the capability in these countries. Kudos to these firms for setting a great example.

Global firms such as these are well positioned for the offshore boom. They have been globalizing their services for a significant period of time and understand the best practices for offshore success. It is decades of experience, not just knowledge, that is accelerating the offshore phenomenon. How much more prudent can a firm be?

The real story behind the offshoring of U.S. jobs is how most firms are approaching their sourcing strategies with prudence and caution. While they see the opportunity, and there is an obvious advantage to moving quickly, they are sophisticated, smart and cautious about filling in the blanks on what to offshore, where to offshore and when to offshore. The real story is about how the smart companies are choosing the right offshoring strategy, the right offshore process, the right country, the right firm for the job or the right ownership option and the right governance structure.

## KEY POINTS

- Futurizing your organization is all about being prepared. Preparation is not about trying to figure out what the future holds and structuring your organization accordingly. Preparation is about being prepared to flourish during rapid change.
- Preparation means managing your risks through diversification of revenue streams, supplier bases, and human resources, even management. It means hedging your cost and revenue structure against potential changes in geopolitics, currencies, economics, cultural clashes, market changes.
- Innovation in everything.
- Three trends that are sure to have a dramatic impact on your bottom line going forward: globalization, outsourcing of services, and the impending labor shortage in many developed nations such as the U.S. and Japan.
- In order to futurize their organizations, smart companies are choosing the right offshoring strategy, the right offshore process, the right country, the right firm for the job or the right ownership option and the right governance structure.

*Chapter* 2

# The Future of Nations

The Offshore Nation is not one country or even one region. It is a world of buyers and sellers of services, all linked by a desire for higher productivity, lower costs and matching supply with demand. It is the United States, which in 2003 spent over $10 billion on outsourced software and IT services alone. It is India, which exported more than $15 billion a year in IT and business process services. The Offshore Nation is the Philippines, an emerging BPO powerhouse where the salary for IT and business

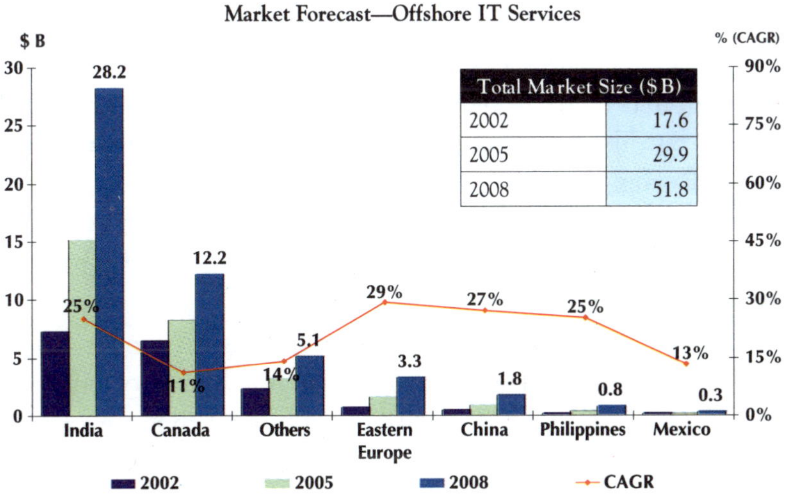


FIGURE 2.1

Contd.

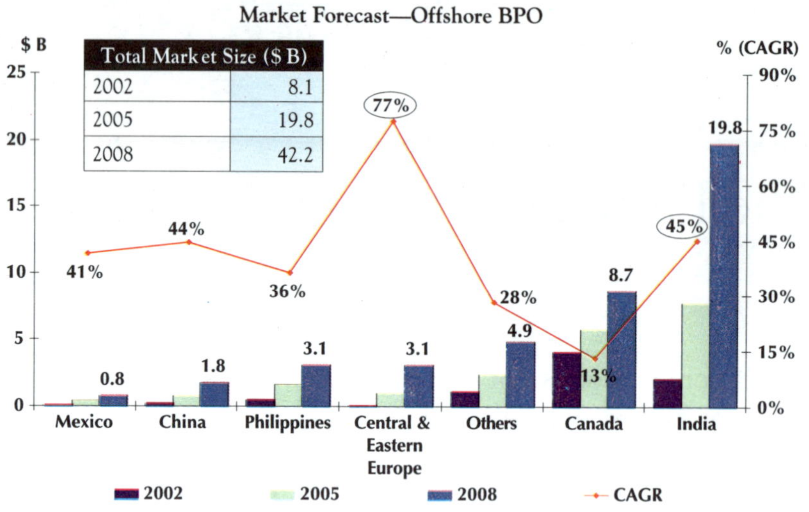


FIGURE 2.1

The rise of offshore services.

process workers averages $5,000 a year, while the per capita income for the nation averages $3,200. It is Canada, which not only sells billions of dollars worth of near-shore services to the United States every year, but also outsources services to countries ranging from Mexico to Russia.

This is not a trend. In an increasingly customer-centric world, the globalization of services is a strategic component in today's successful businesses.

What's more, the globalization of services is no longer about India. While India is far and away the largest source of offshore services, there are at least 20 additional countries that are rapidly building infrastructure and expertise in everything from call centers to IT security. The strategic use of such services to client companies is as much about finding the right location and identifying the right global partners as it is about identifying what products and services are ripe to move offshore.

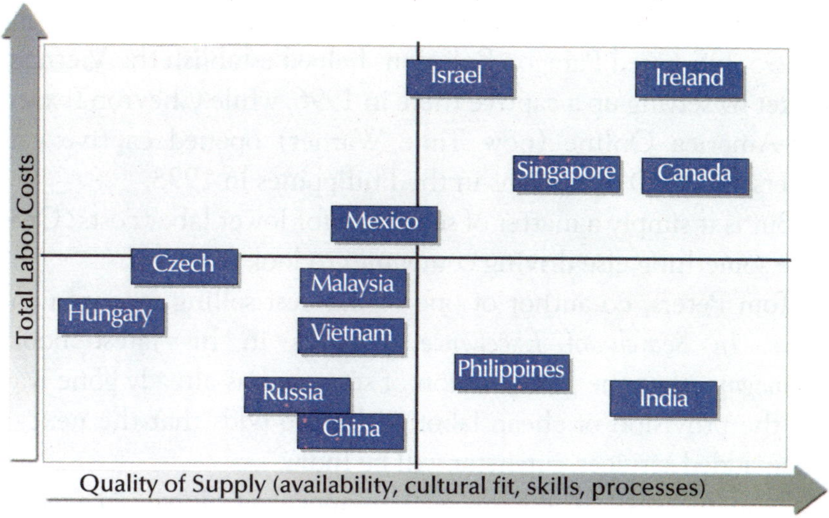


FIGURE 2.2

The largest offshore service exporters.

## THE GLOBALIZATION PROCESS

As the globalization of manufacturing picked up speed in the 1980s, services globalization became the logical next step. Some of the early pioneers in the use of offshore services were the same firms that had been successful on the manufacturing side. Many were companies that already had established sales, service and manufacturing facilities around the world.

The outsourcing of services can trace its roots to India with a few Japanese firms in the 1970s sourcing engineering work, followed by firms such as Texas Instruments, GE and Xerox setting up captive centers in the late 1980s. It was not until the early 1990s that third party vendors like Infosys, Wipro and TCS began to emerge and grow as the dominant offshore IT services suppliers. From the buyer side, another early purchaser of outsourced services was Nortel Networks, both in India and later, in Russia—the Canadian telecom firm engaged four Russian firms for technical development in 1995. US-based Paragon Solutions helped establish the Vietnam market by setting up a captive there in 1996, while ChevronTexaco and America Online (now Time Warner) opened captive call centers and BPO operations in the Philippines in 1998.

But is it simply a matter of searching for lower labor costs? Or is there something else driving companies to look offshore?

Tom Peters, co-author of one of the best-selling management books, *In Search of Excellence*, remarks in his latest book, *Re-Imagine*, that the globalization of services has already gone way past the provision of cheap labor: "I lay 5:6 odds that the next—'value-added services' superstar will be India."

In many ways, it already is. The appeal of globalized service offerings, not unlike the globalization of manufacturing centers in the 1970s, is derived from a multitude of drivers:

- *cost* savings
- *focus* on core business
- *improved* quality standards
- *increased* speed of business
- *flexibility* of business models

Companies that send their services offshore are focusing on the greater value gained by process improvements, service level enhancements, scalability, flexibility and focus on what is core.

"It is not hard to see how outsourcing to India could lead to the next great era in American enterprise," says *Wired* Editor Chris Anderson.

Adds Carol Bartz, CEO of Autodesk, "When you can get great talent at 20 percent of the costs, it isn't about waving the American flag. It's about doing what's right to have a good company . . . I don't want to affect 600 lives. But I want the 3,400 who are staying to be very proud of the company and have it be a healthy company."

## THE STATE OF SUPPLIER NATIONS

As India developed its service outsourcing industry, two simultaneous trends started to take shape. First, other countries quickly saw the value in outsourced services and began to develop their own offerings, and their own niches. Second, India's services evolved and matured, such that the services now offered by India are far more advanced and of much higher quality than they were only a few years ago.

From the supplier side, offshoring has already made sweeping changes in the economies of dozens of countries and in the lives of tens of thousands of people. India, for example, now produces some 2 million college graduates a year, the vast majority of them fluent English speakers. The Philippines, a much smaller country by population, still manages to produce a whopping 290,000 college graduates a year, all of them English speakers. And like India, the Philippines has evolved to the point where it is offering much higher value services than solely call centers and data entry.

What's more, the jobs that are being created by the export of services are raising the standard of living of most of those involved. Many of these jobs are of much higher prestige and social status in supplier countries than they would be in the United States or Europe. As a result, people tend to work harder to keep their jobs and often take more pride in them, which leads in turn to higher quality.

In the Philippines, for example, SPI Technologies is one of the world's largest outsourcers of business processes, from health care and legal documentation services to graphic design and publishing services. While based in Manila, the company has operations at eight locations throughout Asia as well as seven project management and customer support centers in the U.S. and Europe. While this book is being written, they are also evaluating acquisition opportunities in multiple countries.

"The infrastructure we have often blows away what our clients have in their own back-office operations," says Ernest Cu, SPI Tech's CEO, adding that he is often amazed at how little the managers of even the largest U.S. and European companies know about the state and sophistication of many offshore service centers.

"One of our clients, (apparently concerned that SPI Tech might be running some sort of sweatshop operation) asked us to fill out a compliance form stating that our employees had proper desks and air conditioning," says Cu. "Then they came and visited us, and after that the forms never came."

## TECHNOLOGY IS MAKING IT EASIER

Like many people involved in outsourcing, Cu says technological advances have driven growth in the offshore services industry as much as demand for lower labor costs.

> *"Outsourcing is a function of the technology that allows it to happen."—David Frankel*

"Outsourcing is a function of the technology that allows it to happen," says David Frankel, a London-based consultant who specializes in brand and customer strategy.

Both the improved quality of audio and visual communications, as well more bandwidth and connectivity have allowed service providers in remote parts of the world to hook up seamlessly with multiple clients and service partners at the same time, and to share documents in a way that wasn't possible just a few years ago.

"Our clients used to ship us paper documents. Now, they just FTP them over and we work on all electronic files," Cu says.

Video conferencing has made amazing strides in the last two years.

"Video conferencing has allowed companies to get entire project teams with different cultures and languages, in different time zones and geographies, all together in the same virtual room," says Steve Arisco, vice president for operations at Avistar, a video technology firm based in Redwood Shores, California.

Arisco said one of Avistar's clients, a large financial services firm, recently decided to outsource some of its equity research functions to a team in India. With video conferencing, they can get that team together with research analysts in New York and Europe, swapping documents while they're all looking at and listening to each other online. They even play webcasts—such as a recent speech by Federal Reserve Chairman Alan Greenspan—so the whole team can watch and comment on it.

"They can solve in hours what used to take days," Arisco said, adding that the added capability of video conferencing not only makes the process more efficient, but it increases trust among team members when the person on the other end of the line is no longer just a voice with a foreign accent.

Software applications too have made it easier for companies to control and integrate their offshore operations and/or the services of an offshore supplier. In particular, a new category of software called "collaboration software" has grown up to handle just the kind of challenges that companies face when offshoring services.

"Most of the innovations in technology comes in response to people with a need," says Alan Lattaner, CEO and co-founder of Blue Iguana, a software company that does for offshore manufacturing what collaboration software can do for offshore services. "We need to cut costs, so we send things offshore. We need to manage that, so we have collaboration software. Among other things, it allows an engineering team to be developing online in a secure environment together with a remote team."

Figure 2.3 shows some of the ways that real-time software solutions have grown up around new ways of doing business. In many ways, these processes both facilitate and create a need for services globalization:

- Push communications (timing of information delivery determined by the provider rather than the recipient).

| Company | Czech Rep | China | Hungary | India | Philippines | Poland | Russia |
|---|---|---|---|---|---|---|---|
| Accenture | F, C | F, I, C | | I, C, F, H, P, S | C | | |
| Adobe | | | | I, S, E | | | |
| Amazon.com (1) | | | | C, I, S | | | |
| American Express | C | | | , P, I, F, S | C | | |
| AT&T | | | | C, F | | | |
| AXA | | | | P, I, S, C | | | |
| Bear, Steans & Co. | F | | | | | | |
| Bank of America | | | | I, F, C, S, H | | | |
| Boeing | | | | I, S | | E | |
| British Airways | | | | C, F | | | |
| Chevron | | | | I, S, | C, S | | |
| Churchill Insurance | | | | P | | | |
| Citibank | | | | P, C, I, F, H, P, S | | | |
| Computer Associates | | | | I, S | | | |
| Conseco | | | | P, C, F | | | |
| Dell | | | | C | C | | |
| Delta | | | | C | C | | |
| Deutsche Bank | | | | C, F, I | | | |
| Diageo | | | F | | | | |
| EDS | | | | I, S | | | |
| Flour | | | | A | A | A | |
| GE | | F,E, C,I,S | F,E, C,I,S | F, S, E, C, I, P | | | |
| HP | | | | F, E,C,H,I,P,S | | | |
| HSBC | | P | | P,C,I,S | | | |
| INA Schaeffler | | | | | | | E |
| Intel | | E | | E, S,I | C | | |
| Kodak | | | | I, S,C | C | | |
| Lehman Brothers | | | | I, S | | | |
| Microsoft | | I, S | | I, S,E,C | C | | |
| Novell | | | | I, S,E | | | |
| Oracle | | I, C, F | | I, S | | | |
| Philips | | E | | E, S,I | | | |
| Proctor & Gamble | | S, F | | I,S | S, F,C | | |
| Royal Sun & Alliance | | | | I,S,C,F,P | | | |
| Siemens | | | | F,I,S | | | |
| Standard Chartered Bank | | | | H, F, P, I,C,S | | | |
| Sun | | | | I,S,E | | | |
| Texas Instruments | | E | | E, S | | | |
| West Teleservices | | | | C | | | |
| Willis Insurance | | | | P,I,S | | | |

| Center Function Key | |
|---|---|
| A - | *Architecture, Drafting* |
| C - | *Customer Care/Call Center* |
| E - | *Engineering, R&D* |
| F - | *Finance & Accounting* |
| H - | *HR* |
| I - | *IT Development* |
| P - | *Loan/Claim Processing* |
| S - | *IT Support* |

## FIGURE 2.3

Companies that use offshore services, and which countries they use.

Source: Gartner Group

- Individual treatment of events, as opposed to batch handling.
- Simultaneous message delivery to all interested parties.
- Design with explicit focus on events.
- Managing notification systematically, with enterprise-wide dissemination.

## THE GLOBAL PLAYERS ON OFFENSE

If there is a single point of information that one could point to as validation of the future of the global services industry, it would be this: the big multinational IT services firms have finally adopted the offshore resource models. For example, IBM's acquisition of the Indian BPO firm, Daksh.

Offshore players continue to grow stronger by feeding on IT projects normally reserved for the top tier players, nipping away at business once reserved exclusively for the elite cadre of big time global IT services firms. Offshore companies have slowly been competing with IBM Global Services, Accenture, EDS and CSC. In order to remain competitive, many of the large multinational corporations (MNCs) are choosing to offer 'best shore' or 'multi-shore' solutions by partnering with offshore organizations or building their own operations in offshore locations such as India, the Philippines, and more recently China, Poland, Mexico, Hungary, Russia and other such locations.

The result is that it has become increasingly difficult to determine whether the work for any given outsourcing contract is being performed onshore or offshore. And to many client companies, that is a good thing because it puts the onus on costs and service levels rather than time and materials. It also gives clients a choice.

Still, with over a decade of delivering offshore services to global customers, the offshore leaders will continue to be a competitive threat to MNCs. One should also expect to see increased consolidation in this industry.

One of the core reasons companies outsource is to cut costs and increase service levels, especially with the growing interest in BPO. Many offshore suppliers have built their reputation on delivering as good or better quality than can be delivered in domestic markets with significantly lower costs.

## KEY POINTS

- The Offshore Nation is not one country or even one region. It is a world of buyers and sellers of offshore services, all linked by a desire for higher productivity, lower costs and matching supply with demand.
- The globalization of services has fueled growth and change in the offshore services industry, as well as driven change in onshore service providers.
- Offshore players continue to grow stronger by feeding on IT and BPO projects normally reserved for the top tier players, nipping away at business once reserved exclusively for the elite cadre of big time global IT services firms.
- Global IT services firms as well as BPO providers have responded by opening their own offshore operations in markets with varying degrees of maturity.
- The result for the buyer is a plethora of choices, but it also means understanding your own needs and then matching it to the right location and service model options.

*Chapter* 3

# The Good, the Bad and the Ugly

In 1994, Midsize Bank, Inc. (client identity protected) was struggling to bring its new line of consumer credit cards to market against an entrenched competitive landscape that included the likes of Citibank, Chase Manhattan and Bank One. It had a top-notch, highly aggressive marketing plan in place and a financial team that was the best in the business at matching credit products with consumers. Still, as Midsize grew, it was obvious that labor costs were eating away at its bottom line. The customer service required to maintain the credit cards was enormous, and senior management was wary about leveraging the bank's decades-old commercial banking business to finance growth in the new and untested credit card unit.

Then, in 1998, a mid-level manager named Joe Smith approached the director of the credit card unit, Bill Jones, with a bold plan to cut costs. His idea, fostered in discussions with a friend he met in business school, Ravi Patel, was to move customer service to India. At the time, offshoring was mostly still limited to manufacturing and small IT projects, and Jones dismissed the idea outright. How could a Midwestern bank that prided itself on its hometown culture trust its customer service to a team of foreigners half a world away? But Smith was persistent, and as the competition heated up it became obvious that the credit card unit was at risk. Smith approached Jones again, and this time he got the green light to initiate plans for an offshore call center. Within a year, 30 percent of Midsize Bank's customer service had been moved to India, and within three years it was more than half. The average cost of servicing a single credit card user had dropped by more than 70 percent, and Midsize Bank had become one of the largest credit card issuers in the country.

This example is based on the real experiences of not just banks but hundreds of products and services, in dozens of industries that have moved services offshore over the past decade. Most of them have found what they had hoped for—a huge pool of cheap labor. But many have also found something they didn't expect—top engineering talent, attention to detail and quality, sophisticated mid-level and senior level management and even a level of brand identity and loyalty which rivals that of their in-house employees.

Welcome to the Offshore Nation. Each day, innovative companies in the U.S. and Europe are finding new ways to exploit the vast advantages that offshore outsourcing of services offers, and they are using those advantages to leapfrog competition in their respective industries.

These companies also have to deal with an increasing amount of backlash against the transfer of jobs to lower-wage countries like India, China and the Philippines. There's no denying that the upheaval that this trend is causing to the American and European workplace will be difficult, especially in the short term. These are no longer low-skill jobs that are moving offshore. These are white-collar, highly skilled positions that are supplanting people with high five-figure and sometimes six-figure salaries. In the long term, if these jobs don't move offshore, the U.S., U.K., Germany and other developed countries will not be able to compete as nations. Job growth, economic growth, technological progress and offshoring have become mutually dependent.

"The evidence is simply too compelling that our mutual interests are best served by promoting the free flow of goods and services among our increasingly flexible and dynamic market economies," Federal Reserve Chairman Alan Greenspan said in a January 2004 speech.

A study produced for the Information Technology Association of America by *Global Insight* estimated that U.S. companies saved \$6.7 billion from the use of global IT resources in 2003, or 2.3 percent of total IT spending, and that the figure will grow to \$20.9 billion, or 6.2 percent of IT spending, by 2008.

Another study by consulting firm McKinsey & Co. estimates that for every dollar spent on global locations, another $1.45 comes back to the U.S. economy.

There is no disputing the fact that we are playing in an increasingly global market, and competitors worldwide are moving quickly toward the most efficient use of resources. The cost of doing business in places like the United States and Western Europe is growing increasingly higher. Like free trade before it, the globalization of services is a phenomenon that draws loads of controversy. It was not long ago that Ross Perot succeeding in scaring half of America into the fact that the North American Free Trade Agreement was going to create "a huge sucking sound" of U.S. jobs being pulled to Mexico. Perot, of course, was wrong, and history has shown that any short-term displacement of jobs that NAFTA may have caused were more than made up for in other areas that benefited from the agreement, not to mention the vastly lower prices on Mexican goods that consumers have benefited from. Figure 3.1 shows one estimate of how higher economic activity—derived in part from the value gained from globalization—leads to higher net job creation.

But that does not mean that offshore services have been easy to swallow, especially given the difficulties in the U.S. economy in the early years of the 21st century. According to a study by the University of California's Fisher Center for Real Estate and Urban Economics, employment in the sectors most impacted by offshoring plummeted 15.5 percent in the U.S. between the first quarter of 2001 and the second quarter of 2003, and 21 percent in the state of California. While most of those jobs were lost due to the struggling economy, the study hypothesizes that "outsourcing that began as a response to very tight labor markets in the U.S. in 1999–2000 has continued, becoming a factor in the 'jobless' or 'job-loss' recovery of 2003."

A separate study by Forrester Research forecasts that by the year 2015, some 3.3 million jobs will have been irretrievably lost as a result of offshore outsourcing of business processes. The question for U.S. labor markets is how many new jobs will be created in place of those jobs? And how long will that take?

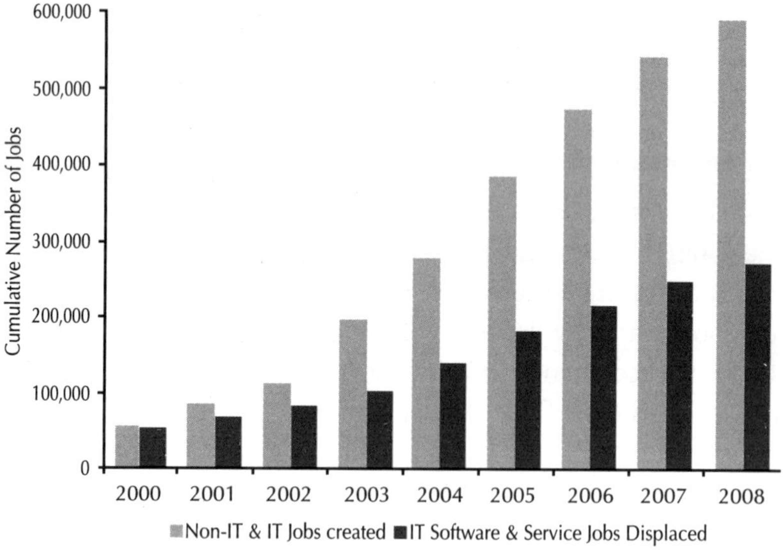


FIGURE 3.1

Cumulative Non-IT and IT Jobs Created Due to Increased Economic Activity vs. Cumulative IT Jobs Lost or Never Created Due to Offshore ITO

Source: Global Insight, Inc.

To illustrate the controversy and perhaps shed some light on the economics of outsourcing, we can point to a recent debate in the New Jersey legislature over a bill that would prohibit the state from buying back-office services from businesses located outside the United States. The sponsor of the bill, State Senator Shirley Turner, argued:

"Neither the people in India who have the jobs, nor the people who are unemployed here in the U.S. are giving anything back in the way of taxes or buying and consuming U.S. goods and services, which is what stimulates our economy. By outsourcing these jobs to other countries we're helping the poor remain poor in this country."

Never mind that a strong case could be made against several of Turner's points, including her allegation that wealthier Indians won't be buying U.S. goods and services. The key to the debate is that Turner is advocating that New Jersey, already faced with a sharp budget deficit, spend more than it has to on services. In other words, she's advocating an inefficient use of resources. Writing in part as a response to such arguments, Deloitte Research's chief economist, Carl Steidtmann, said the case for buying offshore services is clear: "The state of New Jersey benefits from buying lower cost services. In the case of the state, taxes can be lowered, other services can be funded or the gaping budget deficit can be reduced. In all cases, the state of New Jersey is better off. Taxpayers get both the benefits that flow from the outsourced services and a reduction in taxation. Lower taxes stimulate business activity, creating more tax revenue for the state. Productivity growth in New Jersey is enhanced, lifting the standard of living. Everyone in the state of New Jersey is marginally better off in the long run."

And in India, the people who get the jobs are also better off. Economic development there surges, and U.S. companies that export goods and services to India benefit as India's economy improves.

The only people who don't make out better (but only in the short term) are those whose jobs are displaced in the United States. Unfortunately, that is a stark reality of offshoring, and it is one that needs to be addressed. But as we mentioned, those displacements need only be short term.

In the case that prompted New Jersey's anti-offshoring bill, writes Steidtmann, the state would have saved $1.2 million, while 12 jobs would have been lost. "The state can spend $100,000 per worker to retrain them, support them on unemployment benefits, account for the loss in state taxes these workers would have paid and still come out ahead in the first year. Continued savings by the state in subsequent years represent the additional benefits from trade."

Wherever jobs are lost to offshore suppliers, government and the private sector will have to work together to help train these displaced workers to move up the value chain. As the economy changes and adapts to the globalization of services, displaced workers will have three choices:

1. Switch careers to an entirely different line of business or industry.
2. Move up in the value chain from a technical position to management, often overseeing the very processes that are being outsourced.
3. Retrain in the same field but to newer technologies that are more client-intimate and heavily concentrated onshore.

So what are the positions that will remain onshore? Anything that requires a high level of strategy and intimacy with senior management and/or with clients generally is the last to go offshore. Additionally, value-added functions that require special knowledge will remain, as will functions with a certain level of security.

"Because the U.S. IT industry is a value-added industry, it will only maintain its lead in global IT services if it is able to draw on a large, diverse and richly talented domestic IT workforce," the Information Technology Association of America said in a statement in which it embraced the move towards globalized services. "To be the best, U.S. IT firms must continue to perform research, to generate innovative new products and services, to solve customer problems and add productivity, to enhance quality and value."

The problem, says Mimi Strouse, a managing director at Warburg Pincus' private equity unit who is in charge of investments in the outsourcing space, is that "our education system in the United States is in a crunch right now. It becomes hard when you have people who need to be reskilled and there is no money for education."

That problem will need to be addressed by government and the private sector working together.

The displacement of jobs in the United States is likely to be concentrated mostly in metropolitan areas, and in a few areas in particular where there are a high concentration of jobs at risk for outsourcing. As Table 3.1 shows, San Jose, and San Francisco in California stand to lose the most jobs to offshoring, followed by Boston and Atlanta. The types of jobs that are lost will differ from city to city. San Jose, for example, has a lower than average number of office support jobs that are ripe for outsourcing, but has almost four times the average share of computer and math jobs. Cities like Detroit, which lost large numbers of workers during the manufacturing outsourcing boom, are likely to be less affected by the offshoring of services.

*Prices will come down across the board, making many IT services and BPO affordable to many more companies that can't afford them now.*

| Sectors | Employment 2001 | Average annual salary 2001 |
|---|---|---|
| All Occupations (Total US Employment) | 127,980,410 | $34,020 |
| **Occupations at Risk due to Outsourcing** | | |
| Office support | 8,637,900 | $29,791 |
| Computer operators | 177,990 | $30,780 |
| Data entry staff | 405,000 | $22,740 |
| Business and financial support | 2,153,480 | $52,559 |
| Computer and math professionals | 2,825,870 | $60,350 |
| Paralegals and legal assistants | 183,550 | $39,220 |
| Diagnostic support services | 168,240 | $38,860 |
| Medical transcriptionists | 94,090 | $27,020 |
| **Total at risk** | **14,063,130** | **$39,631** |
| **Percent of all occupations** | **11%** | |

TABLE 3.1

US employment in occupations at risk to outsourcing

Source: US Bureau of Labor Statistics.

*Note: Office support aggregates data from 22 office and administrative support categories. Business and financial support aggregates data from 10 business and financial occupations.*

The result across the economies of buyer countries will be that the average business will shrink in size, fueled not only by outsourcing but also by the ever-increasing capabilities of networked technologies. Prices will come down across the board, making IT services and BPO affordable to many more companies that cannot afford them now.

If offshore services follow the example of offshore manufacturing, the resultant long-term impact on prices will be extreme. According to the Institute for International Economics, "Globalized production and international trade made IT hardware some 10 to 30 percent less expensive than it otherwise would have been. These lower prices translated into higher productivity growth and an accumulated $230 billion in additional GDP (U.S. from 1995–2002)." In other words, real U.S. GDP growth would have averaged 0.3 percentage points less per year if globalized production of IT hardware had not occurred.

In the meantime, spending in IT services has increased, growing from 58 percent of total IT spending in 1993 to 69 percent in 2001, according to an IIE white paper by Catherine Mann, a senior fellow with the Institute and former member of the Federal Reserve Board of Governors.

As in manufacturing, the large majority of offshored services will be those that either have become commoditized or are on their way toward eventual commoditization. Offshoring will not, however, be limited to such activities. Already, companies like GE are offshoring cutting-edge design and even strategic technology services that just a few years ago would have been considered too security-sensitive to offshore.

The brokerage industry is a prime example of processes that have, over time, become commoditized and are ripe for offshoring. For trading stocks, for example, a broker that could once charge $1 per share now is lucky to get 10 cents. And the back office processes for brokerages have mostly already been outsourced. Even research is a function that, to a large extent, can be offshored, especially as investors have become sour on the conflicts of interest between investment banks and brokers. Outsourcing research functions to independent offshore suppliers might actually help investment banks win more clients. The final "buy" or "sell" recommendation will no doubt still need final approval from an onshore manager, but all of the fundamental and market-based research that goes into that recommendation can be performed offshore. The cost savings derived from offshoring these functions can be transferred to other sides of the business such as investment banking, mergers and acquisitions, initial public offerings, etc.,—all processes which require personal relationships with clients.

*For enterprises, the lesson is that no matter how compelling your case is for offshoring, you need to consider the internal human resources impact, and how best to manage it.*

Still, regardless of how good offshoring is to the long-term health of both buyer and supplier countries, there will always be vocal opponents on both sides. The 2004 U.S. presidential campaign highlighted these differences of opinion, and the strength that those differences can have on formulating public opinion and shaping policy. For enterprises, the lesson is that no matter how compelling your case is for sending jobs offshore, you need to consider the internal human resources impact, and how to best manage it.

Outsourcing decisions should be based on who can provide the best services for the best price—and that will be the case once the backlash cools down and the long-term positive effects of globalization of services become more apparent.

In summary, the globalization of goods and services is a natural progression of capitalist markets at work in an increasingly cohesive world. Without globalized services, an economy would inevitably be locked into low productivity, low wages and high prices. Globalization allows the more efficient use of resources, drives prices lower, prompts lower tax rates and over time leads to higher job growth. And it still has a long growth path ahead of it. McKinsey & Co. estimated the size of the business process offshoring industry alone at $32 billion to $35 billion in 2002, "just one percent of the $3 trillion worth of business functions that could be performed remotely."

## KEY POINTS

- The globalization of services is a positive for both buyer and supplier countries, fueling productivity growth, cutting costs to corporations, driving down inflation, and creating jobs on both sides.
- Prices will fall across the board, making IT services and BPO affordable to many more companies that cannot afford them now.
- Offshore outsourcing will create short-term job losses for those service workers in buyer countries whose jobs are being exported. Both companies and governments need to work together to ease those displacements and help workers transition into other jobs.
- The current backlash against the globalization of services will ease (but not disappear) over time as people realize that it is inevitable, it is a fait accompli, and it is a positive progression.

Chapter 4

# Integrating Corporate Strategy with Services Globalization

Services globalization is not a one-size-fits-all proposition. In fact, some companies embark upon this endeavor for all the wrong reasons. Companies must consider many issues to determine whether an offshore strategy is an appropriate investment, and this goes beyond number crunching exercises. It requires digging into your corporate culture, your business plan and your strategy for the future.

As companies look to outsource, there are many questions to answer, but first and foremost is to understand your business needs and align them with your goals and objectives. Finding the answer to what type of outsourcing partnership to invest in comes later. In this chapter, we map how services globalization might fit into your overall corporate strategy by using eight key globalization of services factors, in a globalization framework that we refer to as GS8$^{SM}$. We also compare offshore outsourcing to onshore, walk through the process for building a services globalization roadmap, and discuss the decisions that CEOs and other executives face in managing the backlash against offshoring.

## THE FLATTENING OF THE LEARNING CURVE

Fortunately, the learning curve for services globalization is not as steep as it used to be. The pioneers have built the path. The suppliers and markets have developed over time. The infrastructure is in place. The decision about whether or not to offshore has already been made for most of you—by your competition. Now the challenge in front of you is how to maximize the use of offshoring to your strategic advantage. It is about offshoring in a way that will enable your company to seamlessly integrate the benefits of globalized services into your existing infrastructure, to be able to manoeuvre your offshore services from your desktop in real time, to have a product change order relayed instantaneously from Chicago to St. Petersburg or to shift a supply chain in the Philippines with the click of a mouse in Palo Alto. And it is about being able to do all of that without worry!

Whether we realize it or not, we are all part of the Offshore Nation, a nation of buyers and sellers of offshore services. We are a nation of progress for mutual benefit, of the quest for innovation, the perfection of quality and the refinement of the total customer experience.

*"There is no job that is America's God-given right anymore," says Carly Fiorina, CEO of Hewlett-Packard.*

"There is no job that is America's God-given right anymore," says Carly Fiorina, CEO of Hewlett-Packard. "Now more than ever, other nations are developing skills to compete for jobs that would have historically been done by Americans. We shouldn't assume that they won't make an effort to win them. But we should work to keep America what it has always been: the world's most resourceful, innovative and productive country."

As we mentioned in Chapter One, futurizing your company means being prepared for all eventualities. Services globalization is one important tool on the road to accomplishing that level of preparedness.

"When taking outsourcing from a tactical to a more strategic level," says Debashish Sinha, a managing director at neoIT in charge of client engagements, "CEOs need to ask themselves, 'What will my client needs look like five years from now? What geographies and cultures will interface with my organization? What rules and compliance regulations will I have to work with? How will skills be distributed through my organization?'" The GS8 framework as shown in Figure 4.1 will help CEOs answer these questions.

Companies that use the eight factors of the GS8 framework to develop their globalization roadmap will emerge ahead of the competition as they prepare for the future. Cost savings, control, risk, quality, industry activity, social responsibility, corporate strategy and company culture are not only important factors that gauge the integration of services globalization to your overall corporate strategy, but are also critical to the decision of what, who

FIGURE 4.1

The Globalization Strategy Framework (GS8)

Source: neoIT, Inc.

and how to engage: an offshore supplier, an MNC, a multi-supplier strategy or the building of a captive center. And while the answer is not always straightforward, this is a question that needs to be considered carefully.

## Cost Savings

Labor is the biggest fixed cost that most companies face, accounting for approximately 35 percent of the operational budget of the average U.S. company. In the late 1990s, unit labor costs grew at an astronomical rate until peaking in early 2001. Since then, they declined steadily until bottoming out in April 2004. Most economists expect unit labor costs to begin climbing again, with growth likely to continue through the predicted labor shortage next decade as the baby boom generation hits retirement age.

Smart companies are preparing the structure of their labor costs now for that inevitable rise in fixed labor costs. Preparation, however, is not just about reducing the cost of your labor, it is also about diversifying your labor pool and increasing your flexibility to add to or subtract from it at a moment's notice.

Services globalization can not only reduce your overall unit labor costs by 40 percent or more, it can also give you access to a new pool of labor that can be easily tapped once labor costs soar and talent becomes harder to find. Moreover, expanding or shrinking an offshore labor pool can usually be accomplished much faster and cheaper than it would take to reduce full-time staff at onshore facilities—due both to labor laws that are less strict and to the short-term nature of most contracts with offshore suppliers.

Plotting your company's labor costs and adjusting your budget in terms of how much of those services can be outsourced, and how much can be sent offshore is a key first step towards integrating services globalization with the rest of the enterprise.

## Control

How many jobs you *can* outsource is one thing. How many jobs you *should* outsource is quite another. Cost savings is not the only factor in determining what to send outside your firm. Another key criterion is control.

In any outsourcing initiative, some measure of control must be ceded to the company or companies that perform the work. Often, giving up that control is an important first step toward achieving success in services globalization. Still, not all job functions are ripe for outsourcing, even if there are obvious costs savings. Security, risk, ownership and even loyalty issues can sometimes tip the balance in favor of keeping jobs in-house. Any discussion of services globalization must first include a strategic analysis of how much control a company can afford to give up over the job functions that are at stake.

Many ownership models can be used to customize the level of control that an operation or company is comfortable with. These choices include outsourcing, joint ventures, build-operate-transfer and captive centers.

## Risk

To the companies that are doing it now and doing it right, managing the risk of services globalization is part of overall governance. To them, services globalization is about how to leverage the advantages to manage the business and competitive risks of the rest of the firm.

Risks that need to be managed include geopolitical, social, privacy, data security, disaster recovery, business continuity, IP, etc. Financial services firms took the lead in offshoring of services and have been leveraging the advantages for well over a decade. The risks and risk mitigation strategies are well understood.

*Your 1040s are now being prepared in India and the Philippines.*

Nonetheless, there are important additional risks that any outsourcing venture brings to a firm, and offshore outsourcing adds yet another layer of complexity and risk. Having a strong grasp of your firm's current risk management structure and organization is a key first step toward integrating services globalization into that structure in a way that reduces, rather than increases overall risk to the enterprise.

## Quality

An additional point no less important than the others is quality. For every product, process, project and enterprise, there are acceptable and unacceptable levels of quality. Determining what those levels are is a highly strategic decision and one that goes to the core of customer retention and market leadership.

Does it make sense to have a 20-year veteran administrator earning $80,000 a year handling accounts payable? Probably not, especially when someone in the Philippines making one fifth of that salary could handle the same job with an equal or higher educational qualification. By the same token, does it make sense to have a data-entry clerk in India inputting critically sensitive financial information and handling customer service for an institutional client? Again, probably not, especially if you have someone at your home office who has been handling that client for years and has a strong relationship with them.

While quality is a key strategic determinant to what and how much to send offshore, it is also a key driver in determining the right locations and partners when you get there.

## Social Responsibility

One of the typical challenges of services globalization is the impact that it has on employees. In some cases, it leads to job loss in the buyer location and a significant change for the remaining team members. While globalization can have a big personal impact to employees, it can also have a significant impact on communities where these firms may be big employers. The decision to outsource can be even more difficult during an economic downturn.

Social responsibility can have a big impact on a firm's short and long-term globalization plans. It takes into account all stakeholders and the local, national, and international connectedness of businesses and families. Social responsibility does not mandate absolute protection of one group but seeks a social balance. Social responsibility also means ensuring corporate viability; part of your social duty is avoiding bankruptcy.

Socially responsible companies need to deal with emerging issues of worker retraining, unemployment insurance for jobs "transferred offshore," investment in innovation, and other infrastructural changes to enhance local market economic competitiveness. The socially responsible leader will learn from other economies. Social responsibility in globalization involves preserving not only the viability of your enterprise, but also the essence of the Offshore Nation economy.

## Company Culture

Firms have a culture that can aid or create hurdles for globalization. Firms that have never outsourced or do not operate in other cultures can have a very difficult time with their globalization initiatives.

Firms that have not outsourced and do not have much international exposure would obviously approach globalization much differently than an experienced firm. These firms would need to invest heavily in continual learning, research and education. They would need to create executive-led initiatives that create cross-organizational buy-in. In short, these firms would need to look at how this initiative could transform their organization.

Company culture can be a key strategic driver of how to offshore. Understanding the nuances of your internal culture can help you decide whether your organization can support an offshore, nearshore or onshore operation. This factor can also help you determine the ownership model best suited for your culture: joint venture, build-operate-transfer, third-party contract or fully owned captive model.

## Corporate Strategy

Globalization can be a very important part of an expansion or market leadership strategy. If a firm is committed to becoming the low-cost leader in the industry, it behoves them to leverage lower cost locations.

Additionally, many firms that are aggressive growth companies find that globalization of services enables them to serve their growth and clients better, especially in times of rapid growth. A good example of this is Exult, a leading Human Resources Business Process Outsourcing firm, which within a few years of its founding crossed the $500 million revenue mark. A significant portion of the company's growth and operating strategy includes services globalization.

Defining a complementary globalization strategy around your overall corporate strategy enables CEOs to transform their organizations into flexible and client-valued machines. They are futurizing their businesses.

## Industry Activity

Sometimes the firm's choice to offshore is actually determined by competitors or client demands. Today, if you are a software firm in Silicon Valley trying to raise capital, one of the first five questions a venture capitalist will ask is: "What is your offshore strategy?"

Globalization has revolutionized industry segments. In many industries such as logistics and credit cards, if you are not leveraging offshoring, your competitor is beating you in price and eroding away market share. In industries that have become commoditized or are moving toward commoditization, the choice to leverage offshore markets has already been made—it is a must.

Companies in other industries must take time to understand where the industry is headed and what the competition is doing and use that information to develop a services globalization strategy. Do you want to be the leader or have someone force choices upon you and risk exterminating your organization's market leadership?

## OFFSHORE vs. ONSHORE

The guiding principle of outsourcing is that non-core and even critical activities of an enterprise could be handed over to companies with lower labor costs and with expertise in those activities, thereby freeing internal resources to focus on enhancing the value-add of its core business. Over the last decade, the use of offshore resources to support this trend has significantly changed the landscape for outsourcing. Today, offshore outsourcing accounts for nearly five percent of the Global IT services and BPO industry. However, there are some fundamental differences between the traditional onshore outsourcing models and the global delivery model (offshore outsourcing), that significantly impacts planning, sourcing, and management of effective offshore operations.

**Key issue:** What are the key differences that enterprises should be aware of when comparing the traditional onshore outsourcing and the offshore outsourcing model?

By outsourcing, an enterprise aims to target its resources to its core areas of business. This principle has dual objectives:

- Save on cost of operation by acquiring services from a team more productive than the internal resources (based on their

expertise, or their ability to leverage infrastructure across multiple clients); and
- Improve quality and value of operation by acquiring services from an organization with best practices in managing that business activity.

Any outsourcing contract will ultimately be about either or both of these two objectives.

In an *onshore* outsourcing initiative, since the cost basis between internal and external operations is similar, achieving either objective requires the outsourcer to have one of the following capabilities:

- A common IT infrastructure that supports the business function being outsourced, such that it is leveraged across multiple clients, thereby reducing the per-client cost of operation. (e.g. the ADP model for outsourcing payroll, or data center outsourcing to IBM). This model, however, necessitates standardization of processes to be outsourced.
- Very specific process or domain expertise that allows the outsourcer to be significantly more efficient and productive (e.g. marketing departments outsourcing creative to advertising agencies), or
- Operational superiority, that allows the quality and value of the service delivered to greatly exceed any internal benchmarks (e.g. transformational outsourcing services from the likes of Accenture and IBM, or outsourcing auto claims processing to CGI).

In the absence of any of these characteristics, outsourcing can only be more expensive and less valuable than an internal operation. Furthermore, making improvements in existing processes, whether incremental or transformational, creates process stress that can be risky for the enterprise. Since each of these characteristics require large investments in time and resources, it is not surprising that, over the last two years, many seemingly well-structured outsourcing deals have failed to meet expectations.

*Offshore outsourcing, by focusing on changing the cost basis of operations, essentially alters the structure of the outsourcing industry and makes it easier to cost-effectively outsource non-core and even critical business functions.*

Whereas domestic service provisioning is typically assessed on the basis of infrastructure leverage, domain expertise or process knowledge, offshore service provisioning is primarily assessed on the cost basis for consistent quality of service, and capacity to leverage global resources.

Some of the significant differences in the sourcing strategy include:

- **Insourcing vs. Outsourcing.** Managing the complexities of the global delivery model requires a deep expertise in the local environments and experience with cross-border business operation, making the evaluation of whether to outsource a project or leave it in-house very different from a purely onshore sourcing decision.
- **Structure of the solution.** The lack of maturity of the offshore industry requires a significant commitment from the enterprise in supporting the development and growth of the outsourcing solution. Making that commitment, keeping an eye on the long view, necessitates a strategic sourcing decision, distinctly different from a domestic sourcing contract.
- **Due diligence on operating models and supplier selection.** The level of due diligence required, and the types of issues to address during supplier selection are substantially different. For

## CASE STUDY The Brokerage Industry

The first years of the 2000s were difficult ones for the brokerage industry. Merrill Lynch, Citicorp, Goldman Sachs and other large firms faced huge fines and public embarrassment over conflict-of-interest scandals that linked analyst recommendations to investment banking revenue. What's more, the drying up of the IPO market and a rush of new, strict regulations such as Sarbanes-Oxley drove up costs at a time when revenue had shrunk.

For many brokerage firms, offshoring was the solution. Goldman Sachs, facing regulatory actions that forced them to further separate their research arms and accounting from core banking businesses, opened a captive center in India for offshoring accounts payable work and created an RFP for investment research offshore.

J.P. Morgan hired 40 junior analysts in Mumbai to do research functions, while other companies such as Blackrock were also looking into offshoring certain research functions. The booming hedge fund industry also jumped on the bandwagon and is offshoring everything from research to fund accounting.

In all of these cases, offshoring has been a way for companies to take advantage of changes in public policy and regulatory issues by integrating offshore initiatives into overall corporate strategy—solving cost issues, regulatory issues and strategy issues all at the same time.

example, in offshore sourcing for 24×7 process support, it is imperative to check the availability of 100 percent captive power generation. Indeed, it's imperative to check for the level of reserve gasoline available.

- **Resource deployment/redeployment.** Offshore outsourcing transactions rarely include asset and resource transfers from the buyer to the service provider, whereas in onshore sourcing deals that is a common point of negotiation.

- **Knowledge transfer.** The transfer of information and training around the buyer's IT environment and other relationship parameters is very difficult to do in offshore sourcing. Since this has a direct effect on path to productivity for service providers, it becomes an important evaluation criterion, as well as a phase in the sourcing cycle.
- **Portfolio assessment and planning.** The 'offshorability' of an IT service or business process is dependent on many factors, and in most enterprises transitioning to an offshore model requires early planning. The portfolio assessment and planning phase is a critical component of a successful offshore sourcing initiative.

## MANAGING THE BACKLASH

One of the key aspects of integrating offshoring with corporate strategy is to make sure that offshoring does not disrupt your corporate culture or your global image with clients. In an era of increasing resentment of the success of offshore models, companies need to be careful that any backlash is properly managed. Below are some rules for best practices in offshore backlash management. While some may seem obvious, a surprisingly large number of companies violate these rules to their own detriment.

- Take a long-term approach.
- Involve employees in the planning and implementation.
- Create a program to ease the transition of displaced employees.
- Emphasize the economic and business positives that the offshore relationship brings to the company, its workers and society.
- Position offshoring as a part of the solution, not as a part of the problem.

## CASE STUDY — A Good Example of Managing Client Expectations

In early 2004, E-Loan, the Pleasanton, California-based processor of Internet-based mortgage, home equity and auto loans, announced that it would let customers decide if they wanted their loans processed onshore or offshore.

Clearly, the company meant well. CEO Chris Larsen is a vocal critic of companies that "secretly" send processes offshore. Says Larsen: "We don't think we can force that efficiency onto others because of the patriotic and privacy issues."

So, clients were given a choice—onshore loan processing, or offshore loan processing that was two days faster. Surprisingly, 85 percent of E-Loan customers opted for offshore processing. Benefit: Customers decide what they want.

## BUILDING YOUR OFFSHORE ROADMAP

Once firms understand the differences between offshore and onshore outsourcing, the potential for backlash and how the eight factors of the GS8 strategy framework model fit with their corporate strategy, they will have a good understanding of what will work and what won't for their organization.

Integrating the GS8 analysis and market understanding is the key to laying out an executable roadmap. The information in the roadmap should provide supporting information to enable a portfolio assessment and analysis. This analysis will help you choose the most offshoreable initiatives with acceptable levels of cost savings, risk, control and quality. Only when organizations have reached this point is it time to begin due diligence of locations and suppliers to help analyze and tee-up the future phases of offshore outsourcing.

As firms move through the phases of the offshore outsourcing lifecycle they are focused on capturing the returns by mitigating both obvious and unapparent risks. The leaders are approaching offshore from a total cost of ownership (TCO) perspective and following a very systematic method. This systematic method encompasses the entire sourcing lifecycle from planning to services management and receipt. This smart approach to offshoring is what we refer to as the **O4**SM* method, and it involves approaching offshoring in four different phases: *knowledge*, *planning*, *sourcing* and *managing*. You'll read more about this later as we take a look at this best practices approach, and debunk the myth that firms are not being prudent about offshoring.

## KEY POINTS

- The appeal of offshoring comes from many drivers, including cost savings, focus on core business, improved quality standards, increased speed of business, flexibility not provided by onshore or nearshore suppliers.
- The decision about whether or not to offshore has already been made for most of you—by your competition.
- Companies that use the eight factors of the GS8 framework to develop their globalization roadmap will emerge ahead of the competition as they prepare for the future.
- Cost savings, control, risk, quality, industry activity, social responsibility, corporate strategy and company culture are important factors that gauge the integration of services globalization to your overall corporate strategy.
- The differences between offshore and onshore outsourcing are largely due to the differing operating models, financial models and risk profiles.
- Best practices in offshore backlash management may seem obvious; however, a surprisingly large number of companies violate these rules to their own detriment.
- The **O4**SM* method involves approaching offshoring in four different phases: *knowledge*, *planning*, *sourcing* and *managing*.

* GS8SM and O4SM are the intellectual property of neoIT

# Part 2

# The Knowledge of Offshore Outsourcing: Preparation Meets Opportunity

Chapter 5

# Ten Myths of Services Globalization

Any new business model or trend inevitably brings with it confusion and sometimes falsehoods as people who do not understand the trend attempt to make sense of its nuances and complexities. The globalization of services is no exception. In this chapter, we will attempt to dispel some of the myths surrounding services globalization, and discuss the realities of some of the most frequently asked questions surrounding it.

## MYTH 1: SERVICES GLOBALIZATION ADDS RISK TO YOUR ORGANIZATION

**Reality.** It is true that there are some inherent risks that must be managed when moving a service offshore (and we discuss them in detail in chapter 9). But in many cases, the risks are no higher than they are when outsourcing the same service to an onshore provider. Offshoring can actually reduce risk to your overall organization by reducing your cost structure and diversifying your supply base to economies that are removed from the fluctuations of that of your home country and your core markets, and by providing access to a larger and more flexible labor pool.

"One of the things that global sourcing does is it distributes the operations across multiple geographies and multiple teams," says Debashish Sinha, former outsourcing principal analyst at Gartner Group and now a managing director of advisory services at neoIT.

"Globalization actually de-risks the operations of a company by diluting the country risk. It also reduces the risk of not being able to find an appropriate level of talent at an appropriate price point. It improves resilience because it gives companies access to a much larger resource pool."

## MYTH 2: OFFSHORE SUPPLIERS USE SLAVE LABOR

**Reality.** Unlike offshore manufacturing, where in rare cases slave labor and child labor have been found in sweatshops and assembly plants, the globalization of services is typically executed by college-educated workers. The workforce is generally from the middle or even upper-middle classes of their respective countries. While there are some exceptions, the conditions at most of the delivery facilities in countries such as India and the Philippines rival or exceed those of the U.S. and U.K.

What's more, the jobs that are offshored tend to be in the top 25 percent of wage earners in those countries and carry a much higher degree of stature to the people of those countries than they do to people who perform the same functions in the United States or Europe. As a result these workers tend to take more pride in their work and in their job positions.

## MYTH 3: THE INFRASTRUCTURE IS POOR AT OFFSHORE CENTERS

**Reality.** The IT parks in India, the Philippines, China, Hungary, Mexico, Ireland and other big offshoring locales rival those of Silicon Valley in terms of telecommunications, power generation and other infrastructure—and in many cases, even exceed them. For example, the telecom lines in most offshore supplier offices in India have satellite uplinks to North America, Europe and other parts of Asia, and most major buildings have 24-hour instant backup systems. This is something that does not exist in most U.S. cities.

IT equipment and capabilities rival those of onshore suppliers, as offshore suppliers know that speed and processing capabilities are key to winning and keeping new businesses.

"One potential client came to us with some graphic needs and asked if our capacity can handle it? We have 35 G-series Macs, high-end four-color scanners, and handle at least 20,000 graphics a month. Can we handle it? I told him we can handle 10-X that," said Ernest Cu of Manila-based SPI Technologies.

## MYTH 4: YOU LOSE CONTROL WHEN YOU OFFSHORE, OFTEN TO PEOPLE AND COMPANIES IN A FARAWAY LAND

**Reality.** Modern technology has all but eliminated the risk of losing control of offshore processes. New Internet-based technology solutions now make it possible for companies to get a clear view—right on their desktops—of the happenings at their offshore captive centers or at their offshore suppliers.

Supply chains at remote locations can now be managed with the click of a mouse, or in many cases automatically as a new customer order is placed or a process change becomes necessary. Third-party offshore advisory firms can also help add a level of control with people on the ground that understand the market and can verify the credibility of suppliers. Nonetheless, to ensure the clients retain control, appropriate contract language should be built in with any offshore suppliers (see chapters 14 and 15).

To be sure, some loss of control is inevitable when work is moved from within your own walls to any outsourcer, but the fact that the outsourcing is in Russia rather than Boston should no longer make a difference. In recent times, many of the suppliers have incorporated in the United States or other Western nations and are therefore subject to that nation's legal system.

Take Unilever, for example. The London-based consumer goods company—whose brands include Dove, Bertolli, Knorr, Lipton and many more—has both wholly-owned captive offshore centers as well as multiple third-party suppliers across several different countries performing an array of different job functions. Still, Unilever manages to control all of them quite seamlessly.

## MYTH 5: OFFSHORING MEANS LOWER QUALITY

**Reality.** While cheap labor is clearly the biggest driver for moving services offshore, often offshoring brings with it higher quality because of the transfer of non-core services from the client to an offshore supplier that specializes in those particular services.

Sometimes, higher quality is actually the primary driver of moving a business process offshore. And in many cases, quality certifications such as ISO, SEI-CMM Level 5 and six sigma have been the standard for years at major offshore suppliers. In some cases, the process certification at the onshore client facility is lower than that at the offshore location.

Part of the quality difference is because the offshore workers are often much more experienced and educated than the onshore workers who would be performing the same tasks. Data-entry clerks in India and the Philippines often have college degrees, and a slightly more skill-intensive back-office process might require an MBA in India, where in the U.S. even a bachelor's would be a plus.

"The offshore service providers that win out will not just be the low-cost alternatives," says Toby McCullagh, a London-based analyst at Bear Stearns who covers outsourcing companies. "It will be those that can service their global clients and have the project management capacity and workflow methodology necessary to split an engagement into its necessary parts and deliver that solution to its clients on a cost-effective basis."

## MYTH 6: ONLY LARGE COMPANIES OFFSHORE

**Reality.** While offshoring began with large companies, the industry has evolved so quickly that even small firms with less than 50 people can improve their workflow processes and reduce costs by offshoring services.

Thousands of small and mid-sized firms already offshore everything from financial and accounting services to IT, human resource functions and customer service. Some companies are built from day one with offshore outsourcing as a key part of their business plans, and in many cases all their work is performed offshore, with only the management team based in the U.S. or Europe.

"Because of technology, small businesses can now behave like big businesses and can outsource services anywhere—whether it's California, Nebraska or Bangalore," says Fabio Rosati, CEO of Elance, a Sunnyvale, California company that focuses on services procurement and management technologies and whose online marketplace hooks up small companies with outsourcers both onshore and offshore. Rosati says about 60 percent of the work that is contracted through Elance is performed across borders.

## MYTH 7: ALL OFFSHORE SUPPLIERS ARE THE SAME

**Reality.** This statement could not be further from the truth. As in any fast-growing industry, there are those offshore suppliers that were set up to only take advantage of the offshoring trend and there are those that are dedicated to quality service and building long-term relationships. For this reason, it is important to conduct a thorough analysis of your own outsourcing needs and to perform strict due diligence on potential suppliers before making any decisions. And again, hiring a third-party sourcing advisor is tantamount to starting off right.

The crème of the crop of offshore suppliers have billions of dollars invested in planning, infrastructure, recruiting talented management teams and retaining dedicated, highly skilled workforces.

Offshore suppliers vary from country to country. While India currently holds the bulk of the global offshoring business, other countries are catching up and actually growing at faster clips, especially as offshoring expands beyond the traditional software developing and call center functions to include a multitude of other business processes and services. In many cases, as services become commoditized and move down the value chain they are moved to countries where labor is cheaper, allowing higher-end countries like India to move up the chain to more value-added services.

There are already significant offshore service operations in at least a dozen countries, including Mexico, Canada, Brazil, Costa Rica, Ireland, Russia, and throughout Eastern Europe. More countries are developing core expertise each year and increasing their market share of the offshoring services industry.

## MYTH 8: SERVICES GLOBALIZATION WILL ALWAYS SAVE YOU MONEY

**Reality.** It is probably a fair statement that you will almost always be able to find people in other countries that can perform any given task for a less amount of money. But that does not mean that offshoring will always save you money. Sometimes, the cost of managing a contract can reduce or even eliminate the savings from cheaper labor. What's more, sometimes there are services that simply were not meant to be offshored.

The outsourcing of services implies that not only is there a company out there that can perform the services for a lower cost and higher quality, it also implies that your company can transfer those resources to something of higher value.

> *"In order to be good at outsourcing, you also have to be good at innovation."—David Frankel.*

"In order to be good at outsourcing, you also have to be good at innovation," says London-based consultant David Frankel.

Too many companies approach offshoring with the idea that they can "sign the contract, throw it over the wall and forget about it." Offshoring does not work that way. You need constant monitoring, oversight, setting expectations, holding suppliers accountable, and ongoing due diligence. In other words, you have to manage the offshore relationship as you would any other key business partner.

And for those services that are ripe for offshoring, finding the right supplier in the right country and correctly managing that relationship can be the difference between a 40 percent reduction in costs and simply breaking even.

## MYTH 9: OFFSHORING IS A FLASH IN THE PAN

**Reality.** The offshoring of services has been around since the mid-1980s. It is simply a byproduct of a mature, rapidly globalizing IT and business services industry. Offshoring will be around for as long as there are wage and talent discrepancies around the world, and as long as there are companies that can be more profitable by concentrating on their core products and services—and that isn't about to end anytime soon.

"The structure of the world has changed," says Craig Barrett, CEO of Intel. "The U.S. no longer has a lock on high-tech white-collar jobs."

Adds Mimi Strouse of Warburg Pincus: "What has moved offshore so far is insignificant. The big players are going to upscale their outsourcing efforts, and there is a recognition that a lot of this can be done offshore."

## MYTH 10: OFFSHORING IS BAD FOR THE ECONOMY

**Reality.** As we pointed out in Chapter 3, there will be some short-term job displacements caused by the offshoring of services. However, the overall economic impact of offshoring is positive as it creates more profitable companies, drives down prices, fuels progress and over time actually creates jobs in both buyer and provider countries.

While some companies, especially in the United States, have shied away from or downplayed their offshore operations in response to public backlash, others have embraced it to their advantage. British Telecom, for example, is rapidly expanding its use of offshore services in both captive centers and third-party suppliers. Instead of being on the defense, BT officials have publicly stated their plans and have been quick to let the public know of the vast cost savings that have been achieved, which in turn have been passed on to the consumer in the form of price reductions.

In a well-documented study in August 2003, global consulting firm McKinsey & Co. concluded: "Not only is the United States fully able to withstand these changes, as it will be able to create jobs faster than offshoring eliminates them, but the current debate misses the point. Offshoring creates wealth for U.S. companies and consumers and therefore for the United States as a whole: that is why companies choose to follow this course. Offshoring is just one more example of the innovation that keeps U.S. companies at the leading edge of competitiveness across multiple sectors ... Offshoring not only captures every bit of economic value, dollar for dollar, that exists in the U.S. economy prior to the decision to offshore, but it also creates a net additional value for the U.S. economy that did not exist before."

While the buyer country economies stand to gain substantially, the supplier countries tend to gain even more. "We gain, but not to the same degree as poor countries, for which it's a big breakthrough," says Jagdish Bhagwati, international economics professor at Columbia University and author of the book, *In Defense of Globalization*.

Chapter 6

# The Competitive Advantage of Offshore Nations

Traditionally in outsourcing (onshore), the question of location is subordinate to choosing the most qualified provider. For large corporate projects, there is no particular advantage or disadvantage bestowed upon a company based in a particular city, state or province. However, this is not the case in offshoring, as the choice of countries can determine a myriad of unique benefits (or penalties).

Over the past decade, countries have been racing to develop their competitive advantages in services globalization. 2003 witnessed significant growth in services exports in countries such as India, the Philippines and Russia. At the same time countries such as the Czech Republic, Poland, Hungary and Mexico emerged from relatively insignificant markets to legitimate contenders for market share in the growing IT and Business Process Outsourcing market.

Some of these countries have exploited their natural and geographic advantages, while others have developed niches by focusing resources and education on certain areas. For example, one of the biggest drivers of services globalization has been the advent of the 24-hour business cycle. Companies no longer operate in one time zone. As a result, being in a different time zone has in many cases developed into an advantage, whereas just a few years ago it would have been considered a disadvantage.

Similarities in language and culture also distinguish supplier countries. Canada and Ireland hold obvious language and cultural advantages when dealing with U.S. clients, for example, but India and the Philippines run a close second. This has allowed all four of

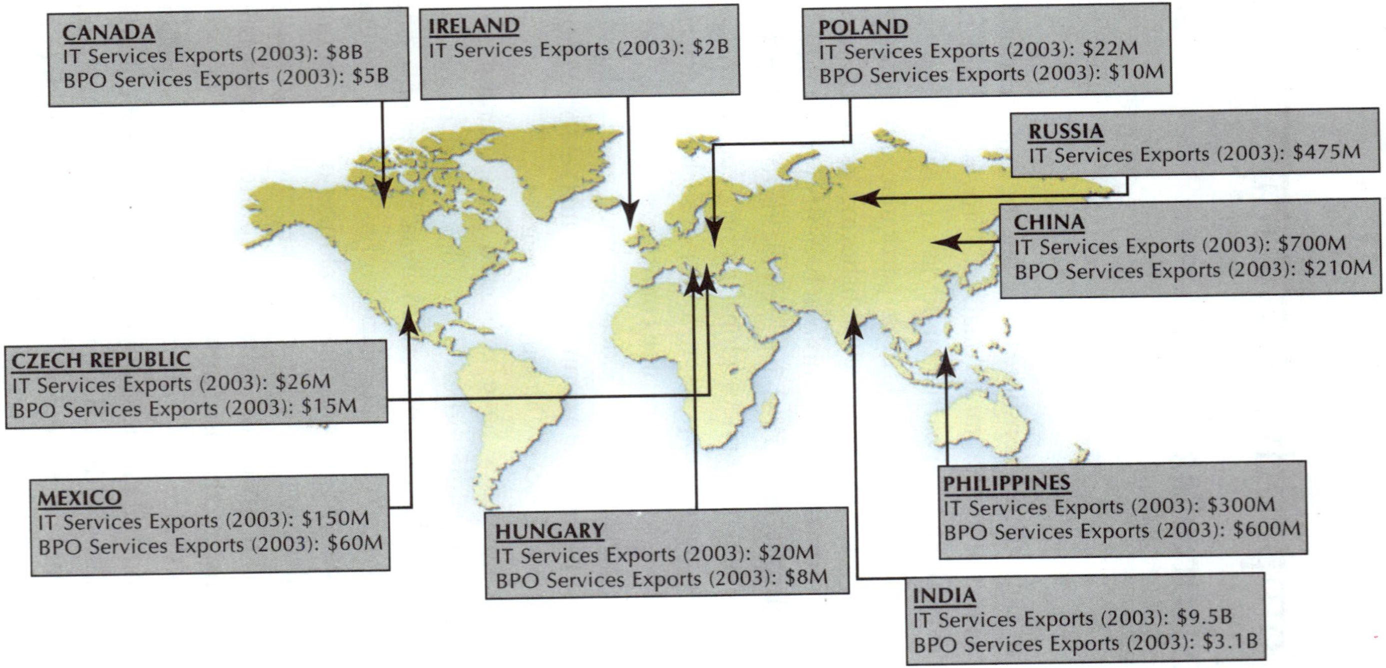


FIGURE 6.1
Key offshore country IT and BPO industry exports.

those countries to develop competitive advantages over other countries in certain services such as call centers.

Technological skill and expertise in advanced sciences, defense communications and other areas has enabled China, India and Russia to gain a competitive advantage in those areas, whereas a long history of software expertise has cemented India's leadership in that sector.

These competitive advantages, however, are constantly changing as new, lower priced labor markets move up the value chain and price other countries out of the market, pushing those countries still further up the value chain.

"The winners are likely to be those that can offer a full range of services, from consulting to systems design, implementation and integration," says Bear Stears analyst Toby McCullagh.

While there are numerous differentiating characteristics of countries, the most important characteristics fall into three categories. **Exogenous factors** are those characteristics that define pervasive environmental factors that any service provider can do little to impact or mitigate relative to the services that they deliver. **Catalyst factors** drive the attractiveness of the location as an offshoring destination. **Business environment factors** define the direct advantages, competencies of suppliers and supportive business issues.

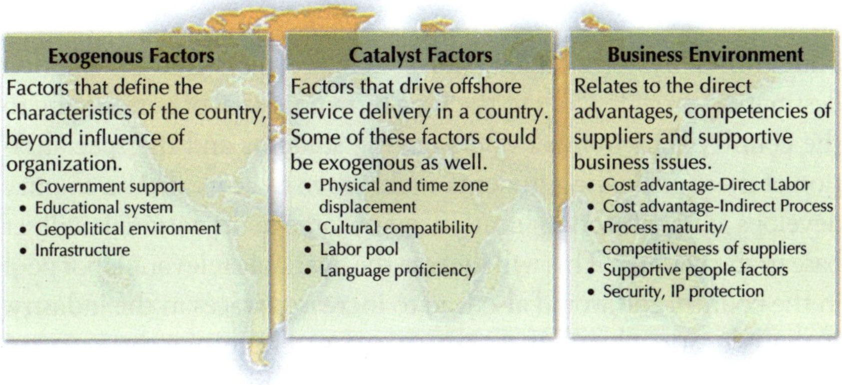


FIGURE 6.2

Factors influencing the selection of the outsourced location.

## EXOGENOUS FACTORS

**Government Support.** Offshoring is a sunrise industry. The advantages of offshoring are proven; furthering these advantages would need support of the local government in terms of providing investment incentives, tax incentives, subsidies, importance given to developing infrastructure, ease of starting a business and intellectual property protection etc. Most local governments in offshoring destinations have realized the importance to give impetus to this industry and have set up special task teams to advice and recommend strategies that need to be adopted. Role of nodal agencies also is key, in lobbying with the government and providing the industry with benefits and incentives. A major reason for the growth of IT and BPO industries in many countries (India, Ireland, Czech Republic etc.) can be attributed to the support provided by government either directly or through nodal agencies and industry associations. China still suffers in part due to lack of rigor in protecting intellectual property. India's highly deliberate and glacial legal system mandates contract enforcement outside of India to ensure timely resolution of disputes. A great example is the trade association in India, NASSCOM. This organization has been instrumental in propelling the Indian software and BPO industry forward.

**Educational System.** Education system prevalent in the offshoring destination provides cues to the long term potential of outsourcing to the country. The number of graduating students and the specialization of these graduating students could prove to be vital. As a country develops as an offshoring location, many large multi nationals will set base in the country. This will squeeze the available relevant labor pool in the country and would also lead to increased wages in the industry. If the educational system is not geared to churn out the required number of graduates in the specialized areas, this hampers the long-term offshore plan of an organization. The quality and depth of education in the specialized streams of study also needs to be looked into. Other than the formal education system, non-formal IT training institutions contribute significantly to the growing demand for skilled manpower for this sector (e.g. NIIT, Aptech, SSI in India).

**Geopolitical environment.** Countries differ in their inherent stability due to exposure to social and geopolitical risks that could lead to unrest, hence disrupting normal business operations. It is critical to note that not just the service provider's competency but factors like geopolitical or social risk impact the success of an offshore engagement. Other than risks, other factors that need to be considered include memberships of the country into unified trade associations with others. Being associated with such bilateral trade treaties provides for easier and profitable trade terms. WTO memberships, EU Accession etc. are some such factors that could help develop a country.

**Infrastructure.** Communications infrastructure enabling both access to and rapid provisioning of high speed digital communications is an important enabler of both IT and BPO offshoring. Such infrastructure is associated with countries that have a deregulated competitive telecom framework. Equally important, though often taken for granted, is a clean supply of continuous electrical power. Countries with superior infrastructure, e.g. Mexico, Canada, Philippines, Ireland, Malaysia, parts of Eastern Europe, and Brazil have the equivalent of the roadways and deep harbors of yesteryear in terms of their impact on attracting international business. On the communications side, service providers can partly address local bottlenecks and shortcomings in the country's communications infrastructure through the deployment of private satellite and microwave communications networks, gain access to international communication networks, and bypass aging local plants. Consequently, India, with a relatively weak infrastructure, has a large number of service providers that have counterbalanced this with sufficient capital investments to enable the continuity of electrical power and high speed digital communications necessary to support the country's offshore leadership position.

## CATALYST FACTORS

**Physical and time zone displacement.** Increased physical distance diminishes the opportunity for personal interaction, direct observation and service provider management, and contract enforcement simply by walking around. Companies concerned with their ability to manage and control service providers within the same city, state, province, or country would be unlikely to consider a superior service provider a great distance away. As physical distance corresponds to time zone displacement and as opportunities for management and control through direct observation diminish, so do opportunities for real time collaboration whether by phone or video conferencing. While both factors are surmountable, albeit at additional costs and personal inconvenience, many firms choose instead to opt for nearshoring as an option. These firms trade higher labor and total costs in favor of greater opportunity for peace of mind with direct management and control.

**Cultural compatibility.** Cultural affinity goes beyond language, enhancing communications and facilitating the formation of strong personal relationships. Consequently, when a high degree of high value-added interaction is required, the nuances of culture differences can be the most critical enabler. For high risk, complex IT development projects where a high degree of trust is required in the relationship between service provider and client, shared culture can accelerate the trust building process. For voice BPO operations culture affinity is especially essential for unstructured, unscripted interactions which require not just information dissemination but empathetic response in employee communications or rapid bonding to drive the trust that can benefit cross selling interactions. For U.S. and U.K. based firms, the Philippines and Canada offer the closest cultural fit. Similarly Eastern Europe is emerging as a strong contender to offshore service delivery for Western European countries. Again, additional investment in employee training, including immersion in popular culture (TV shows, movies, sports etc.), can help bridge the cultural gap.

**Labor pool.** The size of the available labor pool is a direct result of the population in the country. Within the total labor pool, the cumulative base of labor employed in IT and BPO segments right now would only be a minor proportion. The availability of labor for IT and BPO industry is not a factor which would impact the short term plans of any outsourcing organization. But, when the plans are for long term and the organization plans to increase its footprints in the offshore destination considerably in the future, this could become a factor of importance. The total labor pool in China is much more than that of India but the number of people working in IT and BPO industries in India is much higher than that of China. This would continue for the next 4–5 years unless China forays into this industry with higher focus. Availability of IT and BPO labor pool is a major issue for Eastern European countries, Ireland, Canada etc. which could impact the long term prospect of volume driven businesses being offshored to these locations.

**Language proficiency.** Certainly, it is preferable to do business with service providers who speak your language. Yet, communication capability is not just speaking the same language but includes accents, use of colloquialisms and even body language. In IT development, shared language between client and service provider teams is essential when a high degree of interaction is mandated due to loosely defined requirements. In voice-based BPO (customer contact, employee support, telemarketing, collections, financial services etc.) speaking the same language is obviously a requirement that favors the Indian and Philippine BPO providers in securing customers from the U.S. and U.K. respectively.

Language proficiency is not just about English. Requirements for Non-English proficiency to address specific countries/communities also exist. Voice based BPOs in Mexico address the Spanish speaking population in the US; Eastern European countries like Czech Republic, Hungary and Poland have German specialized agents.

## BUSINESS ENVIRONMENT FACTORS

**Cost advantage (Direct and Indirect).** Countries have fundamental differences in their economic structure, gross national product, trade balance, monetary and fiscal policy and other factors that impact the prevailing cost of labor. As cost savings are the major driver for offshoring, the labor arbitrage opportunity is often a key consideration. This is an opportunity largely driven by 'country decision' rather than 'supplier decision'. Once a country has been selected, labor costs for identical roles between companies are trivial relative to the cost savings derived from offshoring to low cost labor centers such as India, Philippines, Russia, China, Vietnam, etc.

Direct cost savings relate to the wage differences between outsourcing country and offshore location for similar profile of employees. Typically, for a US outsourcing organization, the difference in wages could be as high as 60–70 percent when outsourced to India/China and the savings would be in the range of 25–40 percent if offshored to countries like Ireland and Canada. The direct wage differences appear to be extremely attractive to go forward with offshoring. However, there are other costs that are part of any offshoring contract. These would include costs incurred for setup, physical infrastructure, travel, communication/network along with many other hidden costs. Thus any outsourcing organization needs to look at the "Total Cost of Outsourcing" rather than direct cost savings while choosing the offshoring location.

**Process maturity/competencies of suppliers.** Countries differ significantly based on the extent to which they possess distinct competencies. These variances are partly explained by a country's educational system and the existence of proximate industries that can provide fertile training ground and an available pool for the required skills and competencies. For example, Russia and parts of Eastern Europe offer a high degree of technical talent highly useful in engineering driven programming but less relevant to traditional package-oriented business applications. Russia has a large R&D sector, with over 25,000 annual graduates in physics, mathematics, informatics and computer engineering. This background provides Russian computer programmers with more flexibility in crafting software for technical applications. Again, however, companies can address competency gaps by investing in large in-house training programs and through partnerships with universities and individual professors for access to more technically advanced capabilities.

In addition to inherent competencies, experience in handling related projects in the past gives the service providers an extent of competence. The employees, having worked on the project/process, become experts in the domain and are able to be more productive thus resulting in much higher offshoring gains. Less amount of training and hand-holding is required which saves time and cost of the outsourcing company.

**Supportive people factors.** Availability of the labor pool with the required qualifications and skill sets is just one part of the people factor in offshoring. BPO units across the globe are affected by high attrition levels. The reasons for high attrition levels are many; some of it can be attributed to the nature of work (which is repetitive in most cases), increasing number of new setups (poaching from competitors is common), leaving for higher education, problems with working in shifts for long time period etc. The pitfalls of high attrition are many—recruitment and training costs are incurred frequently; affects process maturity; loss of continuity of process, productivity loss etc. are some major issues. Need for specific training (accent neutralization, developing cultural compatibility etc.) to cater to foreign markets is another people issue in this industry.

**Security and IP protection.** One of the major concerns of outsourcing per se, is security. This is more so in the case of offshore outsourcing. Importance of data security is being understood and implemented slowly by some of the offshore locations. Piracy is rampant in most countries that are major offshoring locations. Except for the developed economies, there are no stringent laws for intellectual property protection as well. However, in recent times, most governments have realized the need to formulate and implement these laws so that the interest of the outsourcer is safeguarded. It would take some time for these to come in force operationally.

Based on these factors we can accurately compare the different offshore and nearshore outsourcing destinations.

## THE LEADERS

### India

India has embraced the IT and BPO outsourcing businesses with a fervor that has enveloped the whole country and made it a welcoming environment for companies looking to set up captive centers and find offshore suppliers. Early-mover advantage and critical mass have made it the most attractive global location. India's core capabilities include application maintenance, application development, e-business and packaged software implementation. The growth of the BPO industry has caused a plethora of suppliers to pop up across the nation, although established areas of BPO expertise are yet to mature. Many companies have outsourced business processes such as contact centers, data entry, accounting, credit card processing, collections and data processing services with positive results.

Offshoring experience, a huge English-speaking and college-educated workforce, government support and infrastructure and an inherent cost advantage all make India a top choice, especially for high value-added services.

| ITO Rating | BPO Rating | Risk Factor | Summary |
|---|---|---|---|
| ● | ● | Government Support | India is a favorite outsourcing destination of the Fortune 500, with an appointed national minister specifically for IT. Software Technology Parks of India (STPI: www.stpi.soft.net) provides infrastructure services in over 15 cities around the country.<br>The government has established a policy for no taxes on export profits until 2009 for BPO companies with 100% income tax exemption for the first 5 years and 50% for an additional 2 years.<br>India boasts flexible policies for FDI—100% FDI possible in the automatic route.<br>However, despite all of these advantages red tape still exists in many government and regulatory bodies in the country. |
| ● | ● | Labor Pool | India comprehensively leads other outsourcing destinations in this factor, exhibiting exponential growth in the labor pool in the last 10 years. The IT labor pool alone is expected to touch 2 million within the next 10 years. Over 2,100,000 fresh English-speaking graduates per year including 460,000 IT graduates. |
| ◒ | ◒ | Infrastructure | Infrastructure reliability varies depending upon the region and supplier. For example, the infrastructure is adequately supported and very reliable in IT parks, as redundant telecommunications and power are a standard in the parks. However, outside the parks, the power and telecom is not dependable and may cause interruptions in service levels. There has been extensive commercialization in key cities of the country and privately-owned office space is now readily available. |

*continued*

| ITO Rating | BPO Rating | Risk Factor | Summary |
|---|---|---|---|
| | | | The public utility services are not fully developed. |
| ● | ● | Educational System | India boasts a very good presence of public and private universities with many recognized as global leaders. For example, the six Indian Institute of Technology (IIT).<br>**Top universities for recruiting:**<br>**Technology Institutes**<br>• Birla Institute of Technology & Science<br>• Delhi College of Engineering<br>• Indian Institute of Technology<br>• Indian Institute of Science<br>**Management Institutes**<br>• Faculty of Management Studies, University of Delhi<br>• Indian Institute of Management<br>• XLRI, Jamshedpur<br>In addition, premier research institutions like IISc exist as incubation centers for new technology enterprise development. |
| ● | ● | Cost Advantage—Direct/Indirect | Direct: Typical salaries for a programmer with 2–3 years experience range from $6000 to $12,000 per year while a typical salary in BPO for similar experience would be about $5500 to $7000 per year.<br>Indirect: Telecom and infrastructure costs are relatively lower than other locations. The need for training for process driven work is minimal; accent neutralization is a key training module adopted by most voice based BPO outfits. |
| ● | ● | Quality | Indian companies have a lead over other offshore countries in process-based certification. Over 50 companies have a SEI-CMM 5 level certification out of a total of 74 around the world |

*continued*

| ITO Rating | BPO Rating | Risk Factor | Summary |
|---|---|---|---|
| | | | (October 2002, http://seir.sei.cmu.edu/pml/). Other companies have been early adopters of ISO and neoQA certifications.<br>IT companies in the country have grown profitably and sizably over the years. Repeat businesses and references are a major source of new business growth, due to the proven track record for delivering as promised. Tier 1&2 BPO companies have good quality standards while Tier 3 companies need to bring in more quality focus to deliver consistently. |
| ◒ | ◒ | Cultural Compatibility | Compatibility is good in the major metro areas, but may struggle with cultural nuances in remote locations. In order to reduce some of these gaps, most of the established BPO and IT companies have instituted cultural training and accent neutralization. Once the BPO industry moves into smaller cities these training costs could emerge as a major recurring expense item. |
| ● | ● | Time/Distance Advantage | A 12-hour time difference with North America enables overnight delivery of services. This unique advantage helps American organizations achieve true 24/7 internal operations and customer service. The "time zone" advantage provided by India can also become a strategic enabler for many West Europe and Asia Pacific based organizations. |
| ● | ● | Language Proficiency | English proficiency is excellent in the major metro areas but may suffer as companies look at more remote locations. Indian BPO companies have instituted accent neutralization training as a form of quality control and to continually expose their people to the cultures they serve. |

*continued*

| ITO Rating | BPO Rating | Risk Factor | Summary |
|---|---|---|---|
| ● | ● | Geopolitical Environment | Being the largest democracy in the world the country is host to numerous political parties with contrasting views on economic policies. Over the last 10 years, the effects of such contrasts have been negated by a planned economic reforms approach which was adopted by the parties in power. It is expected that economic policies would delineate from political overtures in the future.<br>The capital market in the country still is closely linked to stability of the government. Political issues with Pakistan and China exist, however, these are not expected to hamper the economic outlook of the country in the short term. |
| ● | ● | Process Maturity/ Competitiveness | India has a well-developed IT/BPO industry with suppliers capable of handling high volume as well as varied technology businesses. Tier 1 and 2 BPO companies have established a stable presence. However, there also exists a large number of small BPO companies that do not have the required competencies to address the outsourcing market. These companies drive down prices to grab projects and fail to deliver.<br>Scalability is not an issue for many companies as investment capability exists and the required manpower is also available. |
| ● | ● | Supportive People Factors | The large pool of relevant workforce does not present many challenges for recruiting employees in the IT and BPO industries. Training needs are limited to accent neutralization and specific process training in the BPO industry.<br>Despite these positive factors, attrition levels in BPO companies are higher |

*continued*

| ITO Rating | BPO Rating | Risk Factor | Summary |
|---|---|---|---|
| | | | (about 25–30% in non-voice and more than 35% in voice based) than other outsourcing destinations. Employee retention is the most critical people issue that BPO companies face today. Anti-poaching agreements, better perks, higher compensation levels, employee satisfaction, scope for higher education-all of these tools are being employed to arrest this aggravated attrition situation. |
| ● | ● | Supportive Economic Scenario | GDP growth was one of the highest ever for the country in 2003. FDI inflows and reserves also touched a record high in 2003. The Indian economy is fast becoming service driven. Special initiatives taken by the IT ministry and nodal agencies for IT have helped foster the growth of the sector. |
| | | | ○ **Low** ◒ **Medium** ● **High** |

TABLE 6.1

Evaluating India as an outsourcing destination.

## Philippines

The Philippines has been a steep success story in the early part of the 2000s, as offshoring of business processes and, to a lesser extent, IT has helped boost the country's economy and increased its awareness among companies worldwide. The Philippines is considered the second most attractive location after India for IT but is on par with India for BPO. English fluency and compatibility with Western cultures explains the Philippines' popularity as a source of call center operations.

The Philippines' strengths are call center operations, business processes such as finance and accounting, sales, human resources and logistics, as well as transcription services and animation. The country's central location also makes it a strategic location for shared services centers.

| ITO Rating | BPO Rating | Risk Factor | Summary |
|---|---|---|---|
| ◒ | ◒ | Government Support | In order to facilitate business growth, the Philippine government has initiated a task force focusing on the development of five specific areas of business process and IT services: BPO (shared services), ASM/ADM, animation services, transcription services and contact centers.<br>Companies setting up in IT parks have an attractive tax holiday for up to 6 years (other advantages include: exemptions from all government fees, licenses, dues, export taxes, etc.)<br>Flexible labor and union rules, deregulated telecom policy etc. are other key support provided by the government for the industry. |
| ◒ | ◒ | Labor Pool | The Philippine education system produces over 380,000 graduates each year, with over 15,000 focused on technology. This has led to a labor force of over 75,000 focused on IT and BPO exports. Despite the large labor pool, companies often find the project manager supply often does not meet demand.<br>Large scale technical training programs that are being started in the country are expected to enhance this labor pool in the future. |
| ● | ● | Infrastructure | The Special Zones created by the 1991 act has enabled a system of IT parks that support the IT export industry. The past presence of USA military bases left behind a solid telecom infrastructure. |

*continued*

| ITO Rating | BPO Rating | Risk Factor | Summary |
|---|---|---|---|
| ◒ | ◒ | Educational System | The university system is very good and is aided by private colleges focusing on IT and BPO related education. Universities churn out 70,000 IT graduates each year.<br>The country has the highest net enrollment in public and private higher education institutions for the age group 17–34.<br>**Top universities for recruiting:**<br>• The University of the Philippines<br>• De La Salle University<br>• Ateneo de Manila University<br>• Mapua Institute of Technology<br>• Far Eastern University<br>• Centro Escolar University<br>The bulk of the new recruits in multinational companies come from the first three and the balance from the rest. |
| ● | ● | Cost Advantage—Direct/Indirect | Average salaries for a programmer with 3–5 years experience range from \$6500 to \$11,000 per year. Average salaries for a call center agent with 3–5 years experience range from \$3500 to \$6000 per year.<br>Labor costs account for nearly 62% of the operating expenditure of call centers in Philippines. Centrally located in the Asian region; comparatively lower travel cost from Europe and North America. |
| ● | ● | Quality | Many Philippine companies have not focused on SEI-CMM but some ISO certifications exist. As a general rule, Philippine companies consistently deliver better quality in BPO than ITO engagements.<br>In order to further develop quality organizations in the ITO/BPO industry, the Philippine government is setting up |

*continued*

| ITO Rating | BPO Rating | Risk Factor | Summary |
|---|---|---|---|
| | | | a program to offer incentives for certification. |
| ● | ● | Cultural Compatibility | Influence from a USA presence since the 1930s has enabled good cultural compatibility. In fact, at one point the Philippines was under US rule for almost 50 years. The political system is one of the oldest working democracies in Asia and is modeled after the United States-including free press. |
| ● | ● | Time/Distance Advantage | The Philippines offers a similar time zone position advantage to India that US firms find convenient. |
| ● | ● | Language Proficiency | Influence from a USA presence since the 1930s has also resulted in very good English proficiency-Philippines is the third largest English speaking country in the world. The overall literacy rate for the country is 94% and the Philippine government claims that 72% of the population is fluent in English. Most service providers are able to hire proficient labor and do not have to offer accent neutralization training. |
| ◒ | ◒ | Geopolitical Environment | Philippines conducted Presidential elections in May 2004. With the re-election of president Arroyo expect additional major economic reforms in the country.<br>However, political insurgency is common in the country and is relatively more prone to domestic incumbency. Even as the country understands the importance of setting up new age businesses, lack of uniformity in policies exists. This could have a direct effect on the business continuity assurance that most outsourcing companies look for. |
| ◒ | ● | Process Maturity/ Competitiveness | Voice based BPO operation is one of the key competencies of the |

*continued*

| ITO Rating | BPO Rating | Risk Factor | Summary |
|---|---|---|---|
| | | | Philippines and contributes more than 50% of export revenues. There are approximately 100 call centers and BPO companies in the Philippines.<br>Almost all call centers in Philippines have only single location operations-low disaster recovery solutions.<br>Since the population as such is small, quick scaling up of operations is a major issue with these BPO companies. |
| ◒ | ● | Supportive People Factors | Availability of personnel while scaling up operations is one of the key HR challenges for BPO operations in Philippines. Thus large-scale BPO operations which require multi-location presence may face challenges.<br>Compared to other outsourcing destinations, attrition rates are much lower in the country, which leads to lower cost for recruiting and training and enhanced productivity levels. |
| ● | ● | Supportive Economic Scenario | GDP grew by 4.5% in 2003, compared to 4.4% in 2002. GDP growth was driven by the services sector, which grew by 5.9%. Due to the political instability and domestic incumbency factors, currency (Peso) has seen a depreciating trend on the Dollar. Domestic inflation was pegged at 3.4%. |

○ **Low** ◒ **Medium** ● **High**

TABLE 6.2

Evaluating Philippines as an outsourcing destination.

## Russia

Challenges still exist as Russia struggles to emerge from the former communist regime, but the country has managed to put together a competitive offshoring industry, especially for many high-level research and development projects. Erratic government, an unstable economy, lack of managerial talent, and poor consumer protection and intellectual property laws continue to cause problems. However, look for Russia to become a more stable business economy in the next 5–7 years (and a more stable choice for offshoring). Over the next few years we expect to see Russian suppliers bidding on more contracts, as they already have more personnel working in R&D than any other country in the world and currently rank third in the number of scientists and engineers per capita. The current cost structure in Russia offers substantial price performance benefits for customers in achieving their software development requirements.

In general, salaries are higher in Moscow in comparison with other cities, but due to the fact that the top companies are from St. Petersburg, Novosibirsk and Nizhni Novgorod this difference is not so significant. St. Petersburg may be considered the most viable option for companies looking for partners in Russia. It is less expensive than Moscow and has a better-developed infrastructure than Novosibirsk.

Russia's core competencies include internet programming, e-commerce, web design, web server applications, web database applications, software/hardware reengineering, CASE systems, telephony based solutions, wireless, radio technology and security systems.

| ITO Rating | BPO Rating | Risk Factor | Summary |
|---|---|---|---|
| ○ | ○ | Government Support | It has only been in the last two or three years that Russia has seen a big turnaround and the government has moved from a course stifling the development of high technology to one that shows an understanding of high-tech's place in the modern world. Old laws and tax structure make doing business difficult, but a new treaty with the US shows some easing of rules and restrictions. |

*continued*

| ITO Rating | BPO Rating | Risk Factor | Summary |
|---|---|---|---|
| | | | The federal program, 'Electronic Russia,' has been made a reality, and the Ministry of Industry and Science has been instrumental in realizing St. Petersburg's first IT-techno park on Vasilevsky Island. |
| ● | ○ | Labor Pool | The third largest pool of engineers and scientists per capita makes Russia an attractive proposition. Top universities are a great source of technical graduates with top skills and new ideas. Currently, Russia has about 20,000 professionals focused on IT exports.<br>Engineering talent is another major advantage that Russia has. Designing of complex and large algorithms and designs in engineering are their competency areas— "a fall out of the defense requirements of the cold war".<br>New locations are competing with Moscow and St. Petersburg for a larger pie of IT services—cities like Nizhny Novgorod where Intel has started a development center due to its cost-effectiveness and considerable talent pool. |
| ◒ | ◒ | Infrastructure | Cost of bandwidth remains relatively high and the infrastructure is poor except in major cities such as Moscow and St. Petersburg. |
| ● | ● | Educational System | Leading universities in the major cities (Moscow, St. Petersburg, Yekaterinburg and Novosibirsk) provide excellent technical graduates. Focus has been given for courses in Math and Physics which augurs well with the need for analytical skills in programming.<br>**Top universities for recruiting:**<br>• Moscow State University<br>• Nizhni Novgorod State University<br>• Novgorod State University<br>• Novosibirsk State University |

*continued*

| ITO Rating | BPO Rating | Risk Factor | Summary |
|---|---|---|---|
| | | | • Penza State Technical University<br>• St. Petersburg State Polytechnic University<br>• Ural State University<br>**Key Research Institutes:**<br>Moscow (Institute for Computer Aided Design, Institute for Problems in Informatics, Institute for System Programming) St. Petersburg (Institute for High Performance Computing & Data Bases, St. Petersburg Institute for Informatics and Automation) Yekaterinburg (Institute of Engineering Sciences) |
| ● | ● | Cost Advantage—Direct/Indirect | Labor costs are moderate and a typical salary for an IT programmer with 2–3 years experience range from $7000 to $13,000 per year depending upon required skills and project size. |
| ◒ | ○ | Quality | ISO adoption is widespread but only 3 SEI-CMM certified companies exist: Luxoft (Moscow, Level 4), Argus-Neva (St. Petersburg, Level 4), Telma (N. Novgorod, Level 4) |
| ◒ | ○ | Cultural Compatibility | Cultural compatibility, especially when it comes to IT is good. Russians tend to be able to work from moderately defined specs and adapt as necessary to client needs. |
| ◒ | ◒ | Time/Distance Advantage | Hour time difference between New York and Moscow/St. Petersburg is 8 hours. Russia has 11 time zones. |
| ◒ | ◒ | Language Proficiency | Top managers typically have a good level of proficiency in English. Mid-level and lower-level staff have less proficiency. This can be a issue but if carefully monitored, can be managed through language training. Proficiency in other languages is low. |

*continued*

| ITO Rating | BPO Rating | Risk Factor | Summary |
|---|---|---|---|
| Medium | Medium | Geopolitical Environment | After the political turmoil in the late nineties, Russia now has a stable government and a firm economic policy. In the initial years, the US found it difficult to tide over the image of the erstwhile Soviet Union as the 'evil empire'. This scenario is fast changing and US clients are currently much more willing to work with Russian service providers. |
| Medium | Low | Process Maturity/ Competitiveness | There are about 200 IT services companies operating in St. Petersburg alone employing more than 5000 programmers. Borland, LG, Lucent, Motorola and Sun are some of the companies that have developed captive operations.<br>Project management skills lack the experience in handling large volume outsourced projects. Intellectual property protection and data security are other challenges faced by US and Western European clients. |
| High | Low | Supportive People Factors | Quality manpower for executing complex IT service assignments available in Russia, specifically higher in St. Petersburg. Russian employees have shown much more loyalty to their employers compared to other IT outsourcing destinations—lower attrition levels. |
| Low | Low | Supportive Economic Scenario | Real GDP growth of 4.3%. High inflationary trends exist in the economy (estimated to be close to 15%—consumer prices). |

○ **Low** ◒ **Medium** ● **High**

TABLE 6.3

Evaluating Russia as an outsourcing destination.

## China

With the support of the Chinese government and rapid economic growth, China could very well be the offshore location of the future. However, until the country strengthens its English-as-a-second-language programs, there will always be limitations to the types of services in which it can be competitive. China's software industry (including exports) is expected to grow to over $30 billion by 2005. Software companies are in China not because of labor quality but because it is a buyer's market. Simpler work that can be done in India can also be done in China, but scalability and value chain growth will take time. Chinese companies have a higher IT spend than Indian companies, and this is fueling the domestic buyer market. Software companies realize that having a presence in China not only lowers their costs but gives them a marketing office to Chinese companies as well.

Currently, some 5,000 software companies employ about 200,000 professionals in China, but most of the business is concentrated among a handful of major firms in each segment. For example, two firms, UFSoft and Kingdee Software, control about 60% of China's $150 million accounting software market. Even in market segments where Chinese firms have been less dominant, the government hopes to strengthen domestic firms rather than hand the market over to foreigners. Only a few Chinese software firms have revenues above $100 million and most have little if any access to capital needed to fund R&D.

China's IT services market has been growing at close to 20 percent a year and is expected to continue that pace, bringing the total value of the country's technology services market to $8.9 billion by 2006. China's growth rate is second only to India.

Much of that growth is due to its vast labor force of 734.3 million people. In spite of this size, only about 10 software enterprises have over 1000 employees, and 55 percent of them employ less than 50 people. Chinese companies account for 32 percent of total software sales, with foreign enterprises covering the remainder. China now has about 160,000 people working in the software industry, with another 300,000 involved in research, applications, and education.

In 2001, the State Development Planning Commission (SDPC) and Ministry of Information Industry (MII) jointly named 10 national software industrial bases (Beijing, Shanghai, Dalian, Chengdu, Xi'an, Jinan, Hangzhou, Guangzhou, Changsha and Nanjing). Located next to universities and scientific institutions as well as some major software enterprises, the industrial bases are expected to become the country's software development, production, service and export centers.

China's core competencies include low-end PC-based application development, application maintenance, QA testing, systems integration, data processing and product development.

| ITO Rating | BPO Rating | Risk Factor | Summary |
|---|---|---|---|
| ○ | ○ | Government Support | Industry growth efforts have been held back because of trade policies, regulations and censorship. Expect the growth issues to slowly disappear as China assimilates with the governing rules of the WTO. The establishment of Special Economic Zones (SEZs) in 2000 gives China a head start on this process, as the five SEZs have been working toward operating in line with international practices. The five SEZs are Shenzhen, Zhuhai, Shantou, Xiamen cities and Hainan Province.<br>• China's 15 Software Industrial Parks<br>• Shenyang NEU Software Park in Liaoning<br>• Changsha Chuangzhi Software Park in Hunan<br>• Jinan Qilu Software Park in Shandong<br>• Chengdu Tuopu Software Park in Sichuan |

*continued*

| ITO Rating | BPO Rating | Risk Factor | Summary |
|---|---|---|---|
| | | | • The North Software Park in Beijing<br>• Pudong Software Park in Shanghai<br>• The South Software Park in Zhuhai of Guangdong<br>• Beijing Software Park<br>• Saiboweir Software Park in Shenzhen Of Guangdong<br>• Nanhai Software Science Park in Guangdong<br>• Hainan Software Industrial Park in Hainan<br>• Software Park in Hangzhou Development Zone of Zhjiang<br>• Jiangnan Software Park in Zhejiang<br>• Xietong Software Park in Xi'an of Shaanxi<br>• Harbin Software Park in Heilongjiang |
| ◒ | ○ | Labor Pool | Over 200,000 professionals work in IT roles. Universities provide a source for excellent technical talent, and produce approximately 50,000 new graduates each year. Unfortunately, many migrate to western pastures. Language and cultural compatibility present barriers to successful engagements.<br>***Expect the 2008 Olympics to greatly enhance the English speaking pool.* |
| ● | ◒ | Infrastructure | Infrastructure in major IT centers such as Beijing and Shanghai is very good. Second tier cities are in the process of significant infrastructure build out. |
| ● | ● | Educational System | Universities graduate very competent technical graduates. Chinese Academy of Sciences is located in over 100 campuses and another 1000 higher education institutions have training programs related to software and IT. is aided by private colleges focusing on IT and BPO related education. Universities churn out 70,000 IT graduates each year. |

*continued*

| ITO Rating | BPO Rating | Risk Factor | Summary |
|---|---|---|---|
| ● | ● | Cost Advantage—Direct/Indirect | Labor rates are very low and present a very attractive value proposition (Think India 10 years ago—low-cost workers and lots of them). Typical IT salaries range from $5500 to $9000 per year for a programmer with 2–3 years experience.<br>Compared to other outsourcing destinations, China has the lowest real estate and power costs. |
| ◒ | ◒ | Quality | Manufacturing quality has not yet influenced the IT sector and quality needs a lot of attention to bring process discipline. ISO certifications have seen the greatest adoption, with close to 58,000 ISO 9000 certifications. China has just one company that has reached CMM Level 5, but has a number of companies certified to CMM Level 3. |
| ○ | ○ | Cultural Compatibility | Isolation and censorship created a void in terms of western influence and knowledge. No strong affinity towards western culture. |
| ● | ● | Time/Distance Advantage | Despite the fact that China's boundaries span five time zones, all of China operates on a single time zone. |
| ○ | ○ | Language Proficiency | Isolation and censorship has not aided English proficiency. English is not the language of choice. An initiative to improve and integrate with western influences, in preparation for the 2008 Olympics, will significantly enhance this proficiency.<br>The Chinese government has taken other proactive steps to bridge this disadvantage—more than $5.4 Billion invested in English education in Universities. |
| ◒ | ◒ | Geopolitical Environment | Being a communist regime, tight political control exists. But of late, relaxed economic initiatives have been |

*continued*

| ITO Rating | BPO Rating | Risk Factor | Summary |
|---|---|---|---|
| | | | taken up by the government. IT industry has been identified for major support in the future. China's government structure allows for significantly faster decision making. Whether the decision is good or bad, the state has the power to enforce the law and the citizens are forced to accept the policies. |
| ○ | ◒ | Process Maturity/ Competitiveness | BPO is a less mature and relatively new industry in China. Chinese BPO industry is well tuned to take advantage of outsourced work from Japan due to its proximity, cultural fit and the low penetration by other BPO industries like India in Japan. Leveraging the image of being a cost effective manufacturing hub.<br>China could be one of the best sources for non-voice transaction processing work in the future.<br>China lacks good quality track record in the IT industry. It has also not been able to leverage the image of volume driven manufacturing base in the BPO space. |
| ○ | ◒ | Supportive People Factors | Relatively small base of English speaking graduates pass out every year in China leading to low availability of personnel for voice based BPOs. High migration rate of English speaking graduates compounds this issue. However, there exists workforce for handling non voice transaction processing jobs. |
| ● | ● | Supportive Economic Scenario | China's GDP (PPP) is around $6 trillion boasting a huge economy, stable domestic market. Even with this large base, the economy has been booming for the last 2 years. The contribution of the services sector in GDP has been increasing consistently. |
| | | | ○ Low ◒ Medium ● High |

TABLE 6.4

Evaluating China as an outsourcing destination.

## Canada

Canada is considered a very safe though somewhat costly nearshore alternative. Outsourcing to this nearshore nation will not save a lot of money but will not present many headaches. With a favorable exchange rate, this option delivers cost savings relative to outsourcing to a US company. It's a good option for companies that are ready to expand outsourcing initiatives to locations outside of the U.S., but are not yet ready to fully manage a more traditional offshore location like India or the Philippines. Canada's core competencies include application development, application maintenance, e-business, call center (basic inbound and outbound; high-end multimedia voice; on-line financial services; and tech support).

| ITO Rating | BPO Rating | Risk Factor | Summary |
|---|---|---|---|
| ◒ | ◒ | Government Support | The Canadian government provides tax breaks for IT related exports and NAFTA enables a free trade market in IT services. |
| ◒ | ◒ | Labor Pool | Technically skilled manpower capable of handling high-end work are available in Canada. The Canadian workforce possesses skill sets comparable to those in the US and Western Europe and superior to countries like Philippines and China. Approximately 35,000 postgraduates specialized in Math, Engineering and related streams emerge every year in Canada. |
| ● | ● | Infrastructure | Canada has a well developed infrastructure, similar to that of the US. Telecom, power and related infrastructure exists in most areas. |
| ● | ● | Educational System | Provincial and territorial governments have the responsibility for the education system. A strong university and college system exist in Canada. |

*continued*

| ITO Rating | BPO Rating | Risk Factor | Summary |
|---|---|---|---|
| ◒ | ◒ | Cost Advantage—Direct/Indirect | Labor rates are attractive compared to the USA, and the favorable exchange rate makes them more attractive. Typical IT salaries range from $25,000 to $50,000 per year for programmers with 2–3 years experience. BPO salaries range from $18,500 to $28,500 for experienced personnel.<br>Infrastructure costs are also lower than US, with cheaper real estate, telecom and power. However, compared to Asian offshore locations, costs are much higher. |
| ● | ● | Quality | Canadians have a strong quality focus. Many companies are ISO certified and many others have SEI-CMM initiatives. CMM initiatives similar to that of the U.S.; 11,635 ISO 9000 certifications. Also important to outsourcing buyers is that many Canadian call center customer service representatives have made it their career. Subsequently, there is a much lower turnover rate for call centers than in the U.S. |
| ● | ● | Cultural Compatibility | Offshore outsourcing service providers in India or Russia offer online training to teach their team about American popular culture, familiarizing them with baseball, soap operas, and popular TV shows. Canadians, however, know about "Survivor," so that type of training is not needed. |
| ○ | ○ | Time/Distance Advantage | If you are looking for the 24/7-time advantage, Canada is not the obvious choice, but if you plan to manage the work through conference calls and daily interaction, the minimal time differences are a lot easier to manage than a 12-hour difference. |
| ● | ● | Language Proficiency | English is the official language—spoken by about 60% of population, with French proficiency among 25% of population. |

*continued*

| ITO Rating | BPO Rating | Risk Factor | Summary |
|---|---|---|---|
| ● | ● | Geopolitical Environment | Good political climate. Capitalistic environment; level of interference in industrial issues low resulting in a self-contained business environment.<br>Its paramount political problem continues to be the relationship of the province of Quebec, with its French-speaking residents and unique culture, to the remainder of the country. |
| ● | ● | Process Maturity/ Competitiveness | Mature IT and BPO industries. Large employee base currently working in these industries. High quality focus.<br>Historic association with companies in the US has helped develop the image that Canada is one of the best near shore destinations for outsourcing.<br>Strong IP protection and data security laws exist. |
| ● | ● | Supportive People Factors | Lower attrition levels as compared to the US and some of the other outsourcing destinations. Need for training low for both IT and BPO operations.<br>However, employable population is much less compared to some other outsourcing locations like India—scaling up operations quickly or setting up large units could be difficult in the long run. |
| ● | ● | Supportive Economic Scenario | As an affluent, high-tech industrial society, Canada today closely resembles the US in its market-oriented economic system, pattern of production, and high living standards. GDP growth rate of about 3.3% (Est.) and Inflation (consumer prices) at 2.2% (Est.) |

○ Low ◒ Medium ● High

TABLE 6.5

Evaluating Canada as an outsourcing destination.

## Ireland

Like Canada, Ireland offers a lot of peace of mind, but is lacking if your primary objective is cost savings. Stability, English proficiency, cultural compatibility and quality processes are Ireland's selling points. This nearshore location is a great option for European shared services centers, but with a small (and talented) labor pool, the large multinationals are eating up this market quickly, saving little resources for smaller, slow-to-move firms.

Ireland's core competencies include application development, application maintenance, call center, customization, translation, production and distribution, technical support, product customization, software testing and fulfilment.

| ITO Rating | BPO Rating | Risk Factor | Summary |
|---|---|---|---|
| ● | ● | Government Support | The IDA and the Ministry of Industry & Trade have been very active in establishing Ireland as the European shared services capital. A $330 million Technology Education Investment Fund was established in 1997, and favorable tax laws have been a great incentive for firms. |
| ○ | ○ | Labor Pool | Ireland produces only about 5000 technical graduates a year. Additionally U.S. companies such as Dell, IBM and Microsoft, with development centers in Ireland, are increasing competition for and cost of labor. This combination makes it difficult for companies to scale up fast. |
| ● | ● | Infrastructure | Very good. |
| ● | ● | Educational System | The university system is excellent, but produces only 5000 technical graduates per year. |
| ○ | ○ | Cost Advantage | Labor rates are attractive compared to the USA. Typical IT salaries range from $25,000 to $35,000 per year. |

*continued*

| ITO Rating | BPO Rating | Risk Factor | Summary |
|---|---|---|---|
| ◒ | ● | Quality | Focus on ISO and Six Sigma has aided in the quality of services, but Irish companies have not invested in CMM certification to the levels that India has. |
| ● | ● | Cultural Compatibility | Very good. |
| ◒ | ◒ | Time/Distance Advantage | Depending upon your coast, Ireland is a 5–8 hour time difference. |
| ● | ● | Language Proficiency | English speaking country. |

○ Low ◒ Medium ● High

TABLE 6.6

Evaluating Ireland as an outsourcing destination.

## UP AND COMERS

### Czech Republic

The Czech Republic offers a great opportunity to set up near shore shared service locations for organizations concentrating in the European markets including Germany and UK. The location is perfect to handle processes that require constant interaction with principals. Compared to Asian locations, wages are higher and if cost saving is the primary objective for outsourcing, Czech Republic may not be the place to set up operations. Government support, English/German proficiency and cultural compatibility are the country's key selling points. Presence of MNC IT majors could drive up wages as well as restrict scope for smaller players who might be left wanting for quality manpower in the future.

The Czech Republic's core competencies include application development, application maintenance, enterprise application integration and maintenance, call center, customization, translation, back office operations.

| ITO Rating | BPO Rating | Risk Factor | Summary |
|---|---|---|---|
| ● | ● | Government Support | The Government of Czech Republic through the Ministry of Industry & Trade provides excellent support for investments in IT and BPO companies in the country. Have an extremely flexible foreign investment policy. Other than tax incentives for investments in the IT industry, the government also provides subsidies to the tune of 35–50% for training and up to 50% on business expenses. |
| ◒ | ◒ | Labor Pool | About 10% of the population is computer literate and about 14,000 students graduate with IT specialization. Total workforce of 11 million across all industries. |
| ● | ● | Infrastructure | Good Telecom. Real estate and public infrastructure present in Czech Republic. Better than countries like Hungary and Poland. |
| ● | ● | Educational System | Strong fully developed educational system. Has the highest completion ratio in Secondary education after US. About 20,000 university graduates with Math, Engineering, IT specialization pass out each year in the country. |
| ◒ | ◒ | Cost Advantage—Direct/Indirect | Comparable wage rates to Hungary and Czech Republic. Average wages in IT range from USD 28–35/hour. |
| ● | ● | Cultural Compatibility | Very good. Proximity to UK helps in being culturally close to countries that outsource. |
| ● | ● | Time/Distance Advantage | Proximity to UK and other Western European countries. Advantages in running operations that need constant interaction with the principal. |
| ● | ● | Language Proficiency | Large English speaking labor pool. Competencies to handle other languages like German an added advantage. |

*continued*

| ITO Rating | BPO Rating | Risk Factor | Summary |
|---|---|---|---|
| ● | ● | Geopolitical Environment | Stabilized government setup exists that gives impetus to industrial growth in the country by way of incentives for investments in the manufacturing and services setup. |
| ◒ | ◒ | Process Maturity/ Competitiveness | Offshore services market growing at more than 10% annually. There are about 300 call centers in the country with close to 9000 employees. Suitable for European organization as they expect service providers to understand their business nature and speak their language.<br>Intellectual Property security is one issue in which considerable amount needs to be done by the country. |
| ◒ | ◒ | Supportive People Factors | Availability of labor for IT and BPO companies is not a major issue in the country. However, the small population of the country could hamper growth of the sector in the long run. Comparable attrition rates with that of other European countries (15–20%). Limited cost of training in voice based BPO centers as need for accent neutralization is less. |
| ◒ | ◒ | Supportive Economic Scenario | Czech economy went through a recession in 1997 & 98 and further has recovered. GDP rose by 3.3% in 2000 and by 3.1% in 2001. The economy slowed down in 2002 due to significant strengthening of the exchange rate and economic stagnation in EU countries. In 2003 GDP increased in constant prices by 2.9%. Recent surge in the industry, albeit slow was fuelled by the growth in foreign investments to the country. |

○ **Low** ◒ **Medium** ● **High**

TABLE 6.7

Evaluating the Czech Republic as an outsourcing destination.

## Poland

The sheer size of Poland compared to Czech Republic and Hungary makes available a large labor pool. In recent times, Poland lost out on foreign investments and the economy was near stagnant. This led to major fiscal problems for home grown IT companies that has adversely affected their plans to expand and scale up. Leveraging the specialized talent available would provide Poland a competitive edge in this industry among other Eastern European countries. Competent labor, linguistic skills, telecom infrastructure, political stability and proximity to Western Europe are some of the factors that could drive the industry.

Poland's core competencies include application management, web-based application development and maintenance, back office operations—HR and Accounting.

| ITO Rating | BPO Rating | Risk Factor | Summary |
|---|---|---|---|
| ◒ | ◒ | Government Support | Recognition of the importance for supporting investments in IT and BPO happened late with the Polish Government. Even as the focus on providing incentives for local entrepreneurship and flexible FDI policies with incentives for investments exists, it is not as high as other European countries. The government needs to take a greater effort specific to these industries and market it well to develop the country as a major outsourcing destination. |
| ● | ● | Labor Pool | Compared to the Czech Republic and Hungary, Poland has the most number of graduates entering the workforce every year. The total available workforce is about 18 million. About 40,000 IT graduates pass out every year from Universities. |

*continued*

| ITO Rating | BPO Rating | Risk Factor | Summary |
|---|---|---|---|
| ● | ● | Infrastructure | Poland has a liberalized telecom policy, well developed public infrastructure with good transport connectivity. |
| ● | ● | Educational System | Poland has a strong fully developed educational system. They have a high number of universities and colleges in comparison with the Czech Republic and Hungary. |
| ◒ | ◒ | Cost Advantage—Direct/Indirect | Charge rates in the IT services business are close to $28–35. This gives considerable savings on outsourcing. Rates are almost on par with that of Czech Republic. |
| ● | ● | Cultural Compatibility | Poland has strong cultural affinity to Germany and rest of Europe. This is expected to further strengthen after accession to the EU. |
| ● | ● | Time/Distance Advantage | Proximity to the UK and other Western European countries support a nearshore advantage in running operations that need constant interaction with the principal. |
| ● | ● | Language Proficiency | English is widely spoken as the second language in the country. A large proportion of qualified manpower is proficient in German while Spanish, Italian and French languages are also prevalent. |
| ● | ● | Geopolitical Environment | A stabilized government setup exists in the country. No major political risk. |
| ◒ | ◒ | Process Maturity/ Competitiveness | Currently there are about 15 companies employing 3000 people in BPO and outsourced IT services operations in the country. These industries are in a very nascent stage and are in the process of acquiring volumes and maturity. |
| ◒ | ◒ | Supportive People Factors | Compared to Hungary and Czech Republic, there is high availability of skilled manpower in Poland. Attrition |

*continued*

| ITO Rating | BPO Rating | Risk Factor | Summary |
|---|---|---|---|
| | | | levels are similar to that of other European countries. Understanding of process issues and legal systems of UK and Germany reduces the cost of training and makes the country more acceptable for HR, Accounting and Legal outsourcing work. |
| ○ | ○ | Supportive Economic Scenario | The GDP (PPP) of the country was about three times that of Czech Republic in 2002. The growth in Real GDP (PPP) was only 1.2% but is estimated to touch 5% mark by 2004. Economic reforms started in the 90's and the efforts taken gained recognition by way of accession to OECD (1996), NATO (1999) and EU (2004). However, in the last two years Poland has been losing out on FDI inflows—average reduction of 1/3 in two years while inflow into Czech Republic and Hungary has increased considerably. |
| | | | ○ Low ◒ Medium ● High |

TABLE 6.8

Evaluating Poland as an outsourcing destination.

## Hungary

Hungary offers opportunity to set up nearshore shared service locations for organizations concentrating in Western Europe. Availability of employable labor in the Industry is one of the key issues that Hungary will have to mitigate. Proximity and access to other European countries need to be leveraged. Domestic IT infrastructure development and the enforcement of IP laws will have to be taken up seriously by the government to foster growth.

Hungary's core competencies include application development, application maintenance, product development, back office operations.

| ITO Rating | BPO Rating | Risk Factor | Summary |
|---|---|---|---|
| ◒ | ◒ | Government Support | Hungary's government has established a separate task force for furthering the growth trends in the IT and BPO industry. Several tax and direct incentives are provided for green field projects with foreign investment. Initiatives to augment the IT infrastructure, e-governance, internet penetration, etc. are also in progress. |
| ◒ | ◒ | Labor Pool | With a total labor pool of about 4.2 million, Hungary has one of the lowest proportions of IT graduates to total graduates in the higher education system. |
| ● | ● | Infrastructure | Liberalized telecom structure. Good real estate availability. |
| ◒ | ◒ | Educational System | Hungary's educational system consists of 89 higher education institutes of which 30 are universities. Universities provide a solid background in theory, while colleges give more practical and short-term courses. Approximately 10,000 engineering and IT graduates every year. |
| ◒ | ◒ | Cost Advantage—Direct/Indirect | The average monthly salaries for an IT programmer with 2–3 years experience ranges from $13,000 to $14,000 per year. The average fully loaded charge rates range from $15 to $18. |
| ● | ● | Cultural Compatibility | Cultural affinity to Germany and France. Compatible with other European countries. |
| ● | ● | Time/Distance Advantage | Ideal to serve Western European markets as a nearshore location. |
| ○ | ○ | Language Proficiency | Hungarian primary language. Use of English as a medium in higher education. Other languages are German and French. |
| ● | ● | Geopolitical Environment | Low/moderate political risk. No major violence threats. |

*continued*

| ITO Rating | BPO Rating | Risk Factor | Summary |
|---|---|---|---|
| ◒ | ◒ | Process Maturity/ Competitiveness | Recession in the economy in general and the resultant lack of demand for high end products have driven local IT firms to reduce prices following which many firms had to realign scales and operations. This has mostly affected the SME IT firms. Low process maturity. |
| ○ | ○ | Supportive People Factors | Limited number of IT and engineering graduates passing out every year. |
| ◒ | ◒ | Supportive Economic Scenario | Hungary has made the transition from a centrally planned to a market economy, with a per capita income one-half that of the Big Four European nations. Inflation has declined substantially, from 14% in 1998 to 4.7% in 2003; unemployment has persisted around the 6.4% level.<br>Germany is by far Hungary's largest economic partner. GDP growth at 3.5% (2002) and 2.9% (2003); FDI—$1.3 billion (2002) spurred by Greenfield investments. Growing budget and current account deficits. |

○ **Low** ◒ **Medium** ● **High**

TABLE 6.9

Evaluating Hungary as an outsourcing destination.

## Mexico

Mexico's proximity to the USA and participation in NAFTA is helping to position this country as a strong nearshore option for US companies. The wage structure is very attractive but weak government support and few service providers of significant size and scale have inhibited strong growth. Companies that are risk averse and looking to lower geo-political risk or especially interested in satisfying Spanish-related needs, will find Mexico a good alternative.

Mexico's core competencies include application development and maintenance, Spanish language call center, and data processing.

| ITO Rating | BPO Rating | Risk Factor | Summary |
|---|---|---|---|
| ◒ | ◒ | Government Support | Headed by the Ministry of the Economy, the Mexican government has defined a comprehensive program to support and grow the local IT Industry. ProSoft is the government's multi-lateral initiative to stimulate growth among existing IT companies and encourage the creation of new ventures. Designed with input from local companies, IT associations, educational institutions and entrepreneurs, ProSoft is currently in its early stages of execution. |
| ◒ | ◒ | Labor Pool | Total labor pool of about 40 million. IT and engineering graduates amount to 20,000 per year. Mexico has approximately 110,000 highly educated, bilingual resources currently employed in the private and public IT industry. |
| ● | ● | Infrastructure | Although the market was deregulated in 1994, Mexico's telecommunications infrastructure remains dominated by the former state monopoly, Telmex. The overall quality and availability of telecommunications infrastructure in Mexico is quite good. The infrastructure in major cities such as Mexico City, Guadalajara, Monterrey and the key resort destinations tends to be on par with US cities. |

*continued*

| ITO Rating | BPO Rating | Risk Factor | Summary |
|---|---|---|---|
| ◒ | ◒ | Educational System | The Mexican university system consists of both public and private universities with campuses in most primary and secondary metropolitan areas. |
| ◒ | ◒ | Cost Advantage—Direct/Indirect | The average salary for a Mexican programmer with 2–3 years of experience in Mexico City would be approximately $1,500 per month, or $18,000 annually. The average, fully-loaded charge rates for the same programmer would be $18–26 per hour. Average salary for BPO employee with 2–3 years experience ranges from $3000 to $15000 per year. |
| ● | ● | Cultural Compatibility | Mexico has very close commercial and cultural ties to the US. Liberal visa norms allow Mexicans to frequently travel to the US. |
| ● | ● | Time/Distance Advantage | Compatible time zone with US. |
| ○ | ○ | Language Proficiency | The primary language in Mexico is Spanish, however, English is commonly used in the IT industry, especially in the key industry centers such as Mexico City, Guadalajara and Monterrey. |
| ● | ● | Geopolitical Environment | Low political risk. No major violence threats. A stable government is in place which is aiming to increase the inflow of FDI into the country. Combating the vastly prevalent corruption in the system has also been identified as a key issue to be managed. |
| ◒ | ◒ | Process Maturity/ Competitiveness | The export market for IT services in Mexico is still immature, with few companies that have any significant portion of revenues attributed to services exports. Of the top three domestic IT services firms, not more than 40% of their revenues are attributed to services exports. Low process maturity. Best for low-end jobs. |

*continued*

| ITO Rating | BPO Rating | Risk Factor | Summary |
|---|---|---|---|
| ◒ | ◒ | Supportive Economic Scenario | Mexico over the years has registered slow growth in economy. The key reason for this is the slowdown in the US economy which is the biggest trade partner. GDP growth at 2.9% (2003 Est.); FDI—$13 billion (2002). |

○ Low ◒ Medium ● High

TABLE 6.10

Evaluating Mexico as an outsourcing destination.

## Malaysia

Malaysia, as a country of approximately 22 million people and a low wage structure, is a good location for smaller operations, although scaling up can be difficult. This market will definitely be a better prospect over the next five years.

The government has made significant investments in improving the infrastructure, especially in and around Kuala Lumpur with projects such as developing Cyberjaya and Putrajaya as "intelligent-cities." The Multimedia Super Corridor project and other government investments have enticed firms such as Motorola and IBM to set up IT and shared services operations. Many global players such as CSC are active in the country. Local companies such as MayBank and global companies such as BASF are beginning to outsource for local operations and boosting prospects for suppliers.

Malaysia's core competencies include application development, application maintenance, e-business, multimedia & animation, and data processing.

## THE LATE STARTERS

### Vietnam

Vietnam has one of the cheapest labor forces in the world, with thousands of programmers who are eager to work for less than $5,000 a year—well under the going rate in India. It also has a fairly good educational system. However, the infrastructure in Vietnam leaves a lot to be desired in terms of electrical and telecommunications systems, roads, buildings, banking, etc. Vietnam also got a late start in offshoring, and its government is only now getting behind it full force. English proficiency is a big problem too, and the 14-hour time difference with California hasn't helped. But Vietnam shows promise, and its goal to enter the World Trade Organization in 2005 could provide a significant boost to its offshoring industry.

Vietnam's core competencies include applications development and maintenance.

### Singapore

Singapore is one of the leading locations for Asian headquarters for many global firms. Its high quality telecom infrastructure and good technical talent has also made it a preferred destination for data centers, but compared to other Asian locations, Singapore is expensive.

Singapore's core competencies include application development, application maintenance, and systems integration.

### Central America/Caribbean

Companies that are looking to manage risk through diversification of supplier bases, or those that are particularly interested in satisfying Spanish language-related needs, will find Latin countries as good alternatives.

We are seeing a growth in call centers in this region, especially in Costa Rica and some Caribbean Islands. A leading U.S. call center company, Tele-Tech, has multiple locations in this region.

Core competencies for Central American and Caribbean neighbors include application development, application maintenance, data center outsourcing, and Spanish language call centers.

## Brazil/South America

Brazil is a sleeping giant that is beginning to be recognized as a large potential pool of offshore labor. While not quite as inexpensive as India and China, it is substantially cheaper than Canada and Ireland and also offers several other advantages over its offshore rivals. For one, the time zone is only one to three hours later than New York (one is off daylight savings when the other is on). With 180 million people, it is the world's fifth largest country in terms of population and has a robust education system that churns out tens of thousands of IT graduates each year. English language skills are fair—not as good as India but better than Mexico—and cultural compatibility with the U.S. is high. What's more, it is politically stable and has a sound infrastructure in Sao Paulo and Rio de Janeiro, the hubs of the offshoring industry.

Among the companies with major offshore initiatives in Brazil are GE, Goodyear and Xerox, and IBM announced in 2004 that Brazil is one of three countries in which in plans to build major offshoring centers.

Core competencies in Brazil include application development, application maintenance, web development, and systems integration.

Chile and Argentina are also rapidly ramping up on their offshoring industries. Argentina has a high number of English speaking residents and a large number of college graduates, while Chile offers a modern infrastructure and a stable political economy. Both of them have high IT talent pools and time zone advantages.

However, the labor pools in both countries are smaller and more expensive than Brazil's.

## Israel

Israel is another up-and-coming offshoring hub. In spite of its small size, the country churns out thousands of IT graduates each year, and has a workforce of about 30,000 software engineers. Software exports are close to $1 billion a year. The country offers several key advantages including strong government support, ample infrastructure, proximity to Europe, high English language skills and cultural compatibility. However, political instability and terrorist activity have increased the perceived risk of offshoring to Israel. In spite of this, several major companies including IBM, Microsoft, Motorola and HP have offshoring initiatives in Israel.

Israel's core competencies include application development, application maintenance, and high-end IT programming.

## South Africa

South Africa has a low level of outsourcing penetration, and internal problems persist, hampering real growth. Still, South Africa has some advantages. Several local companies have evolved into booming technology enterprises, although for the most part IT talent emigrates elsewhere. Native English is a huge plus and a 30-mile stretch between Johannesburg and Pretoria is evolving into the country's first technology hub. A Presidential Task Force has been formed to consider ways to improve IT infrastructure and industry support, including a $23 million investment in a technology park in Pretoria.

South Africa's core competencies include call centers, e-business, application development, IT security, low-end contact center and data processing.

## KEY POINTS

- Offshoring represents a distinct sourcing challenge, and selecting a location—or at least narrowing it down to a small list—should be made prior to making a decision about a specific supplier.
- As this chapter has shown, there are a number of viable offshoring locations. The choice of geography need not default to India, the most popular low cost offshoring option. Numerous other locations are emerging as viable offshoring centers, each with their own competitive advantages, including China, the Philippines, Russia, Vietnam, Mexico, Hungary, Czech Republic, Poland and other countries.
- Where to offshore depends not only on cost considerations but on a variety of other criteria as well, including risk profile, project type and the importance of skills such as English language proficiency, IT expertise and cultural compatibility.
- Before answering the question of where to offshore, your firm needs to fully understand its own requirements, its risk tolerance, and the three factors (exogenous, catalyst and business requirements) of potential offshore destinations.

Chapter 7

# Offshore Models

The next step in ramping up the globalization knowledge curve is to gain an understanding of the various types of offshore models. The two obvious types are the offshore supplier model and the wholly owned captive center. But there are a number of other models in between the two that may be the best strategy for your company. Determining which ownership model is best can be just as important as choosing a country and choosing a supplier, if not more so.

The choice of an offshore model depends on a number of factors, especially your goals and objectives for services globalization. Are your outsourcing needs long-term? How much flexibility do you want for future downsizing or expansion? How important is security? How much risk is your company willing to take on by itself? Are proprietary technologies needed to develop the product or service? Are there special skill sets that only your company can teach? How much control is desired?

And if your choice of model is a captive center, then you have another decision to make—do you build it from scratch or do you acquire it?

In the chart at the end of the chapter, we have outlined the advantages and disadvantages of the various types of offshore models. First, let's look at what each type of model entails. We will also give you some examples of companies that have experimented with each type.

## SUPPLIER DIRECT

The advantages of choosing an offshore supplier rather than building your own offshore center are in many ways similar to the advantages of outsourcing rather than keeping the function in-house. Using an offshore supplier brings all the advantages inherent in offshore outsourcing—including low cost—while allowing you to concentrate on your core business. In many cases, these suppliers are better at the outsourced service than your own internal staff, as it is their core business and they want to retain you as a customer.

Over the long term, the average cost of using a supplier tends to be higher than building and running your own offshore center. However, the startup costs tend to be much less, as the infrastructure and facilities are usually already in place by the supplier, and the costs involved with the selection and hiring of staff has already been done for you.

By signing a long-term contract with an offshore supplier, you will in most cases have a designated account manager and a well-defined relationship that maintains a tight focus on the scope, goals and objectives of the project.

Plus, if you later decide that a captive center is better, there are ways of structuring supplier contracts that allow the client to acquire the resources if desired at a later date.

There are hundreds of such relationships already successfully operating in offshore locations around the world, ranging from simple data entry and call center tasks to high-level BPO and IT service agreements. Clients range from Fortune 500 firms to small business owners with IT or BPO needs. Some of the leading users of this model include GE, American Express, Verisign and Abbey National, with suppliers such as Accenture, IBM, Keane, TCS, Wipro, Patni, WNS, SPI, Neusoft, Luxoft and others.

## DEDICATED CENTER

If quality control issues preclude you from hiring an offshore supplier, or if you would rather have a tighter hand over cost issues but are not quite ready to make the leap to build your own offshore center, a Dedicated Center relationship is a viable alternative. A Dedicated Center is operated by an offshore supplier, but the staff, equipment and facilities are all exclusively dedicated to your company. These centers tend to involve some shared processes, and some long-term risk sharing, including co-ownership or co-leasing of facilities in some cases. Such relationships are becoming more popular, and tend to be favored by some of the major offshore suppliers such as Wipro and Infosys.

For example, Wipro runs the "Orbit," a highly technical developer assistance center for Sun Microsystems' Solaris Operating System. Now in its tenth year of operations, the center has access to Sun's Wide Area Network and troubleshoots developer needs from around the world. Wipro explains the Sun contract as addressing "the peculiar demands of the developer community, which cannot be addressed by the traditional product support centers and whose requirements are not big enough to be classified as consulting opportunities. Developer support while being complex needs a mix of engineering, troubleshooting and customer interaction skills." Other examples include JPMorganChase which opened a dedicated center in Mumbai, India in 2002 to perform research, loan processing and customer care and Dell Computers which opened a dedicated center in Bangalore, India in 2000 to perform level 1 and level technical support for its customers.

## JOINT VENTURE

Offshore joint ventures can take many different forms. In some cases, the service that is being outsourced is something with its own revenue stream that can be separated out from the rest of the company's business. As a result, and in order to reduce risk, the company will invite an offshore supplier to partner with them in a joint venture relationship in which they each share a percentage of revenue. In other cases, a joint venture can be between two or more global companies, with or without local partners, with the goal of building an offshore center with multiple owners so as to reduce startup costs and operating risks. And in still other cases, the company will spin off whatever unit it is offshoring, and that unit will form a joint venture with local and/or foreign partners.

One example is the strategic joint venture formed in 2000 between Hyderabad, India-based Satyam and U.S.-based TRW to provide IT services to the automotive industry. The venture was 76 percent owned by Satyam and 24 percent by TRW initially, with Satyam managing and operating the venture. From the start, it won a $200 million 5-year contract to service TRW and Northrop Grumman units with enterprise resource management, supply chain management, information systems, e-business applications, and engineering services. After three years, Satyam bought out TRW's share and has since won extensions on long-term contracts with both Northrop Grumman and TRW Automotive. Other examples include Cadmus and Datamatics, which created a joint venture in 2003 to perform a variety of publisher support services and Carreker and Mastek, which created a joint venture in 2003 to perform financial processing services.

## THIRD PARTY TRANSPARENT

Another fast-growing type of offshore relationship is one in which a third-party, rather than the company itself, builds and maintains the offshore presence. In many cases the company is already outsourcing onshore work to the third party, and the move offshore is a natural progression aimed at either reducing the cost to the client, or improving the profit margin to the third-party outsourcer, or both. In most cases, third parties will not attempt such relationships without the complete knowledge and approval of the client company, and will often even involve the client company in planning the offshore center and choosing the location. A disadvantage to this type of relationship is that the costs to the client company tend to be higher than if they were to build the offshore presence themselves, but it does reduce the headaches involved in setting up offshore and can reduce some of the political backlash to the client company.

Accenture has made good use of such models, allowing its client companies to leverage low-priced labor in China and Eastern Europe, for example, without going through the normal pains and risks of starting up in those markets. Accenture accepts the risks, forges all the relationships and establishes the offshore centers, gaining economies of scale by servicing multiple clients either from the same facilities or nearby. Other examples include Keane, which set up operations in Canada in 1997, and in India in 2002 to perform application development services and BearingPoint, which has set up operations in India and has recently expanded their operations in China to perform software development services.

## BUILD-OPERATE-TRANSFER (BOT)

A BOT relationship is one in which the entire offshore center is built by one entity—usually a major offshore supplier—and then transferred to another—usually the foreign buyer. In many such cases, these centers are built specifically for that one client with the intention to transfer ownership as soon as it is complete. In other cases, an existing center is simply sold to a foreign buyer, complete with staff and equipment. The typical scenario, however, is one in which an offshore supplier has been operating a Dedicated Center on behalf of the client, sometimes for several years, and the client decides it wants to own it and run it themselves. Many offshore suppliers would prefer to sell to the client rather than risk losing the contract entirely and seeing the client open its own offshore center.

Aetna and AIG are both examples of major multinational companies that now own their own captive offshore centers, initially built by offshore suppliers. British Airways is one of the few that has actually gone the other direction. After establishing its own offshore center and successfully operating it for several years, the entire operation was acquired by India's WNS, which is in majority owned by Warburg Pincus' private equity unit. Other examples include Aviva, a UK-based insurance company that set up BOT's with both EXL and 24/7 Customer in 2003 to perform both voice based and back office work, as well as Cadence which, in 2003 exercised the transfer option on a Russian operation set up by Mirantis. The Cadence operation performs both software development and research services for the company.

## CAPTIVE CENTER

The ultimate do-it-yourself method is to go out and build your own offshore captive center. This tactic was initially used by companies that already had large physical presences in the countries involved—Citibank's commercial banking in Brazil and Poland, for example, or GE Capital's operation in India. But lately some companies have been building captive centers from the start without any prior experience in the country and sometimes without even a prior offshoring relationship. Hiring a strong third-party consultant with previous experience in the local market can help with the details of how to begin.

The advantage to opening your own center is, if done right, it can help you quickly gain more cost efficiencies and stricter quality control. As a result, the company can often retain more of the profits from the enterprise. This option is usually taken by companies that consider the service they are offshoring to be a core function of their global operations—IBM's systems integration offerings, for example. The disadvantages are high startup costs, a steep learning curve, a high degree of risk and the political difficulties involved with the loss of jobs in the company's home country as job functions are transferred overseas.

A variant of this model is to build your own captive center and then invite third-party suppliers to augment that center in different ways. Agilent Technologies, for example, leased a building in Delhi and set up its own captive, inviting suppliers to participate. In such models, one supplier might be responsible for workforce training, while another might contribute to the startup process and still another might provide resources in a given area of expertise.

In the end, deciding which model to run with is a highly strategic decision and not one to be taken lightly.

"The decision on which model to use depends in large part on the process and the customer," says Warburg's Strouse. "To set up a captive center is not a trivial undertaking. To compete against companies that are established and to find senior level management offshore is a challenge. Many end up sending over expats, and the expats don't know how to manage the local market."

Table 7.1 illustrates the common requirements for choosing an ownership model. In the next section, we discuss each requirement in more detail.

**Control.** Captive is an obvious choice if the company has a need to have total control over the quality, timeliness, process, security, data privacy, etc. of the process in question. With a captive model, companies will have the advantage of offshore operations without the management challenges of working with a third-party.

**Risk.** Captive is a strong choice if the company needs to aggressively manage and retain control over its risk profile, although using a supplier direct model can transfer some of the risks to the supplier and reduces startup risks. Many firms that are tightly regulated tend to manage their offshore business processes in captive centers, especially for critical business areas.

**Higher Start-up Costs.** Typical investments in infrastructure, hardware, software and facility service provisioning require high initial setup costs. These costs are usually significantly higher in building a captive center when compared to outsourcing to a third party who can spread their costs and risks over a wider client base. Also, while the client has to bear all the costs as it occurs in a captive scenario, in a third-party situation the supplier can spread it over the terms of the agreement. Thus, a client will need to have a larger amount of capital available in order to invest in building a captive center.

| Model | Definition | Pricing/ Cost | Control | Management Effort | Operational Risk | Financial Risk | Scalability |
|---|---|---|---|---|---|---|---|
| Supplier Direct | Contract directly with a supplier | Medium | Medium | Medium | Low | Low | High |
| Dedicated Center | Supplier operated, dedicated to your company | Medium | High | Medium | Low | Low | Medium |
| Joint Venture | Split investment and revenues between client and supplier | Medium | High* | Medium* | Medium* | Medium | High |
| Third-Party Transparent | Integrator deal who contracts out to offshore | High | Low | Medium | Medium | Low | Medium |
| Build-Operate-Transfer (BOT) | Supplier build, operate, transfer | Low | Initially Medium, High after transfer | Initially Medium, High after transfer | Initially Medium, Low after transfer | Medium | Very Low |
| Captive Center | Do it yourself | Low | High | High | Low | High | Low |

TABLE 7.1

Common requirements for choosing an ownership model.

**Level may change due to ownership stake*

**Long-Term Cost Reduction.** One of the biggest drivers behind the growth of captive centers is the desire to reduce long-term costs. Doing it yourself can eliminate the mark-up charged by an offshore supplier. However, this is not always the case, as a third-party supplier can have certain economies of scale, local knowledge and domain expertise that can sometimes keep their mark-ups low enough to rival the costs of operating a captive center.

**Location Scale.** When choosing an ownership model it is important to understand the economic feasibility for the location in question, which includes the resource availability, infrastructure, etc.

**Domain Knowledge.** A captive is often the best option when there is a high need for industry or domain-specific knowledge that suppliers in the offshore location do not have.

## DECISION INFLUENCERS

The following criteria may also influence your decision in selecting an ownership model.

**Process Improvements.** Sourcing complex business functions across multiple cultures presents multifaceted challenges. These facts force many companies to look at a long-term globalization strategy, driven not solely by labor arbitrage but also by potential for increased quality and process improvements or business process reengineering.

**Recruiting Benefits.** Historically offshore outsourcing has involved moving work from a developed nation to a developing nation. In this situation, the offshore talent pool often looks fondly on working for a large multinational company headquartered in a developed nation. Hence, attracting the right talent, which is crucial to the success of an offshore BPO center, becomes easier.

**Proprietary Processes.** With captive centers, companies can have more control over proprietary processes or technologies that require greater assurance of security/data privacy than could be provided by a third-party service provider.

**Geographic Shared Services.** When there is a need to coordinate disparate processes serving similar product lines across different geographies, companies will often use offshore captive centers to create a shared services environment. By nurturing this environment, companies can enhance global service levels across functional areas.

**Expansion Opportunities.** A third party supplier will always include a margin for future growth plans of their organization. Client companies may find it advantageous to invest the money in growing their own operations.

**Social Responsibility.** Although not the primary reason for choosing a captive operating model, social responsibility can play a role in the decision process.

## KEY POINTS

- There are two key types of offshore models—the supplier direct model and the captive center—but there are several other in-between models that can be easily adapted to a firm's particular needs and interests.
- Among the other popular types of offshore models are the Dedicated Center, the Joint Venture, the Third Party Transparent and the Build-Operate-Transfer models.
- The choice of an offshore model depends on a number of factors, especially your goals and objectives for services globalization. Several of the key questions surrounding which type of offshore model best suited for your company's strategy include: How long-term are your offshoring needs? How much flexibility do you want? How important is security? How much risk is your company willing to take on? And how much control is desired?

*Chapter* 8

# Supplier Models

As the offshore business models of buyer companies have evolved, so have the models offered by service providers. Recognizing a need for flexibility among clients, suppliers have been highly accommodative of the changing needs of global industries. Pricing models, ownership models, sourcing models and partnership models have all been in a constant state of evolution. Many suppliers have formed strategic ventures with other suppliers to leverage each other's expertise in different areas, or to leverage cross-border competitive advantages.

The management of offshore suppliers has also matured substantially. Back in the late 1980s, some of today's largest offshore service providers started out by providing technical resources onsite to clients in the United States and Europe, in essence providing skilled foreign labor under work visas. This trend progressed to supplier relationships where the work was performed offshore, and later developed into dedicated centers.

Today's dedicated centers are generally physically segregated from the rest of the supplier's operations and from the operations of other clients, with separate networks, secure firewalls and access restrictions.

Supplier models have also become increasingly global in their scope and appeal. Competition from multinational service providers (MNCs) has driven a large part of the global supplier expansion. Most large-scale offshore suppliers now have major presences near their clients, offering consulting services, customer service, marketing and sales; while the MNCs in turn have moved large amounts of their operations offshore in order to compete on price with the offshore suppliers.

Marketing and sales by suppliers is now predominantly U.S. based, and increasingly, so is the delivery side of the business. Offshore suppliers typically will put a client manager on their own payroll, or if the client is not willing to transfer employees will go out and find their own project manager, preferably with client-specific experience or at the minimum with similar project experience. This managerial person will be located near the client, hold responsibility for delivering the services to the client, and will operate separately from the sales and marketing personnel.

Consulting services are also being offered by an increasing number of offshore service providers such as Wipro, which entered consulting through acquisitions, and Infosys, which built its own consulting unit. The message that these firms are trying to send to their clients is that they do not have to give up the strategic aspect of the service offerings when using an offshore supplier as opposed to an onshore vendor such as EDS, Accenture or IBM.

Increasingly, offshore suppliers are also becoming multinational as they realize the changing face of competitive advantages among nations. Tata Consultancy Services (TCS) for example is based in India but now has operations in China where it can take advantage of still lower labor costs for certain tasks that may not require English speakers. Leading offshore service providers such as Cognizant have locations in India and China while TCS also has operations in India and China and a strong operation in Hungary as well.

## MNC OR OFFSHORE SUPPLIER?

How do the service offerings of the large multinational companies (MNCs) compare to the pure-play offshore suppliers?

Currently, the outsourcing of applications support, maintenance and development by client firms is a significant part of the revenue that large services firms generate.

## CASE STUDY Wipro

India-based Wipro was not always an offshore outsourcing firm. It began two decades ago as a manufacturer of computers at a time when IBM and other major tech firms had left the country. For years, Wipro and others enjoyed a protectionist environment, but in the early 1990s the likes of IBM and others came back, and Wipro had to reinvent itself. Rather than confront the competition, Wipro worked with it, and India's offshore outsourcing industry was born.

Wipro's revenue has shot up from $150 million four years ago to $1.02 billion in fiscal 2004. While IT services is still its bread and butter, the company now attains more than 10 percent of its revenue from BPO and is the largest third-party BPO provider in India. It also obtains a fast-growing 4 percent of its revenue from consulting services. The company acquired Boston-based NerveWire, a financial consulting firm, as well as the energy consulting unit of American Management Systems. Says a senior Wipro official: "We plan to continue with our string of strategic acquisitions." Wipro's business has also evolved along with client needs, and more than half of its services are now performed onsite at client facilities—both offshore and onshore. As Wipro's services have moved up the value chain, the company has also fostered an integral relationship with clients in everything from change management to strategic human resource planning.

The larger players have implemented aggressive strategies aimed at lessening the impact to their bottom line and delivering global service offerings to their clients.

*Mainstream IT services suppliers recognize that they cannot continue to charge high daily consulting rates and be price competitive at the same time.*

Mainstream IT services suppliers recognize that they cannot continue to charge high daily consulting rates and remain price competitive at the same time without reducing costs. The result is a race to the middle ground, as high-end onshore suppliers expand their offshore delivery capabilities into application development and maintenance (ADM) while offshore suppliers continue to work to solidify their outsourcing capabilities and their consulting presence in client countries like the U.S. and the UK—moving from project-based work to larger, full-service ITO and BPO outsourcing delivery models. In fact, IBM, Accenture, CSC, EDS, CGE&Y, Deloitte Consulting, Bearing Point, Perot Systems and Keane, among other brand-name companies, all maintain offshore development centers (ODC's) and/or subcontract work to offshore companies.

Beginning with IT, this movement is now starting to gain momentum in the BPO space as well, although it is a lot more immature offshore. As the market evolves and supplier service offerings mature, buyers need to be aware of the pros and cons of using one model over the other. Accenture has developed BPO groups in locations such as the Philippines, India and the Czech Republic while other large services companies have added locations in Poland and the Caribbean. However, for MNCs to achieve scalable and economical offshore delivery models they need to increase the percentage of global staff in offshore locations.

Many MNCs have entered the Indian market by partnering with top firms (i.e. Satyam Computers, Mastek, HCL, Cognizant Technologies) as part of their delivery model, and have found they are often competing with their partners for the same deals.

The MNCs are faced with tough competition from strongly developed offshore-founded operations (i.e. TCS, Wipro, Infosys). This competition is mature, has brand presence, and is often more cost-competitive.

Pricing battles are already well underway in some areas. The difference in pricing in various supplier hybrid models can be attributed partly to high combination rates for delivery—MNC

| Companies | China | Russia | Philippines | U.S. | India |
|---|---|---|---|---|---|
| Accenture | Present | Present | Delivery Center | Headquarters, Consulting, Delivery Center, Sales & Marketing | Consulting, Delivery Center |
| IBM | Present | Present | Consulting, Delivery Center & Marketing | Headquarters, Consulting, Delivery Center, Sales | Consulting, Delivery Center |
| Wipro | Not Present | Not Present | Not Present | Sales & Marketing, Delivery Center, Consulting | Headquarters, Delivery Center, Consulting |
| Infosys | Delivery Center | Not Present | Joint Venture | Sales & Marketing, Delivery Center, Consulting | Headquarters, Delivery Center, Consulting |
| TCS | Consulting, Delivery Center | Not Present | Not Present | Sales & Marketing, Delivery Center, Consulting | Headquarters, Delivery Center, Consulting |
| CSC | Consulting, Delivery Center | Not Present | Not Present | Headquarters, Consulting, Delivery Center, Sales & Marketing | Consulting, Delivery Center |
| EDS | Consulting, Delivery Center | Not Present | Delivery Center | Headquarters, Consulting, Delivery Center, Sales & Marketing | Consulting, Delivery Center |
| Satyam | Consulting, Delivery Center | Not Present | Not Present | Sales & Marketing, Delivery Center, Consulting | Headquarters, Delivery Center, Consulting |
| ACS | Not Present | N/A | N/A | Headquarters, Consulting, Delivery Center, Sales & Marketing | Consulting, Delivery Center |
| HP | Delivery Center | N/A | N/A | Headquarters, Consulting, Delivery Center, Sales & Marketing | Consulting, Delivery Center |

TABLE 8.1

Sample of multinational IT Firms' Offshore Relationships/Presence.

US + MNC India (MNC direct presence) or MNC US + One of India Centric Suppliers (MNC partnership presence).

Some MNCs are new to offshore delivery models. Their offshore maturity in many cases is behind that of mature offshore players, or their delivery centers have traditionally focused on servicing clients in the local offshore markets (i.e., Brazil's office serving Brazilian companies). Despite these issues it won't take long for the leading MNCs' offshore offerings to mature.

MNCs are paying attention to the qualifying moves such as SEI-CMM certifications. For example, Accenture, IBM and CSC have shown rapid progress by achieving coveted Level 4 and Level 5 in some of their offshore locations. Within less than a year of operations, CSC's center in Indore, India was certified at SEI-CMM Level 5.

## WHAT IT MEANS FOR THE SUPPLIER

Existing customers will continue to put pressure on the MNC supplier to reduce prices. While offshore suppliers will face this challenge as well, it is much less for the ones that clearly demonstrate deep domain expertise and productivity improvements. Suppliers need to focus on increasing their quality of delivery and the overall customer experience rather than pure price. Suppliers willing to lower price may achieve short-term gains, but may damage themselves and the market long-term. The winners will be those that clearly demonstrate gains in productivity and service levels beyond any labor arbitrage.

Brand building is important. MNCs have an edge here, but a few offshore suppliers are shining in this area. Suppliers need to continue to appropriately invest in this area. Firms should join up with industry associations, government agencies and other global influencers to promote the offshore maturity of their country in large buying markets (U.S./Europe).

During client acquisition, it is imperative that the client clearly understands potential and proposed delivery models (i.e.

pure offshore or a hybrid), and that the supplier help the client understand its role in creating a win-win relationship. Pure-play offshore suppliers need to realize that because MNCs have a client presence at a senior level they can be a serious threat, as client loyalty is strong. This is a key advantage for MNCs as many have relationships at a higher level than the offshore firms. However, offshore players are beginning to develop strong client relationships as well and should not underestimate their own unique capabilities and the varying client requirements.

*Offshore firms have to demonstrate stability and maturity in order to successfully compete.*

The MNC brand name also enables success, and relative size denotes stability. Offshore firms have to demonstrate stability and maturity in order to successfully compete. MNC experience plays well in large deals as they have deep experience in managing long-term and client-intimate projects/processes. Some offshore suppliers have more experience in discrete projects and need to demonstrate skills in on-going relationship and outsourcing management.

## HOW BPO DIFFERS

Many people see Business Process Outsourcing (BPO) as a company's natural evolution from IT Outsourcing. And while it may be the logical next step, BPO presents distinct opportunities and challenges. Like ITO before it, offshore BPO will evolve through three distinct phases of increasing complexity, from managing transactional to area to comprehensive services.

Transactional processes are single, simple and can easily be handled by one supplier. Examples would be payroll processing or benefits administration. Area processes may include several inter-related services and are slightly more complex to manage. A good example of an area process would be workforce management, including both recruiting and staffing. Comprehensive processes are the transactional and administrative processes of a functional department, like HR or finance and accounting.

Offshore BPO has been around for a number of years disguised as simple, low-level, labor-intensive work like teleservices, application processing, medical transcriptions, etc. The market is still immature, and while many clients have become sophisticated with their approach to offshore, there is still a lot of confusion as to who the suppliers are and how BPO will vary from their offshore IT operations. As the offshore market moves on from transactional to more area and comprehensive services, we anticipate many hiccups along the way.

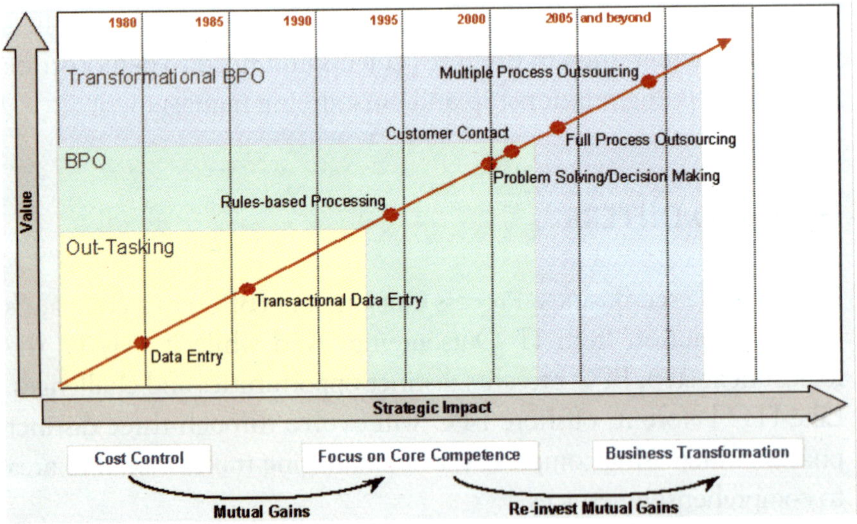


FIGURE 8.1

The Evolution of Offshore Business Process Outsourcing (BPO).

Nonetheless, there are several aspects of BPO that make it at an attractive offshoring alternative:

**The economic reason is strong.** No one can debate that cost pressures will continue. BPO is the next level of opportunity for companies after outsourcing manufacturing and IT. Over the last few years, companies have demonstrated 40 percent 60 percent cost savings over their existing operations.

**The outsourcing process is continuous.** Outsourcing has traditionally followed the renegotiation and expansion model. As companies become more comfortable with their offshore ITO models, BPO is the logical next step.

**Extension of existing supplier relationships.** Many of the large, traditional outsourcing suppliers (IBM, EDS, CSC, Infosys, Wipro, TCS) have invested heavily in expanding their global delivery models. Companies that trust these organizations want to leverage their offshore capabilities to expand their relationship into offshore BPO services.

**Infrastructure maturity.** Advances in communication technology for data and voice and other elements of infrastructure, improvements in overall technology, and investments in training and language development are allowing even more complex processes to be handled from offshore.

**Knowledge of offshore markets.** Whether through the web or interaction with experts, the amount of readily available information on offshore markets has increased dramatically, thereby reducing perceptions of risk caused by fear of the unknown.

**New markets provide new ways to leverage old investments.** Markets where manufacturing has been mastered (i.e. China, Mexico) are enticing companies to take a closer look at how they can leverage these markets for services outsourcing.

**The shared services center opportunity.** Rather than continue to invest in shared services centers, companies are now thinking about how to transition the centers to external service providers.

Others are developing strategies to leverage the centers as a potential source of revenue.

**Resourcing flexibility.** Offshore BPO investments allows enterprises to develop a flexible resourcing model for managing growth.

**Speed of operation.** The differences in time zones across multiple offshore locations has the potential to allow enterprises to significantly speed operations, and provide 24/7 coverage to their constituents.

Offshore BPO will continue to grow steadily for years to come. In light of such phenomenal growth and competitive opportunities that offshore BPO provides, there are basic preparations and investments that companies can make before they take the next step. Here are some recommendations in preparing for BPO:

**Invest in management.** Management of offshore BPO requires a different approach. Offshore BPO is not as mature as offshore ITO; therefore there are less experienced managers. Companies need to focus on not only program management (relationship, performance, resource, contract and financial), but also transition management and change management.

**Help build the market.** The offshore BPO market is changing rapidly. Companies that are serious about the opportunity should figure out ways to help it mature.

**Know your own service levels.** Before building an offshore strategy, companies need to fully understand their process improvement opportunities and create the metrics to gauge success. As offshore BPO is relatively new, industry best practices are yet to be established.

**Use an expert.** Whether internal or external, someone who has been there before can prevent many of the unexpected challenges along the way.

## KEY POINTS

- The supplier landscape has changed dramatically for the better, driven both by client demands and by competition among offshore providers and MNCs.
- Most major offshore suppliers now have a major presence near their clients; while the MNCs in turn have moved large amounts of their operations offshore in order to compete on price with the offshore suppliers.
- BPO, while relatively immature, will evolve through three distinct phases of increasing complexity, from managing transactional to area to comprehensive services.

Chapter 9

# Identifying and Managing Offshore Risks

As we mentioned in the previous chapter, the cost savings that offshoring can bring is important but is only one of several factors that should be considered when implementing an offshore outsourcing plan. Companies also need to focus on the greater value gained by offshoring in terms of process improvements, service level enhancements, scalability and incorporation as a comprehensive strategic business model. To do this, it is critical that a company identifies the risks, executes due diligence and forms a strategy for effectively managing its offshore partnerships.

In this chapter, we outline the possible pitfalls on the road to achieving a cost effective, long-term and scalable offshore solution. We classify the risks into three broad categories: *Strategic*, *Operational* and *Financial.*

## STRATEGIC RISKS

Offshoring transfers operational control and accountability for specific business functions into the hands of an external entity or remote operation. The outsourcing or offshoring organization faces new challenges to yield the returns envisaged by such an arrangement, including risks in the following areas.

## 1. Offshoring Destination

Choosing the most appropriate country is as important as choosing the most appropriate supplier. The company should analyze the political stability of the country in question and compare other factors such as:

- ***Social/political risk:*** Many countries see the American way of life as contrary to their beliefs. These could be high-risk locations especially if the government is unstable or controlled by extreme wing segments.
- ***Government support:*** Special concessions to stimulate business may ease the administrative aspects of the relationship (e.g., tax holidays, easier terms for import of equipment, etc.).
- ***Country laws:*** A study of relevant legal provisions is essential for engineering an appropriate contract, and to avoid unknown complications due to use of foreign country resources.
- ***Cultural compatibility:*** Depending on the degree of interaction between the people of different nationalities, cultural sensitization plays an important role. This oft-ignored factor is most vital during critical phases of contract execution, such as knowledge transfer and milestone delivery. Third party advisors are assuming larger roles in bridging this divide.

## 2. Intellectual Property

Offshoring invariably involves sharing proprietary information with the supplier. While the contract terms bind the supplier to protect that information, very often data protection practices on the supplier side fall short of the client's expectations. Stipulations upfront in terms of the proprietary nature of the information and supplier members' utilization of such data are encouraged to avoid any misunderstandings.

## 3. Ongoing Process Improvements

Process improvements used to be considered as "extras" to external partnerships. Over the past few years this has changed. With offshoring turning into a strategic initiative, many corporations are using the process and domain maturity of suppliers as a key tool for incorporating best practices internally. Although potentially requiring extra diligence upfront and higher price tags, buyers should ideally look to suppliers who support the sharing of skills, process excellence principles, and domain knowledge to reap the full benefits of the offshoring relationship.

## OPERATIONAL RISKS

Inadequate planning and insufficient diligence can expose an offshoring initiative to a variety of operational risks. It takes a deep knowledge of the offshoring lifecycle to avoid mistakes in identifying appropriate business areas to offshore, developing proper supplier candidates and selecting the best supplier fit, and managing the ongoing offshoring relationship.

## 1. Planning

Planning what, when, where and how to offshore is a critical component to a company's overall outsourcing strategy. Companies need to ask if the organization is mature enough to source to an offshore location. Before an offshoring initiative can even be construed, the targeted business segment must have clearly established processes and documentation that highlight management reviews, define roles and responsibilities of involved personnel, succinctly outline the intended results, and analyze other organizational areas that may be impacted before bringing the process to an external entity.

## 2. Sourcing

Most offshore suppliers will claim to have expertise in whatever service a customer needs; however, the sophisticated outsourcing company will see beyond the marketing pitch and understand real capabilities and processes for supporting the contract.

Parameters such as ISO and SEI-CMM certifications can help, but experience has shown a large variance in the delivery capabilities of the suppliers who pass these tests. Beyond process certifications, the company needs to evaluate more parameters to ensure against operational failures related to domain knowledge, infrastructure, quality processes, risk and delivery management, and the financial stability of the company.

## 3. Delivery Management

- ***Transition:*** Offshoring presents a radical change within the internal operations of an organization. These changes may not be as much business process related, as they are people related. Employees with in-depth knowledge of the services being offshored are invaluable to educating the suppliers on the current and future processes. Besides reviewing existing documentation, meeting and sharing knowledge with buyers who have unique experiences and information that has yet to be captured organizationally will greatly benefit the transition process.
- ***Communication:*** The organization needs to establish a clear communication framework in terms of the type of medium, tone, forum and frequency for the information flow regarding objectives, impacts, issues, updates, and results achieved. Extinguishing small issues that often arise during the initial phases of the engagement will lead to better chances for future success.

- ***Cultural incompatibility:*** This is not as much a risk in itself, as it is a potential cause for misaligned expectations. Cultural barriers cause a lot of implicit communication to be lost or misinterpreted. Results range from misunderstood needs to the more extreme scenario of client and supplier resources not being able to work together. Being aware of cultural and communication differences will reduce the likelihood of misplaced expectations about critical deliverables.
- ***Implementing process improvements:*** Process improvements form one of the key long-term deliverables of offshoring contracts. However, once steady state is achieved there is an understandable reluctance on both sides to diverge away from the status quo. Developing a plan, evaluating metrics, and receiving management commitment form the basics for incorporating a process for continuous improvement.

## FINANCIAL RISKS

The motivations behind offshoring are primarily associated with cost savings. The risks here fall at opposite ends of the spectrum:

### 1. Inflated Pricing

Inexperienced buyers may fall prey to contract structures that require a premium to be paid over the term of the deal, suppliers that include incentive credits based on attainment of misconstrued performance metrics, or simply paying above known market rates. There is no substitute for experience and knowledge of a specific market, and buyers are well served to seek guidance in segments that are new to them.

**CASE STUDY** **Cor–Pay**

For years, Cor-Pay Solutions of Levonia, Michigan, was a successful provider of third-party financial and accounting services to major U.S. corporations. Ford was one of its biggest clients. Cor-Pay had longstanding relationships with Ford and others to provide accounts payable, accounts receivable, financial statement operations, cash flow management and other business processes. Then, in 2002, Ford—itself seeking ways to cut costs amidst a struggling market for auto sales—asked Cor-Pay to cut its prices. But Cor-Pay, already at low margins due to the slumping U.S. economy, was not able to do so.

In late 2002, Cor-Pay lost the Ford contract as the automaker set up its own BPO center in India. Too late, Cor-Pay finally started making plans to set up its own offshore center, but instead was acquired by one of India's largest software companies, Datamatics.

## 2. Undervalued Pricing

In a competitive scenario, suppliers often quote extremely low prices, driving down their margins to virtually nothing. There are several reasons why a supplier might low bid, but most common are to enter new markets, or the opportunity to associate with a big client. While this initially seems beneficial for the buyer, the old adage 'you get what you pay for' comes into play beyond the short term. The initial bubble of huge savings almost invariably gives way to sub-optimal client service, reluctance to ramp up, and a net negative to the buyer. It is imperative that the buyer understands the ramifications of low-bidding suppliers and the impacts it may have on quality delivery.

While the risks we have outlined here may or may not be pertinent to your company and your situation, we cannot stress enough the importance of knowing what you are in for and how to manage

## CASE STUDY Capital One

Capital One has long been one of the most aggressive U.S. banks in terms of services globalization, with both captive centers and supplier relationships, mostly in India. Wipro has been one of Capital One's biggest and most trusted suppliers. However, in early 2004 Capital One was forced to cancel the outbound telemarketing portion of its contract with Wipro after at least 30 overzealous employees were caught making offers to customers that they had not been authorized to make.

To its credit, it was Wipro itself that first discovered the discrepancies and brought it to the attention of Capital One. While Capital One continues to offshore thousands of jobs—and continues to use Wipro for inbound customer service—the incident is a good example of what can go wrong in an offshore contract, the importance of selecting a quality supplier, and the urgency of routine governance once the contract has been awarded.

| Offshoring Risks | Impact to Your Operations |
| --- | --- |
| **Minimal Offshore Planning**—business necessity can push a company to move ahead without an adequate offshoring strategy, which is the key element to de-risking an offshore sourcing transaction | • Without Engineering an Offshoring Solution, which includes determining on/offshore mix, phasing of offshoring and process alignment as per a firm's specific business requirements, a company cannot understand its internal capabilities, current costs, resources, and potential impacts from offshoring<br>• Potential to offshore the wrong functions with little opportunity to maximize returns; further in not setting appropriate targets can get irrational expectations in setting savings and timing targets<br>• Ensuring buy-in and communication across key areas of your organization greatly increases the chance of a successful offshore engagement |

*continued*

| Offshoring Risks | Impact to Your Operations |
|---|---|
| **Limiting Scope of Geographic Areas**—countries have a predominant composition of skills and capabilities based on culture, infrastructure, economics, business risk, and government factors | • Not including the right destinations can both limit the strategic benefits achievable and incur unnecessary risk from the outset of an engagement<br>• Extensive knowledge is needed to tie supplier capabilities back to a clients' unique requirements in all the leading and emerging countries, including India, China, Philippines, Russia, etc.<br>• Since specific country attributes influence many supplier capabilities, not selecting the right locales increases chance of incurring delays and additional costs to deal with legal, cultural, and infrastructure issues |
| **Non-comprehensive RFP**—many RFPs focus solely on business and technology requirements, instead of being based on offshore-specific productivity and service-level metrics | • A robust, detailed RFP is the framework for all future engagement activities<br>• Bad RFPs can lead to disastrous results, increased costs, failed projects, and misaligned expectations<br>• Sufficient performance-based detail is key so that deep visibility is given to what suppliers commit to deliver to the deal |
| **Non-optimized Time Acceleration**—significant loss of offshore value occurs without the right sourcing management, transition plan and engagement schedule | • Understanding an organization's internal capabilities is critical to create an optimized, company-specific timing and transition plan<br>• Moving too quickly can cause internal chaos and disrupt mission critical operations<br>• Moving too slowly prevents value optimization |
| **Inadequate Due Diligence and Supplier Knowledge**—without extensive knowledge and experience, it is difficult to conduct deep due diligence and fully understand key supplier-specific risks and capabilities | • Many companies forced to evaluate a deal largely based on supplier size and marketing presence<br>• Companies can overpay for required capabilities or often be limited to suppliers with basic or broadly defined abilities and not deep expertise<br>• Hidden costs, performance failures, and business risks often not identified until too late |
| **Supplier-Driven Pricing**—difficult to compare complex contracts using the typical marketing-based "offer" approach | • The offer approach, where the RFP states the problem and suppliers offer back a complicated mix of solutions, prices, and alternatives that too often are largely supplier-benefiting |

*continued*

| Offshoring Risks | Impact to Your Operations |
| --- | --- |
| | • Suppliers should respond back to a set of specific structured arrangements with pre-defined best practices alternatives to ensure comparable bids are submitted with well understood pricing and service delivery expectations |
| **Inefficient Negotiation**—many negotiations focus on driving down rates without understanding the Total Cost of Offshoring (TCO) | • Driving down costs too low ensures problems for both the supplier and client down the road and ultimately result in longer-term cost increases<br>• Fact-based negotiations by knowing current market cost, performance, and supplier benchmarks allow all parties to have a common understanding on the deal requirements and bid appropriately<br>• A variety of offshore contract alternatives (multi-supplier, functional or technical segmentation) should be considered to maximize flexibility |
| **Non-comprehensive Contracting**—not incorporating the unique terms and conditions (T&C's) needed for an effective contract | • A weak contract can leave a client's business operations critically at risk<br>• Contracts that do not include offshore specific T&C's (performance audits and bonds, buffer staff, retention incentives, experience profiling, tax, currency clauses, etc.) greatly increase the risk of performance, financial, relationship or contract management delivery issues |
| **Inadequate Offshore Program Management**—beyond traditional oversight, specific offshore issues often are not proactively addressed | • Without offshore program management, much of the value negotiated and planned for during the sourcing phase can be lost<br>• Structured, performance-based reviews prevent service levels identified in the contracting phase from being missed<br>• Cultural, geographic, and offshore specific issues must also be addressed to ensure maximum value and operational efficiency |

TABLE 9.1

Offshore Risks and the Possible Impact to the Organization.

the risks. Table 9.1 outlines some key risk and value factors that your company should be addressing in its sourcing process, and their subsequent impact to your organization.

## KEY POINTS

- The actual value received from offshoring can vary significantly based on how well offshore and supplier knowledge is understood and leveraged, key offshoring risks are mitigated, and detailed sourcing and program management plans are put in place.
- Putting these types of plans in place will initially take more time, resources, and commitment. However, the benefits can mean the difference between a sub-standard sourcing engagement full of hidden downstream costs and an engagement that leverages best practices and delivers maximum value for your business.
- Before beginning an offshoring engagement, your organization should take a detailed look at the issues and risks raised above, and feel confident in your ability to effectively identify, prevent, and manage each of them.
- Offshoring is a bit like treading on unfamiliar territory, where financial, operational and strategic risk can, if not addressed properly, sabotage an otherwise effective offshore relationship.
- The solution lies in being able to visualize the process in its entirety, identify potential minefields, and to take preventive measures.
- Do not rely on one past outsourcing experience as the foundation for building an entire offshore strategy. Companies need to look at offshoring as a lifecycle with risk factors that need to be considered in each stage and for different offshoring scenarios.
- Qualified third-party advisors are in the best position to help mitigate these risks since in many instances they have onshore experience in the countries of interest, and an understanding of the specific nuances associated with them.

# Part 3

# The Planning of the Offshore Journey: The Offshore Road-Map

Chapter 10

# The Offshore Maturity Model

Even if services globalization fits well into the overall corporate strategy, many companies are not prepared to execute. Strategically, financially, technologically and culturally, services globalization requires a certain level of preparedness that will allow you to work better with offshore operation or partners, and maximize return on investment.

Over the next three chapters, we will discuss how to determine when your company is ready to execute a services globalization plan, or what we refer to as an organization's level of offshore readiness. This chapter looks at readiness from an industry-wide and enterprise level. We will answer questions such as, is your company ready for services globalization, and how mature is the industry itself? Then, in the subsequent two chapters we will look at readiness at a more granular level, answering the questions of, what services and processes within the enterprise are ripe for offshoring, and when should the process begin?

In preparation for the offshore journey, companies need to first develop a roadmap borne of deep analysis and knowledge. The following three chapters will help you understand the type of knowledge and analysis you will need to begin building your offshore roadmap.

## MEETING GLOBAL STANDARDS

It would certainly be risky to go offshore if the market or suppliers had no experience with a particular service, or with managing service delivery. However, many markets offer strong business process outsourcing opportunity and offshore suppliers have created a strong value proposition in the IT software and services arena. India in particular enjoys advantages of people sophistication in terms of a very large pool of English speaking scientific personnel, varied and extensive skill sets, and globally competitive costs. India also boasts of vendor sophistication, with more than 200 companies quality accredited and serving the needs of over 255 Fortune 500 companies. Today, the world looks to the Indian software industry as a good frame of reference for an offshore maturity model. It is the most mature of the offshore service sectors and has the highest levels of standardization in place.

In 1991, the Software Engineering Institute at Carnegie Mellon University, with the help of the industry and federal research grants, released a Capability Maturity Model (CMM) for software developers. The system rates companies in terms of their organizational maturity and capability to execute software development, evaluating factors such as how well their processes are defined, do they have a well-established organizational matrix, is there a process in place for continuous improvement, etc. The CMM is a framework that describes the key elements of an effective process. It provides a foundation for process improvement. The CMM describes an evolutionary improvement path from an *ad hoc*, immature process to a mature, disciplined process. The highest rating is a Level 5, typically reserved for the cream of the crop of IT service providers, both onshore and offshore.

The CMM rating provides good insight into the maturity level of the offshore service provider and their capability to perform different services. The CMM framework can also provide great insight into the maturity level of your own organization. Client companies that are planning to go offshore should recognize that it would be risky to engage in offshore outsourcing if their own internal processes were in disarray and they lacked the capability to manage service delivery. If companies want to extract the maximum benefit from an offshore engagement, they need to ensure that their own internal processes are in order.

CMM, therefore, can be used as a self-diagnostic checklist for determining gaps in the offshore readiness of the enterprise and in building a roadmap as to what processes make the most sense to move offshore and in what stages.

The CMM framework is not the only tool companies can use to determine offshore readiness, but it is the basis for developing similar outsourcing standards for other areas of IT and BPO. Another standard measure is the Six Sigma rating, a rigorous and disciplined methodology that uses data and statistical analysis to measure and improve a company's operational performance by identifying and eliminating "defects" in manufacturing and service-related processes. External auditors typically award the Six Sigma rating to a services firm that approximates zero defects per one million transactions in any given process.

Three similar diagnostic methods are fast becoming the industry standard for recognizing excellence in IT and business process outsourcing. One, COPC, applies to call centers and is awarded by Amherst, New York-based Customer Operations Performance Center. COPC is the equivalent of CMM for call center suppliers and measures companies by the criteria of customer service, customer satisfaction, and operational efficiency. San Ramon, California-based neoIT has developed the neoQA methodology to assess a service provider's expertise and ability to effectively deliver services. A neoQA rating demonstrates that the supplier adheres to capability parameters (Key Performance Indicators) that directly affect the quality and timely delivery of an outsourced project. So the focus is not just on process documentation but on performance. Carnegie Mellon, meanwhile, is developing a similar methodology that could be applied across the BPO industry, tentatively referred to as e-Sourcing Capability Model, or eSCM. Table 10.1 compares the various services qualifications standards available in the market today.

| | Features | COPC | ISO 9000: 2000 | CMM | neoQA | eSCM |
|---|---|---|---|---|---|---|
| 1 | Outsourcing capability orientation | No | No | No | Yes | Yes |
| 2 | Dynamic approach of the standard | No | Slow | Slow | Fast | No |
| 3 | Customized standard for different industries | No | No | No | Yes | No |
| 4 | Detailed audit report | Yes | Yes | Yes | Yes | Yes |
| 5 | Network of the auditors | No | Yes | Yes | Yes | No |
| 6 | Levels in certification | No | No | Yes | Yes | Yes |
| 7 | Third party periodic audit/assessment | Yes | Yes | Yes | Yes | Yes |
| 8 | Applies to IT, BPO or Both | BPO | IT | IT | Both | BPO |

TABLE 10.1

A Comparison of Services Qualification Standards.

Regardless of whether you use a services qualification standard mentioned above or an internally developed standard, your company should use some type of self-diagnostic checklist for determining gaps in the enterprise before you begin to build your offshore roadmap.

## THE BIG PICTURE

Too often, companies look at services globalization as a short-term fix to a cost problem. In a typical inexperienced company scenario executives would see a need to reduce costs, quickly identify a process that they see others outsourcing, and simply send out an RFP (Request for Proposal). They would not seek outside expertise, nor would they conduct a careful analysis of the organization and its processes. When companies use this haphazard approach, they often identify the wrong processes, select the wrong supplier and could even increase their overall costs.

The larger, and more serious players are looking beyond cost savings and quick fixes. They have identified services globalization as an integral part of their long-term corporate strategy. They understand the potential impact a well-executed plan can bring to the organization and have recognized the need for a staged roadmap.

"You can globalize demand or you can globalize supply, but for the most part you should be globalizing both at the same time," says neoIT's Debashish Sinha. "Instead of looking at near-term offshoring of current operations, you should be sitting down and thinking about what is the most appropriate way to look at operations in order to meet the company's goals over the next three to five years."

"What's beginning to happen," Sinha continues, "is that as the economy improves and as organizations begin to hold back a little on aggressive outsourcing initiatives, more organizations are beginning to realize the value of offshoring as a long-term strategic initiative to improve the value and competitiveness of the enterprise. Developing the offshore strategy is now being led by the CEO or CFO's office, instead of the procurement director."

Good planning can also go a long way toward alleviating some of the risks we talked about in Chapter 9, and it can reduce risks to the enterprise as a whole. Indeed, for the more long-term, strategic-thinking firms, one of the biggest drivers of establishing offshore operations and suppliers has been to tap into new pools of resources.

In the late 1990s, when labor was suddenly scarce and expensive, companies woke up desperate to find new pools of talent. The Y2K problem confronted companies with the prospect of having to pay $300 an hour to COBOL programmers to perform Y2K remediation work. Companies began to source projects to offshore suppliers and some imported workers by leveraging the H1B and L1B visa programs. If those same firms had operations in India and China, they would have been able to find those same resources much easier, much quicker and much cheaper.

## CASE STUDY The Big Picture for P&G

In 2001, Procter & Gamble (P&G) began a pilot global sourcing program for its information technology work, particularly software development. The goal was to create $100 million worth of capability around the world that could be leveraged on-demand by its individual business units. Through the pilot, approximately 600 full time employees (FTE's) were relocated to lower-cost P&G shared services locations such as Manila, Philippines and Warsaw, Poland. Additionally, several hundred contractor positions were consolidated and sourced offshore through third-party engagements.

P&G found that offshore labor rates were, on average, about one-fifth of the cost in the U.S. and other more advanced economies. For example, a contract Java programmer that might cost $98 an hour in Cincinnati cost $20–$22 dollars per hour in India and the Philippines.

P&G also found that it was not only lower local labor rates that created the cost difference; it was also the competition between outside organizations bidding for P&G's work.

The company determined that productivity differences were an important contributor, as well. These highly educated and well-trained individuals were extremely motivated to work hard to improve their standard of living—individually, for their families and for their countries. They were often on the job at 7:00 a.m. handling emails before beginning their regular work at 8:00 a.m. Similarly, internal meetings and training were typically deferred until the evening hours in order to maximize productive time during the day.

In other words, it was the lower charge rates, competition and the work ethic that combined to create the offshore cost advantage.

Other advantages were also found. P&G was able to build a more dynamic operating structure. Resources could be added and removed quickly. Flexibility, as measured by the percent of the company's IT workforce that could be ramped up and down

*continued*

**CASE STUDY** ***Continued...***

on short notice, increased. Economies of scale were created because the program centralized purchasing for skills that could be leveraged across multiple business units. With the ability to objectively measure a provider's processes against standard industry benchmarks, quality increased.

Overall, during the first twelve months of the program, P&G saved an estimated $28 million dollars—a relatively small number given the total information technology spending of a Fortune 500 company, but still an important benefit in any economy. Expansion of the program is underway.

Those that established offshore operations are well ahead of the competition. These organizations will have access to new and untapped pools of resources when the economy recovers and the labor market reverts back to where it was in the late 1990s. They will be perfectly positioned to excel in their industry.

## LOOK WITHIN

Beyond determining strategy and standardization, companies need to assess their maturity levels for services globalization in eight strategic areas. These eight components, introduced in Chapter 4 as the Globalization Strategy (GS8) Framework can help you determine your organization's offshore readiness. Preparing your organization for globalization can have a big impact on whether your initiative will survive or thrive.

To assess an organization's globalization maturity, it is important to review an organization across the eight components of the GS8 Framework. The GS8 Framework can identify three distinct stages of

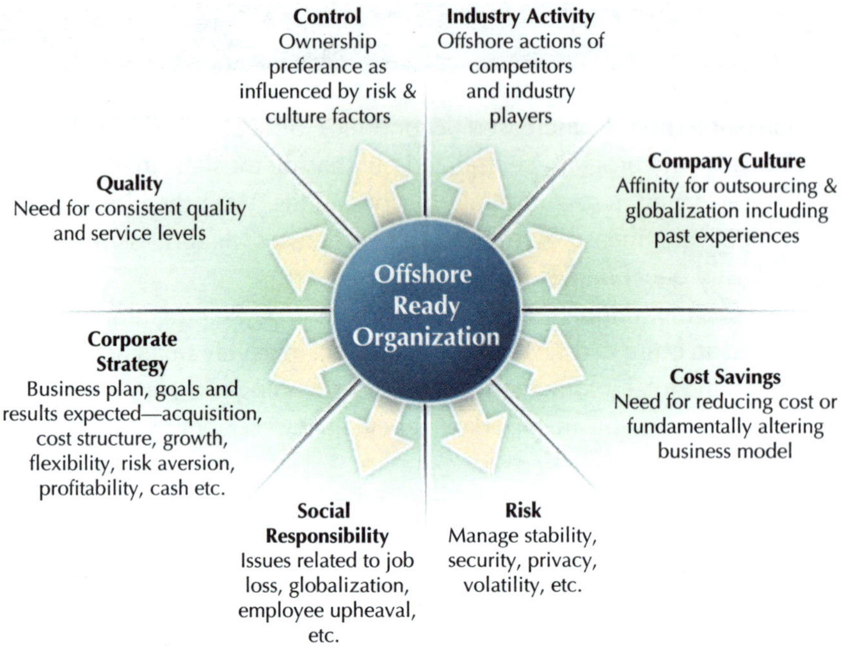


FIGURE 10.1

The Globalization Strategy Framework (GS8).

organizational maturity—expert, practiced or novice. This evaluation can quickly identify the internal readiness of an organization for services globalization initiatives. The result is that not all organizations have the same ability to globalize their services, nor should they try a cookie-cutter approach.

The first stage of offshore readiness is the novice organization. This organization is just beginning to explore the full possibilities of globalization. They probably have experience with domestic outsourcing and/or leveraging staffing models to meet resource shortages, but they have not engaged in large-scale offshore initiatives. They have no experience managing highly complex end-to-end initiatives. In general, their outsourcing has been limited to application maintenance (and occasionally, development) characterized by high definition, clarity of task and technology, and simplicity. From a business perspective, the work was almost invariably of low complexity and low business impact. Nevertheless, the talent availability and quality of the finished product, coupled with the capability to ramp up quickly, has caused the offshore service concept to grow. This phase is what one might call the "Our competitors are outsourcing, we better hurry up and find our strategy" approach. In order to expand globalization across the organization, a novice organization would need to make significant knowledge and process investments.

The second stage of offshore readiness is the practiced organization. In this organization, globalization may have the attention of a few top executives. They have experience dealing with offshore operations and may have several contracts with offshore suppliers. Despite the contracts, the globalization initiative is fragmented across the organization. Each department has their own goals and objectives. Many of the initiatives across the organization are driven by cost reduction, with other objectives taking a back seat.

In this second stage of offshore readiness the firm is sourcing work with a high business impact but is, of necessity, of low complexity. While the quality of the work done offshore is high, the lack of a strong governance framework may be making their current offshore initiatives more difficult than desirable. This organization needs to invest time and energy on a strategy to expand globalization across the organization. Executive sponsorship, divisional alignment and a consolidated strategy are key.

The third stage of offshore readiness is the expert organization. In this organization, globalization has the attention of top executives. Globalization is a way of life for this firm, the culture embraces it and their competitive advantage shows. These firms have a local presence in key offshore markets not only for onsite project management and problem resolution, but also as their own delivery centers. Their strategy crosses departments, divisions and countries. In order to further leverage the benefits of globalization, this organization needs to further invest in strategy and on-going management to make sure that risks are mitigated.

Undertaking a services globalization effort needs vision, commitment and proper planning. It should not be taken lightly and in fact if done properly provides a great opportunity to fundamentally

| Category | Criteria | Expert | Practiced | Novice |
|---|---|---|---|---|
| **Globalization Alignment Index**<br>*Indicates the company's ability to implement globalization best practices* | | | | |
| **Company Culture** | **Change Management:** Does the company have experience managing international operations? | Y | Y/N | N |
| | **Infrastructure:** Has enough investment and time been allocated to develop the infrastructure needed for services globalization? | Y | N | N |
| | International Operations: Does the company have experience managing international operations? | Y | Y/N | N |
| **Corporate Strategy** | **Goals and Objectives:** Is there clarity around globalization plans? | Y | Y/N | N |
| | **Executive Champion:** Does the initiative have C-level support? Will it be sustained? | Y | Y/N | N |
| | **Cross-Organizational Buy-in:** Have necessary steps been taken to ensure buy-in across divisions/organization? | Y | N | N |
| **Industry Activity** | **Competition:** Are your globalization plans competitive with the competition? | Y | N | N |
| | **Industry:** Are your globalization plans competitive with the industry standards? | Y | N | N |

*continued*

| Category | Criteria | Expert | Practiced | Novice |
|---|---|---|---|---|
| **Globalization Objectives Index**<br>*Indicates clarity around the benefits of offshoring and the factors that influence globalization decisions* | | | | |
| Control | **Governance Framework:** Does your organization have a governance framework in place? | Y/N | N | N |
| | **Audit Environment:** Do you conduct internal and/or independent audits of divisional processes? | Y | Y | Y |
| | **Escalation Procedures:** Are strong, documented escalation procedures in place? | Y | Y | Y/N |
| Cost Savings | **Desired Cost Structure:** Does the company want to move from a fixed cost to variable cost structure? | Y | Y | Y |
| | **Investment Choice:** Does the company have a good understanding of the global ownership models and how they might be leveraged to improve the current business situation? | Y | Y/N | Y/N |
| Quality | **Onshore Productivity:** Is the current level of process maturity high for onshore productivity? | Y | Y | Y |
| | **Offshore Productivity:** Is the current level of process maturity high for offshore productivity? | Y | Y/N | N |
| | **Onshore Service Levels:** Is the current level of process maturity high for onshore service levels? | Y | Y | Y |
| | **Offshore Service Levels:** Is the current level of process maturity high for offshore service levels? | Y | Y/N | N |
| **Globalization Risk Tolerance Index**<br>*Indicates the organization's ability to prepare for, mitigate and possibly withstand potential risk factors* | | | | |
| Risk | **Security Policies:** Does the organization have a strong | Y | Y/N | Y/N |

*continued*

| Category | Criteria | Expert | Practiced | Novice |
|---|---|---|---|---|
| | global security policy? Is it enterprise-wide? Does it cover external service provider and/or JV relationships? | | | |
| | **Disaster Recovery/Business Continuity:** Does the company have an industry best practice DC/BC plan in place? | Y | Y/N | Y/N |
| | **Audit Environment:** Does the business conduct regular and consistent audits for process improvement, compliance, etc.? | Y | Y/N | Y/N |
| **Social Responsibility** | **HR Policies and Practices:** Will the company still be able to have a fair and productive workplace as it relates to: communication, severance practices, retraining, outplacement services, reorganization, etc. | Y | Y | Y |
| | **Business Ethics:** Will outsourcing negatively affect the expectations of our government regulations, consumers, shareholders, stakeholders, etc. | N | N | N |

TABLE 10.2

Applying GS8 to determine offshore readiness—sample analysis of the eight factors that determine an organization's offshore readiness.

enhance the cost and delivery structure, re-evaluate the status quo and make improvements to some major processes and procedures. Firms that are disciplined in understanding their own organization and put a strong focus in planning the offshore roadmap will find that the benefits for offshoring are fully realized. The complexities in going offshore (services globalization), whether it is to set-up a captive or a third-party sourcing relationship, requires the firm to plan for these activities ahead of time thereby reducing some of the risks involved in such a drastic change to the organization.

## KEY POINTS

- Companies need to be prepared strategically, financially, culturally and technologically before they embark on services globalization.
- Meeting industry standards, and knowing what processes are likely to have suppliers that meet those standards, is a first step towards offshore maturity.
- Looking at services globalization from a long-term, big-picture perspective can help increase savings, reduce risks and prepare companies for economic changes in the future.

*Chapter* 11

# Portfolio Assessment and Analysis

At times, although the enterprise itself may be ready for services globalization, the processes or services that it plans to offshore are not ready. Perhaps they are not mature enough to withstand the rigors—either because those services do not have enough of a foundational base within the client company or because the offshore market for those services is not mature.

How does a firm begin the process of evaluating offshore outsourcing? How do you know what product or service lines are mature enough for offshoring? What criteria and factors should be evaluated to make decisions on the potential scope for offshoring?

This chapter outlines a framework to help companies make these decisions in a systematic way to ensure alignment of offshore and corporate strategies. With the proper alignment in place, companies will have a roadmap to ensure success throughout the lifecycle of their offshore engagements.

## THE SERVICES PORTFOLIO ASSESSMENT

A logical starting point for understanding the opportunities that offshoring affords is through a services portfolio assessment. In any business venture, companies execute fundamental analyses to support a proposed concept. In offshoring, a portfolio assessment provides this foundation. A services-based assessment examines the Information Technology (IT) applications, IT infrastructure

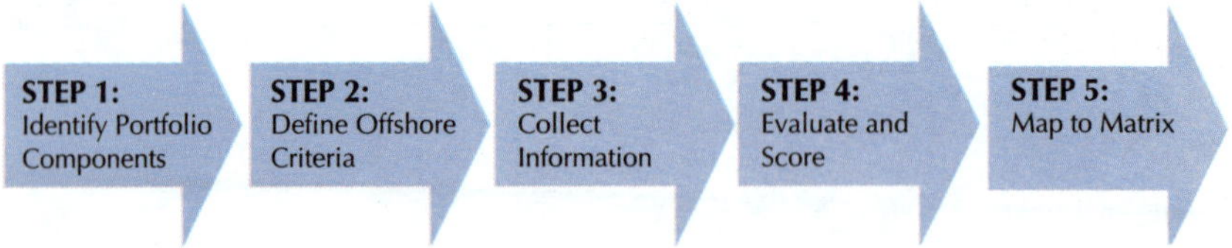


FIGURE 11.1

A5 Assessment Methodology for defining what processes are most suitable for globalization.

components, and Business Process (BP) components of existing and future operations within a particular business unit (or the entire enterprise). An outline of the major steps of the assessment process is shown above in Figure 11.1.

Each step in the assessment process is critical for companies to achieve clarity around the best service areas to send offshore. The assessment must balance both objective and subjective data in order to gain insight into the company's present set of services and take into consideration any future plans. As companies compare their needs against services available in the market (through service providers), a scoring of the most applicable areas for offshoring is computed. This scoring is heavily dictated by the weights applied to selected key criteria. As the assessment is completed, a clear picture is presented of the levels of opportunity in each service area, and an initial road map is constructed that presents a business case for further exploring the offshoring market.

The overall assessment process outlines a rigorous methodology that must be followed and tailored for each client. A key decision that must be made is how to approach the assessment in terms of using a top-down or bottom-up approach. The key determinants include the magnitude of resources present within the client company, and the number of applications or business process events that are present. Theoretically, regardless of the initial starting point, the assessment should find itself at the same position—a middle point that balances the need for high-level groupings of service areas but with enough detail that makes them clearly distinguishable. In that way, the data is both manageable and meaningful, and can be represented simply in graphical format within the offshoring potential matrix.

## STEP 1: IDENTIFY PORTFOLIO COMPONENTS

The first step of the assessment process involves collecting high-level data about the company's service areas. The intent is to understand the nature of the client's business and overall internal environment, and hone in on the key service areas that make up the portfolio. Ideally, this first step in the knowledge sharing process begins with a meeting of key executives to understand both the high-level overview of the major components of services that are being delivered and how the organization is structured. At this time, the executives also can pinpoint the primary players for each service category, highlighting key contacts that will provide the best information and insight to additional discussion areas, such as employee personalities, organizational politics, or even one-off service models.

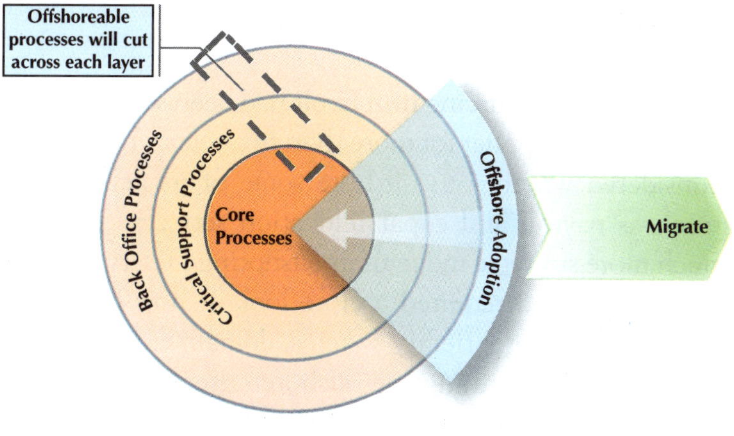


FIGURE 11.2

Defining the offshoreable processes. All organizations have three levels of processes: back office, critical support and core processes.

## STEP 2: DEFINE OFFSHORE CRITERIA

As information is attained in regard to the high-level portfolio components, the appropriate offshore factors to consider while collecting, evaluating and analyzing data from each of the service areas are selected. For example, a client with a high-degree of proprietary systems will require information that examines protection of informational property, data privacy, and the amount of documentation available. These factors are quite different from ones that would be applied to packaged software applications.

Business rationale underlying a decision to outsource an organization's business process will vary from industry to industry and from organization to organization.

Some common drivers and inhibitors that all organizations weigh are:

- Is the process a core competence?
- Is this function core for the company?
- Customized or standardized?
- Low or high variation in demand?
- Highly administrative task or not?
- Low volume or high volume?

For example, HR outsourcing firm Exult had been sending its IT services to an offshore supplier for more than two years when, in late 2002, it considered whether to offshore some of its actual BPO processes such as payroll and expat relocation services. This was clearly a much more strategic move than offshoring IT services, and the decision to go ahead required a close look at how offshoring would impact the firm's proprietary systems, domain expertise, and customer relationships. Defining the offshore criteria early on not only helped Exult make the right decision as to whether or not to offshore business processes, but also helped identify which processes were ripe for offshoring. Those same criteria also helped lead to the firm's subsequent decision—which offshore model to use (See

Chapter 20 for a case study on how Exult build its own Captive Center).

## STEP 3: COLLECT INFORMATION

While capturing data is not considered a glamorous task, its significance is paramount since it provides the foundation for all subsequent steps. Step three begins heavy data collection, the majority of which is quantitative, but some is qualitative. Quantitative data must be evaluated and assigned a ranking that is consistent across each factor. To understand the 'real' details of the IT applications or BPO events, companies need to look to the employees who make it happen.

Talking to IT and BPO leads and other integral team members performing the day-to-day work will uncover the intricacies of each operation and answer the key factors that drive the assessment results. A detailed data template should be utilized to guide these discussions; furthermore, there is no substitute for being able to witness the service offerings in action if given the opportunity.

While data about the applications and processes are vital to the assessment, a heavy factor that influences the offshoring opportunity is the number of Full-Time Equivalent (FTE) resources involved per service area. The analysis should include more than FTE numbers, but should also distinguish FTEs by their different roles within the IT development or BPO event lifecycle. Knowledge of FTE segmentation across the different major roles will bring light to the different resources that may be affected by offshoring initiatives and enable preparation of appropriate change management techniques to lessen the associated human elements.

## STEP 4: EVALUATE AND SCORE

Before the data collection process is complete, rationalization of the data must take place. The reason is that employee responses will

| Weighting Percentages | 60 | 40 | 15 | 15 | 15 | 15 | 10 | 10 | 10 | 10 | | |
|---|---|---|---|---|---|---|---|---|---|---|---|---|
| Application Name | Total FTEs | Investment Required | Domain Knowledge Required/Available | Human Resources Factors | Customer Sensitivity | Access/Response Requirement | Standardization | Quality/CoQ | Process Improvement Potential | Regulatory/Compliance | Cumulative Weighted Score | Offshoring Potential Benefit (H/M/L) |
| New Business Acquisition | 25 | 1 | 3 | 2 | 1 | 3 | 3 | 3 | 3 | 2 | 79 | H |
| Claims Adjudication | 158 | 1 | 3 | 2 | 1 | 3 | 3 | 2 | 3 | 2 | 77 | H |
| Policy Maintenance | 25 | 2 | 2 | 2 | 2 | 3 | 3 | 2 | 2 | 3 | 64 | M |
| Data Analytics | 9 | 2 | 2 | 2 | 2 | 3 | 3 | 2 | 2 | 3 | 64 | M |
| Collections | 30 | 3 | 3 | 2 | 2 | 1 | 3 | 3 | 3 | 1 | 63 | M |
| Billings | 25 | 1 | 2 | 3 | 3 | 3 | 3 | 1 | 1 | 3 | 61 | M |
| Financial Analysis | 15 | 1 | 2 | 3 | 2 | 1 | 3 | 2 | 1 | 2 | 60 | M |
| Payables | 39 | 2 | 2 | 3 | 1 | 2 | 3 | 2 | 2 | 2 | 59 | M |

TABLE 11.1

Example of data template used to collect services information for the insurance industry.

reflect both factual data and individual perspectives. In addition, considering the nature of the exercise, employees may bias the information they provide to lessen or strengthen the evaluation of their service area. Therefore, the data collected must go through a high-level validation check against other company service offerings and relevant market data to balance out fact from fiction and provide integrity and consistency across services activities. An additional way of assisting in the data rationalization process is to re-involve the executive team to confirm or enhance aspects of the data collected that seem to be deviations from the norm.

Once the data is validated for consistency and relevance across service areas, the overall scoring and ranking of each service area can take place. Again, while a template can be leveraged, the way the information is utilized must be tailored to each client and represent their environment.

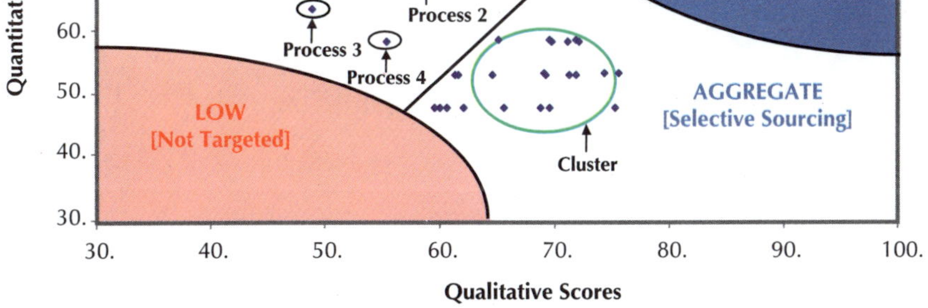


FIGURE 11.3

Identifying, evaluating and scoring target processes.

## KEY POINTS

- Conducting a strategic assessment is an important ingredient to justify leveraging the offshore market.
- The approach must be a disciplined process that evaluates the data collected and analysis performed.
- Assessment is a five-step process that involves identifying the portfolio components, defining offshore criteria, collecting information, evaluating and scoring the data, and mapping the scores to the assessment matrix (see Chapter 12).
- Performing each step of the assessment will ensure that the proper analysis has been accomplished and the real opportunity revealed for offshoring. The assessment will be the building block for further analysis and execution of the offshore strategy.

Chapter 12

# When to Offshore: Utilizing the Offshore Waves

As we mentioned, knowing what to send offshore and where to send it are essential cogs in the services globalization analysis process. Equally important, however, is knowing when to send processes offshore. Too many companies have offshored the wrong services at the wrong times.

A laddered, or "waves" approach to services globalization is usually advised. This transition methodology can provide a complete schedule of what activities will go offshore and the exact timing of the transition.

Continuing from where we left off in Chapter 11, in the final phase of assessment a graphical matrix relates a service area's financial impact to its ability to be offshored. The ability to offshore a certain service area or subset is reflective of the criteria gathered in step two of the previous chapter. Using information about the company and its internal climate for services globalization, each factor is assigned a weight to give more credence to the most influential ones. Much of the weighting percentages can be derived from reflecting the current market norm and past client experiences and applying them to the client situation at hand. Then, depending on the make-up of qualitative to quantitative factors, an algorithm that calculates the overall score for a service area's potential to be offshored is derived and converted, as needed, into a value with the highest possible score being 100. With all the service segments rated in a cumulative score fashion, grouping of relative scores from highest to lowest can be performed to delineate areas of High, Medium, and Low potential.

The other component of the matrix graphic, financial impact, is directly related to the FTEs currently performing a particular services function. It is imperative to note that part of the assessment assumption is that not all FTEs will undergo an offshore transformation, and secondly, the assessment results are for the purpose of conducting further analysis in areas that have the most potential. Therefore, it is common that only portions of a particular service area will have FTEs transferred to offshore resources. Table 12.1 and Figure 12.1, is an

| Technology Platform | Technical Area Complexity | Supplier Maturity/Capability | Business Criticality | FTEs | Adjusted Package or In-House Domain | Cumulative Weighted Score | Offshoring Potential Benefit (H/M/L) |
|---|---|---|---|---|---|---|---|
| **Document Management** | 3 | 3 | 3 | 3 | 3 | **270** | H |
| **DBA** | 2 | 3 | 2 | 10 | 3 | **260** | H |
| **Access** | 3 | 3 | 3 | 5 | 1 | **250** | H |
| **Web** | 3 | 3 | 3 | 2 | 1 | **250** | H |
| **Microsoft** | 3 | 3 | 3 | 2 | 3 | **240** | H |
| **EDI** | 3 | 3 | 2 | 10 | 1 | **235** | H |
| **SAP** | 2 | 3 | 1 | 2 | 2 | **235** | H |
| **Peoplesoft** | 2 | 3 | 2 | 4 | 2 | **220** | H |
| **SQL** | 3 | 3 | 1 | 1 | 1 | **190** | M |
| **ADC** | 2 | 2 | 1 | 2 | 2 | **185** | M |
| **SQR** | 2 | 3 | 2 | 1 | 1 | **180** | M |
| **Process Cntl** | 1 | 2 | 1 | 1 | 2 | **130** | L |
| **VAX/VMS** | 1 | 1 | 1 | 1 | 3 | **120** | L |

TABLE 12.1

Scoring applications for offshoreability.

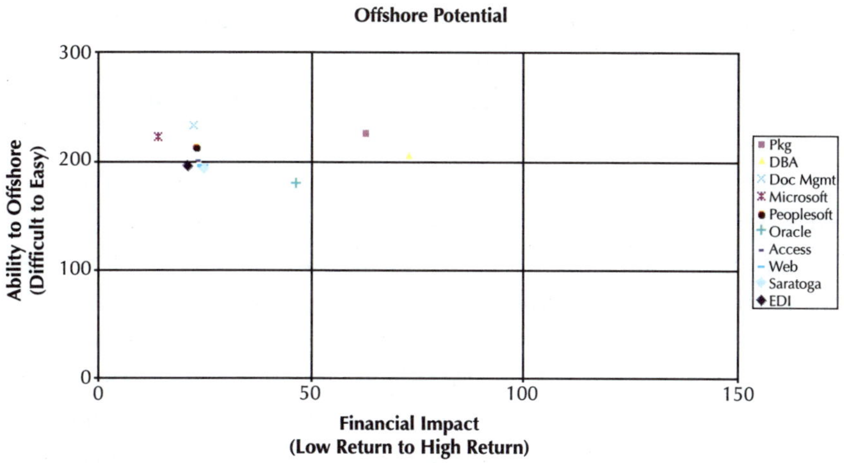


FIGURE 12.1

Identifying the offshore potential of target processes.

example of the scoring and resulting matrix plots that highlight the areas of high, medium, and low potential for offshoring.

With a thorough assessment complete, it is noteworthy to highlight the meaning behind the overall scoring and ratings:

- Results highlight the general areas where data reflects the most potential for offshore concentration; however, another level of detail is required to extract the specific segments of service areas that are recommended to be offshored.
- The assessment is only one factor that contributes to the final decision of what to offshore and when.
- The assessment is combined with the factors of the GS8 framework, such as corporate priorities, industry activity, degree of executive support, level of aggressiveness and risk allowance of the company that will impact the strategy and scope going forward.

As you'll notice from Table 12.1, your own readiness for services globalization is just part of the equation. Supplier Maturity is the other major part. As the market for such services is constantly changing and improving, this criteria is best determined through a complete market analysis that looks at the various offshore locations and suppliers in detail.

Now that we have collected, analyzed and scored the data relating to each service area, we are ready to determine which service segments are appropriate for offshoring, and in what order. The wave strategy breaks the offshoring initiative into 6–18 month segments that provide a definitive timeline for offshore activities to be performed and potential savings to be evaluated. In essence, the most likely candidates for offshoring will go in wave 1, and the next likely in wave 2, and so on. The wave strategy provides a complete schedule of what activities will go offshore and the exact timing of the transition.

## HOW IT WORKS

To give a concrete example of how a wave strategy might work in real life, we can look at IT application development support and maintenance. There are generally several processes involved in this, chief among them requirements capture, high level design, low level design, coding, design testing, integration testing, systems testing, acceptance testing and delivery. The first step is generally low-level design, and a first wave strategy might also include coding and design testing. This is both because the supplier needs to get accustomed to the business and the application, and because the client itself might not be ready to send the entire process offshore, either for control, financial or other reasons.

In wave two, as the supplier and client both become more comfortable with the relationship, high level design and integration testing can be added. And in the third phase, the client might involve the supplier as part of the team that does requirements capture and also participates in system testing and acceptance testing. Beyond that, in some cases a fourth wave might take the supplier through a more advanced involvement and to actual delivery to the end user.

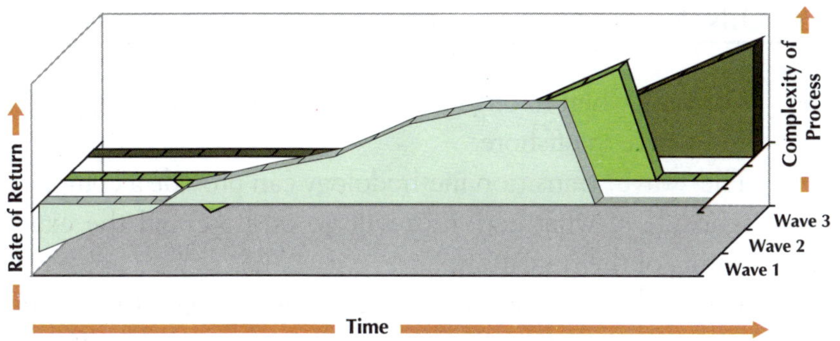


FIGURE 12.2

Example of a three-phase wave strategy.

The wave strategy works the same way in BPO. In call centers, for example, the type of call can often be classified into three tiers. A tier one call would be, for example, a credit card holder calling to check their balance, or an employee calling to find out how many vacation days they have left. If, however, the employee is calling to ask why the new benefits they signed up for did not get added, a tier one service provider might not be enabled with that capability and responsibility, so they will send the call to a supervisor and it becomes a tier two call. Now, let's say that the supervisor tells the employee that they are not eligible for that benefit, and the employee refutes that decision and presents a case for eligibility. The supervisor may send the call further upstream to someone who is responsible for actually determining eligibility, and it becomes a tier three call. These are all calls that offshore providers can handle with varying degrees of efficiency, but in most cases it makes sense to move them offshore gradually, in waves.

The same thing works for document processing—an insurance claim form needs to be scanned, indexed, processed, verified for accuracy and completeness, reviewed by someone in authority for approval, and then the payment must be processed and a check is cut. All of these are processes that may or may not be offshore mature, and which can and should be done in waves.

## KEY POINTS

- Knowing when to offshore is as important as knowing what and where to offshore.
- The "wave" transition methodology can provide a complete schedule of what activities will go offshore and the exact timing of the transition.
- The results of a strategic assessment can highlight the general areas whose data reflects the most potential for offshore concentration.
- The assessment is only one factor that contributes to the final decision of what to offshore and when.

Chapter 13

# The Total Cost of Offshoring

Cost optimization is one of the primary objectives companies have in developing a global sourcing initiative. With so much media discussion of the wage rate differences that form the basic leverage in global sourcing, enterprises frequently set expectations of cost savings entirely on wage rate arbitrage. This assumption can easily lead to a false sense of anticipated savings. When companies recognize the prospect of lower savings, they lower investment in appropriate risk mitigation strategies. This sets up the initiatives to fail or not meet expectations.

It is very important to ensure that in pursuit of lower costs, enterprises are realistic about the cost and direct financial benefits of offshore sourcing, and manage all components of cost, not just the one or two obvious ones. There are several components of cost that are inevitable in a global delivery model, and others that are elective, but critical in managing the risk and complexity of the global delivery model.

On an average, clients achieve savings ranging from 25 percent–50 percent annually over a three-year period, not 70 percent–90 percent, as the pure wage rate differential would suggest. In this chapter, we take a look at the other components of cost that impact the financial base case for global sourcing. The total of all these costs is called the Total Cost to Offshore (TCO).

Any Financial Base Case analysis of the impact of offshore outsourcing must take into account all the costs associated with an offshore initiative. The Total Cost to Offshore has the following key components:

1. Wage Rate
2. Communication Systems
3. Physical Infrastructure and Support
4. Transition
5. Governance
6. Resource Redeployment
7. HR Change Management
8. Training and Productivity
9. Disaster Recovery and Business Continuity Capabilities
10. Offshore Knowledge Development/Advisory Services
11. Travel Costs
12. Exchange Rate Fluctuations

Even though, under typical outsourcing contracts, several of the above components are included within the "charge rates" quoted by service providers, it is important for enterprises to understand the various cost lines in order to negotiate appropriate charge rates, and manage the balance between different cost components. Understanding total cost is also important to ensure that the service providers are adequately budgeting their investment in infrastructure to support the needs of the enterprise.

In the section below, we describe each component in detail.

## WAGE RATE

The wage rate differential between countries is the most important cost savings opportunity, and drives the market for offshore sourcing. Wage rates for similar skill sets in different geographies is shown in Table 13.1. However, the wage rate is only one of many costs that make up the total. For example, in offshore Call Center Outsourcing, direct labor costs account for less than 30 percent of the total cost of operations.

| | Programmer (2–3 yrs. experience) | | | Call Center Agent (2–3 yrs. experience) | | | Programmer AVG. |
|---|---|---|---|---|---|---|---|
| India | $6,000 | to | $9,000 | $5,500 | to | $7,000 | $7,500 |
| China | $5,500 | to | $9,600 | N/A | | N/A | $7,550 |
| Philippines | $6,500 | to | $10,900 | $7,600 | to | $9,200 | $8,700 |
| Russia | $7,000 | to | $13,000 | N/A | | N/A | $10,000 |
| Ireland | $21,000 | to | $28,000 | $16,000 | to | $25,500 | $24,500 |
| Mexico | $18,000 | to | $23,000 | $3,000 | to | $15,000 | $20,500 |
| Malaysia | $8,700 | to | $12,800 | N/A | | N/A | $10,750 |
| Brazil | $9,000 | to | $16,000 | N/A | | N/A | $12,500 |
| Vietnam | $2,850 | to | $4,100 | N/A | | N/A | $3,475 |
| Singapore | $27,300 | to | $34,600 | $22,300 | to | $28,400 | $30,950 |
| Canada | $25,000 | to | $50,000 | $18,600 | to | $28,300 | $37,500 |
| United States | $45,000 | to | $85,000 | $25,000 | to | $40,000 | $65,000 |

TABLE 13.1

A comparison of wage rates in different countries for similar skills.

*Note: Salary range depends on Supplier Tier (1,2 or 3) and City of Operations (tier 1, 2 or 3)*

## COMMUNICATION SYSTEMS

Offshore outsourcing requires a significant investment in reliable communication infrastructure. Typical components include leased circuits with enough dedicated bandwidth to carry simultaneous voice and data traffic between countries without latency. Typically, with appropriate compression, a 2Mbps IPLC (IP Leased Circuit) can support a team of 80 simultaneous voice and data channels. In the Application Development and Maintenance space, the number of supported resources can be higher. These costs, while they have come down significantly over the last two years, are still relevant. For example, a dedicated line from a POP (Point-of-Presence) in the U.S. to India costs approximately $6000–$8000 per month. To ensure business continuity, most organizations need to develop redundant communication links, thereby doubling the investment.

In addition, the offshore facilities need to invest in routing equipment (switches, routers, LAN infrastructure, etc.) to direct the communication lines to each desktop. Since the operating model for offshore deals is based on dedicated VLANs (Virtual LAN), there is an additional cost allocated to the outsourcing contract.

The communication costs offshore can be 30 to 60 percent higher than U.S./U.K. costs. The good news is that the cost of bandwidth is constantly dropping.

## PHYSICAL INFRASTRUCTURE AND SUPPORT

The cost of the physical infrastructure and other support is usually an additional redundant cost. In most cases, the offshore outsourcing initiative does not lead to a substantial reduction in the physical infrastructure (buildings, power, etc.) at the enterprise. In the case of offshore (captive, wholly-owned) BPO or Call Center operations, these costs can be substantial. The lease rates of Class A buildings continue to rise amid competition for infrastructure, and most BPO operations require additional expenditure on meals, transport, concierge services, etc. for their employees who need to work at night. These costs are very location specific and vary between locations within countries too.

## TRANSITION

One of the key components of cost associated with offshore sourcing models (whether they be outsourcing contracts or captive operations) is the cost of transitioning from locally deployed to globally deployed operations.

A typical transition timeline for an Applications Outsourcing project is 3–4 months. BPO Outsourcing contracts take anywhere from 5–7 months for the first process outsourced to complete transition. This is the time between a signed outsourcing contract and achieving steady state of operations at the outsourcer or captive center.

During this time, all resources need to be in place, and additional supplier resources are required for documentation and training. Enterprise employees need to work overtime, and are likely to receive bonuses for that work. All of these costs associated with these tasks can add a heavy burden to the cost of offshoring if the transition is not managed efficiently, or the project does not achieve steady state within the expected timelines.

## GOVERNANCE

Similarly, project governance also requires additional resources. Efficient management of the offshore sourcing process can be one of the greatest sink-holes of cost in an offshore initiative. While it appears somewhat obvious, enterprises (especially those embarking on large, complex initiatives) often under-invest in this area. It is important to ensure that there is a clear and well-articulated process for moving forward with an offshore initiative that covers the lifecycle of the program. All too often, enterprises get caught in 'analysis paralysis'—going around in circles looking for information without a clear understanding of how to use it. Alternatively, they adopt the opposite 'Ready-Fire-Aim' approach in hopes of achieving a quick hit and then figuring out what to do next.

Both approaches can lead to significant remedial costs that ultimately get allocated to the offshore initiative. In the former case, the knowledge acquisition cost is much higher than necessary. The latter can lead enterprises to additional sourcing costs or be held hostage by the 'Power of the Incumbency,' so common in offshore outsourcing. Power of the incumbency is the bias enterprises have towards their existing service provider.

These resources, primarily those involved in managing the offshore projects, are typically more expensive than project lead resources. In addition, program management resources from the enterprise need to be available frequently at the offshore outsourcer's location. Large enterprises with significant offshore presence develop expatriate resources for this, while smaller initiatives rely on employees to travel frequently. In either case, the cost of resources can be substantial. As a rule of thumb, resources that cost an enterprise $200K in the U.S. will have a total cost to the enterprise of $500K on an expatriate basis.

## HR CHANGE MANAGEMENT

As the transition to the global delivery model is completed, and organizations enter operational steady state, there is invariably a cost of internal change management. If the enterprise plans to internally redeploy resources, there are costs typically related to retraining and redeployment. If layoffs become necessary, costs of severance and assisting in job searches can be a significant component of costs.

In addition to direct resources costs, there are the costs associated with modifying HR plans to reflect the new roles and responsibilities of internal resources. For example, if an Application Engineer's role changes from primary involvement in technology development to vendor management of an outsourced contract, the change will impact compensation structures and HR metrics, and require training and development to ensure continued productivity.

## RESOURCE REDUNDANCY

Most types of offshore outsourcing deals require a program structure that creates a certain level of redundancy in resource utilization. Since the cost savings from wage rate differentials is high, this redundancy can be ignored as minor. However, it is important to realize that an offshore outsourcing initiative will have a larger number of FTEs than a similar sized initiative managed purely onsite, especially within the first 18 months of a contract.

As the outsourcing transactions get more complex, the redundancy increases, largely due to additional requirements in governance, and retention of core intellectual capital.

As an example, when an offshore applications outsourcing contract is instituted, there are project managers associated with the program, both from the enterprise as well as from the service provider working onsite. Some of the effort of these resources goes to managing the global delivery model itself (culture, communication, performance management, quality assurance, etc.). This is also true for the technical workers, who begin to take on vendor management roles, while their previous technical roles are adopted by the offshore outsourcer.

## TRAINING AND PRODUCTIVITY

Among the most important considerations in measuring the Total Cost of Offshoring is the level of productivity of the teams. Drivers of productivity include:

- Level of training of offshore resources on the enterprise's business environment
- Quality of resources available
- Capability of enterprise IS/business managers to manage offshore outsourcing initiatives, and develop comfort with the global delivery model
- Maturity of the communication infrastructure and processes
- Complexity of the program

Each of these can significantly impact the productivity of the resources and thereby dilute the overall cost effectiveness of the delivery model.

## DISASTER RECOVERY AND BUSINESS CONTINUITY CAPABILITIES

The development of a Business Continuity Plan (BCP) and a Disaster Recovery Plan (DRP) can be a significant additional cost to the initiative. Both include taking regular back-ups in a facility not likely to be affected by any broad force major event. Both also require some built in redundancy in people, technology and processes. These may be created through a mature sourcing model with multiple facilities, or as an investment in back up facilities and a 'hot site' in the U.S.

## OFFSHORE KNOWLEDGE DEVELOPMENT/ADVISORY SERVICES

Enterprises need to tie in the cost of knowledge acquisition on offshore outsourcing, whether it is independently conducted, or by leveraging industry experts.

Within the cost of knowledge acquisition is embedded the cost of leveraging an external knowledge base for tools, templates, processes and best practices to help plan, develop and manage their offshore initiatives. This cost item includes the time and effort tied up in internal readiness assessments, portfolio planning, site visits, due diligence of the supply landscape, and contracting.

## TRAVEL COSTS

A global sourcing initiative requires substantial travel by various people as the initiatives progress through the offshore/global lifecycle. While many sponsors and process owners may travel during the knowledge phase, the program managers and process leads travel significantly during the transition stage.

International travel can be expensive, with business class tickets from the U.S. to India and China ranging from $4000 to over $7500 and economy class prices hovering around $1500. These expenses can add up quickly.

Also, the budget needs to ensure that ongoing team meeting and operations reviews are accounted for.

## EXCHANGE RATE CHANGES

Exchange rate changes are often not included in even detailed assessments of cost. However fluctuations in exchange rate can be an important contributor to the overall financial impact. For captive centers and long-term outsourcing contracts, changes in exchange rates are built into renegotiation of wage rates (or charge rates) and other costs. A foreign currency strengthening against the dollar will increase costs, reduce interest among offshore outsourcers to export and in general soften the market for offshore sourcing.

Table 13.2 shows a case study that demonstrates the relative percentage of different components of cost on the Total Cost to Offshore.

In taking a typical offshore scenario, lets assume the following sample cost, timing, and deal attributes:

- Fortune 1000 firm with IT operations in three U.S. locations
- Three-year deal for applications support and maintenance (ASM) of Peoplesoft HR, SAP financials, and some legacy mainframe applications
- 150 FTE being offshored; current loaded-labor rate (LLE) of $120,000 per employee; offshored to India at competitive market rates
- Total deal value of $38 million, as resources transitioned offshore over time.

| BPO | % Cost | ITO | % Cost |
|---|---|---|---|
| Wage Rate | 42% | Wage Rate | 46% |
| Communication System | 5% | Communication System | 3% |
| Physical Infrastructure and Support | 17% | Physical Infrastructure and Support | 18% |
| Transition and Governance | 8% | Transition and Governance | 7% |
| Resource Redeployment | 3% | Resource Redeployment | 4% |
| Resource Redundancy | 2% | Resource Redundancy | 1% |
| Training and Productivity | 10% | Training and Productivity | 9% |
| Disaster Recovery and Business Continuity | 5% | Disaster Recovery and Business Continuity | 3% |
| Advisory Services | 2% | Advisory Services | 4% |
| Travel costs | 3% | Travel costs | 3% |
| Exchange Rate Changes | 2% | Exchange Rate Changes | 3% |

TABLE 13.2

Typical percentage breakdown of the Total Cost of Offshore.

With these aspects, the outcomes and actual value captured can vary widely depending on how well the deal is planned up-front, executed during sourcing, and then delivered over the duration of the contract. For example, with the same base and offshore rates, the table below illustrates three very different potential TCO results based on the deal described above.

As the three deals in Table 13.3 show, capturing the highest value in an offshore deal is about much more than finding a good offshore rate. The savings are significant in any of the scenarios above, and therefore why almost any offshoring deal initially looks attractive. What makes the difference in these scenarios and how can your company achieve maximize value, decrease risk, and minimize operational disruption? In short, the answer is, the devil is in the details. To holistically evaluate an offshoring initiative in

| Offshore Deal | Representative Offshore Sourcing and Results | Savings Potential (%) | Value of Savings ($) |
|---|---|---|---|
| **Base Offshore** | **Sourcing**—Quick evaluation to send functions / resources offshore. Selected provider from a couple of offshore firms that have previously called and pitched; firms did not necessarily have best industry, functional, or technical expertise in key disciplines.<br>**Results**—Most savings delivered from lower cost wages, but results leave significant value unrealized and many risks not fully addressed. | 10%–15% | $3.6–$5.4M |
| **Average Offshore** | **Sourcing**—An internal 'expert' or offshore 'consultant' helped put together an RFP and run a competitive bidding process; limited time spent in evaluating process and cultural fit of firms; limited due diligence conducted, resulting in elimination of one potential firm but no deep understanding of comparative capabilities.<br>**Results**—Significant value delivered, but many key risks and delivery issues not identified until post-contract. Inefficient transition plan results in operational challenges and some delays. Key requirements not fully understood during sourcing, requiring resource re-allocation from supplier and significantly increased resource dedication from client. | 20%–35% | $7.2–$12.6M |
| **Best Practices Offshore** | **Sourcing**—Formal planning process ensures business strategy aligned with offshoring requirements and eventual RFP; deep supplier knowledge and due diligence ensures optimal suppliers considered and selected; potential delivery, culture, process, and communication issues addressed up-front.<br>**Results**—Comprehensive approach with strategic plan, sourcing process, and program management plan put in place. | 40%–60% | $14.4–$19.8M |

*continued*

| Offshore Deal | Representative Offshore Sourcing and Results | Savings Potential (%) | Value of Savings ($) |
|---|---|---|---|
| | Program management plan based on contractual service levels result is maximizing savings captured and minimizing many offshore-specific risks. | | |

TABLE 13.3

Total Cost of Offshore Scenarios.

light of your specific business environment, your company has to have detailed information and knowledge on its side.

However, getting this detailed offshoring information is only part of the solution to executing an effective offshore deal. This knowledge must then be leveraged throughout the engagement to minimize risks and prevent value destruction. Different than maximizing value, value destruction occurs when negotiated savings and risks, initially thought to be mitigated up-front, were not either fully understood or not properly managed over the key steps of the offshoring lifecycle. The result can be an offshoring engagement full of misaligned expectations, offshoring results that do not meet initial savings projections, and unnecessary business risk.

The total cost of offshoring is not a fixed amount either. It can change both on an actual and on a relative basis. For example, as efficiencies are worked out and processes improved, the TCO might become less. On the other hand, unforeseen problems might arise that lead to additional expenses, inflating the TCO. And even if the TCO remains stable, it might change on a relative basis in relation to what could be garnered in the market as competitive pressures drive down prices.

## KEY POINTS

- Wading through the thousands of offshore suppliers and the new ones that pop up every day can be a daunting task.
- Be careful of supplier claims about cost savings.
- The Total Cost of Ownership is not just the initial price, but also the entire range of direct costs and indirect business changes, and potential risks.
- The difference between the Base Offshore TCO, the Average TCO and a Best Practices TCO can be huge, and can determine the success or failure of an offshore engagement.

# Part 4

# The Sourcing and/or Building of the Offshore Presence: Ground Zero

*Chapter* 14

# Sourcing to Third Party Service Providers

Once the Knowledge and Planning stages of the offshore process have been completed, it is time to move on to the Sourcing Process, the actual building of your offshore presence.

The difference between a good offshore experience and a poor one typically resides in the choice of the third party service provider. And yet, surprisingly little research and due diligence is done by most firms prior to selecting a service provider. This chapter is designed to help you understand how to choose an offshore service provider, and to guide you in managing your selection process.

## COMMON CHALLENGES IN SUPPLIER SELECTION

Offshore deals that will either fail or not live up to promised results are generally predictable. To reduce the inherent risks, certain steps are necessary in offshore transactions. The client must have a high degree of visibility of the supplier's capabilities, understand the supplier's culture and background, understand the various offshore models and must choose a supplier that aligns strategically with the organization.

Most clients notice very little difference in the sales presentations of suppliers. However, actual experience, company culture, and capabilities vary. It is important that a client understand the strengths and weaknesses of each supplier to help ensure low-risk, high-value, long-term partner relationships.

Even the large integrators who operate in developing nations face the same challenges in transitioning work and maintaining high productivity.

Other key challenges include:

- Finding the right suppliers with the right capabilities.
- Socio-cultural differences.
- Immaturity of the offshore supplier market.
- Growth dynamics and constantly changing focus of offshore firms.
- Lack of understanding of supplier reputation and history.
- Over reliance on supplier-provided information.

Prior to formal due diligence, the mining of data on offshore service providers generally can be broken down into three key processes:

- Visiting Offshore Suppliers.
- Asking the Right Questions.
- Managing Service Provider Responses.

The offshore supplier visit is a critical step in the Sourcing process, and yet too few companies prepare enough prior to the visit. An ill-prepared visit can lead to a fumbling of the supplier selection process by failing to identify important attributes of a supplier, both positive and negative. Also, a well-prepared visit can drastically reduce the time and money you spend later on due diligence.

In Appendix B, we have outlined what we call a "Best Practices Supplier Visit," which is designed to assist you as a buyer in achieving an objective understanding of a supplier's capabilities. Given the limited client time of the visit, this process is designed to be informative, structured and efficient. By the end of the visit you will have a deeper understanding of:

**Supplier Capabilities.** Companies need to drill below the surface of the supplier's operations to understand the actual ability to perform within the scope of the agreement. Do not just list–to sales presentations, talk with and see the personnel performing the work. It is advisable to have a local neutral sourcing expert help sift through the key strengths of each supplier and the areas of concern.

**Offshore Models.** It is important to analyze the logic behind various operating models. At the end of the visit, companies should understand options and models that are right for their environment. Companies should have a clearer understanding of financial structures, pricing and savings opportunities. This can change rapidly too and so needs to view latest data.

**Supplier Reputation.** Companies should understand the background and qualitative capabilities of the potential suppliers.

**Competitive Landscape.** During the visit, companies will gain an insider's view on the strategic landscape with discussions about near-term and long-term outlooks among the prospective supply base. This understanding will help place the buyer company on equal footing with the supplier.

**Geographic Factors.** The visit will also assist with the learning process about the cultural and socio-political factors associated with the offshore location.

## SERVICE PROVIDER DUE DILIGENCE

While a client visit and a carefully chosen list of questions and answers are important, the choice of an offshore supplier does not end there. Managing the supplier responses and careful follow-up due diligence are essential. One of the biggest challenges is how to perform due diligence with suppliers as far away as India, Hungary, Russia, Philippines and China given the tremendous geographic, cultural, and time constraints. A reliance on supplier-provided information given in RFPs is simply not enough, and can lead to a myriad of problems down the road. Due diligence is a critical step that should be performed to clarify and validate supplier capabilities, and can ultimately lead to better deals and relationships. Without the proper validation, many risks and weaknesses are not uncovered until after the deals are signed and critical problems arise.

During 1999–2001, IT service suppliers were excited to adopt process-oriented quality management system certification models, as many buying organizations started using this as a qualifier to bid on a project. The reason for adding industry certification as a qualifying criterion was very simple—clients wanted to reduce risk associated with outsourcing, especially offshore agreements. These process-oriented quality management system certifications gave some amount of assurance to buying organizations that the supplier they were partnering with had a minimum set of processes in place. However, over time these same buying organizations found that even suppliers with these process-oriented certifications were not always able to deliver on service level agreements (SLAs). As illustrated in Figure 14.1, the results the buyers received were variable. While the certification had measured a supplier's ability to follow a documented and stringent process, the capabilities of the provider and their ability to deliver on specific requirements had not been addressed.

Organizations began looking for a different set of parameters relevant for outsourcing capabilities to create better partnerships with their suppliers. However, these parameters remain loosely knit, and every organization uses a different set of criteria. For many organizations, the outsourcing due diligence model has yet to mature.

FIGURE 14.1

Organizations accepted variable results from their sourcing engagements, as they relied solely on verifying vendor processes.

Some of the challenges faced by these organizations during the due diligence process include discovery of the following information about the supplier in question:

- Breadth and depth of supplier domain knowledge.
- Mature infrastructure and technology to support requirements.
- Business continuity plan, disaster recovery, data privacy, security and confidentiality.
- Project and program management skills.
- Customer and partner satisfaction.
- Management skills (geography, project size, project type, experience).
- Transition process and management.
- Financial stability.
- HR environment—including cultural fit, experience levels, buffer management, attrition rates and HR initiatives for improving retention, transition team, implementation team, etc.
- Flexibility—comfort level and experience in various pricing models and service level agreements.

Since 2001, San Ramon-based, neoIT and other leading advisory players have formulated what is rapidly becoming an industry standard in performing offshore due diligence. Customer focus groups from the U.S., Europe, and other key global markets brought attention to the need for an outsourcing assurance program. Buyers from the Global 2000 were demanding a comprehensive process for qualifying and assuring the capabilities of service supplier companies before outsourcing their projects. neoIT's initiative, neoQA, was the industry's first outsourcing assurance and offshore supplier due diligence program.

## DUE DILIGENCE WITH neoQA

neoQA is a methodology to assess a service provider's expertise and ability to effectively deliver services. A neoQA rating demonstrates that the supplier adheres to capability parameters (Key Performance

FIGURE 14.2

Organizations now achieve desired results from their sourcing engagements, as they rely on capabilities due diligence programs such as neoQA.

Indicators) that directly affect the quality and timely delivery of an outsourced project. So the focus is not just on process documentation, but on performance. As shown in Figure 14.2, buyers can be confident that suppliers with the neoQA stamp have undergone rigorous due diligence, have met high standards of services delivery and can be expected to produce the desired results.

As opposed to some standard industry certifications that are centered around inward looking business capabilities, neoQA reviews outward looking business capabilities, and includes the deliverable parameters that are direct indicators as to whether a supplier can deliver on service level agreements required for a specific deal. For example, it will show not only that a call center company follows a specific process for answering customer issues, but how many calls the supplier can handle, scale up to and how quickly customer concerns can be answered. neoQA covers a number of infrastructure and program-specific elements such as team experience level, manager experience level, relevant project experience, depth and breadth of domain knowledge, technical skill set, project risk and reward pricing model, customer orientation, and HR competencies. A sample comparison of neoQA and some of the leading process-centric audits is illustrated in Table 14.1.

The following two examples illustrate the advantages a third-party due diligence program, such as neoQA, can deliver to buyers.

| | Features | COPC | ISO 9000: 2000 | CMM | neoQA | eSCM |
|---|---|---|---|---|---|---|
| 1 | Outsourcing capability orientation | No | No | No | Yes | Yes |
| 2 | Dynamic approach of the standard | No | Slow | Slow | Fast | No |
| 3 | Customized standard for different industries | No | No | No | Yes | No |
| 4 | Detailed audit report | Yes | Yes | Yes | Yes | Yes |
| 5 | Network of the auditors | No | Yes | Yes | Yes | No |
| 6 | Levels in certification | No | No | Yes | Yes | Yes |
| 7 | Third party periodic audit/assessment | Yes | Yes | Yes | Yes | Yes |
| 8 | Applies to IT, BPO or Both | BPO | IT | IT | Both | BPO |

TABLE 14.1

A Comparison of Services Qualification Standards.

## EXAMPLE ONE: CALL CENTER

A global BPO firm wanted to outsource a significant portion of its call center operations offshore. Some of the key business requirements included significantly reducing costs (over 50 percent), while still finding a supplier with a highly educated workforce and a strong telecommunications infrastructure. Suppliers bidding on the project needed to have reference accounts, a proven track record and the ability to handle a high volume of calls per day. The suppliers needed not only to be able to meet the current call volume, but also adjust to forecasted growth patterns. During due diligence, the client needed validation of a low risk, high cost savings scenario for choosing an offshore supplier as a partner.

**Risk Scenario.** During preliminary due diligence stages, the suppliers validated their capabilities, including the buying organization reviewing the standard industry certifications such as SEI and CMM. Yet, the details of these third-party certifications only provided process data such as, "yes, the supplier has a process in place to enable them to answer calls in 5 seconds or less." But, what was more important to the buyer was a validation that the service levels of the deal would be met: would the supplier have the proper language and cultural training? Would the suppliers' resources and infrastructure be able to scale quickly enough to meet the buyer's growth needs?

**Third-Party Assessment.** The neoQA detailed capabilities assessment provided the due diligence necessary to actively address the client's concerns. With this information, the client was able to pinpoint the partners' weaknesses early on and proactively ask the right questions, uncover issues, and confirm satisfactory solutions were in place. Armed with this information, the client ended up choosing a Tier 2 firm and more importantly the right supplier for the job. Without the information provided by neoQA, the client would have chosen a Tier 1 firm that may have lead to higher cost investments in the long term. The resulting data was also instrumental in negotiations to ensure that the client and the supplier were satisfied with the deal.

## EXAMPLE TWO: APPLICATIONS PORTFOLIO

A Fortune 500 healthcare services company needed to reduce costs and change from the current state of fixed cost management to variable cost management. The desired solution was to outsource the applications management of non-core, but critical functions such as hospital management, patient care and billing management. With that in mind, the company made the decision to look at offshore and nearshore sourcing solutions, specifically in Canada and India.

**Risk Scenario.** Canada would provide a low-cost solution with minimal risk factors. India on the other hand provided an even greater cost advantage, but the client was hesitant and unsure of the associated risks. While a standard, detailed due diligence had been performed, the client was still not assured of the level of quality that would be provided or that the proposed service levels and pricing agreements could be met.

**Third-Party Assessment.** Again, the neoQA detailed capabilities assessment provided the additional due diligence to measure delivery-critical supplier capabilities. From a third-party offshore advisory firm, the client was also able to obtain data points to compare country infrastructure and stability. As a result of the neoQA program, the client was able to see that all of the companies profiled were proven able to produce the desired results as outlined in the contract. With the neoQA information, the client was able to pick the obvious choice, the lower cost Indian firm, and was able to leverage the data to negotiate better SLAs and pricing terms.

## PRICE NEGOTIATIONS

One of the biggest stumbling blocks in the offshore process is the cultural differences inherent in price negotiations. Clients should look at price negotiations as extremely malleable, and avoid the tendency to say, "This is my final price." Indian suppliers, for example, typically won't even consider the fact that a price may be final until many rounds of negotiations.

In bidding, the various supplier models result in tiered pricing. MNCs are usually higher priced than the offshore suppliers. And, the top-tier offshore suppliers are typically higher priced than the increasingly competitive second-tier offshore suppliers. It is foreseeable in the near future that the pricing gaps between the tiers will close and they

> *Many offshore suppliers have built their reputation on delivering as good or better quality than can be delivered in domestic markets.*

will bid head-to-head on offshore deals focusing more on delivery capability than price.

India's trade association for the IT services industry, NASSCOM, has a strong U.S./European presence to assist with the global development of their suppliers. Other offshore country leaders will follow the example of NASSCOM. For example, the Philippines recently launched an industry organization with government sponsorship, Outsource Philippines.

Many of the larger Indian, Philippine and Russian suppliers have established global offices in their buyer markets and are also expanding, much like the MNCs, into other lower-cost supplier markets.

Pure offshore-based operations (i.e. India-based operations—TCS, Wipro, Infosys) are mature, have developing brand presence, and are often more cost-competitive. Niche players in certain vertical markets have deep domain knowledge and a solid track record such as Cognizant and iFlex in financial services and WNS and eXL in BPO. Many of these have displayed pricing stability in an extremely competitive environment.

## CONTRACTS

As we have stressed throughout this book, the actual contract with the service provider is an extremely important document that should not be taken lightly and requires professional legal assistance from an attorney schooled in offshore outsourcing. For this section, we enlisted the help of Daniel Masur of Mayer, Brown, Rowe & Maw LLP, who has worked on numerous such transactions.

Offshore sourcing contracts have evolved significantly over the past decade, usually with the intention of trying to make wary onshore clients more comfortable with the whole process.

"Contracts are one way to address or mitigate the actual or perceived risk of offshoring," says Masur. "Clients should view it from the perspective of doing a deal that makes sense now but that can also evolve as the industry evolves along with it."

A contract with an offshore supplier should seek to accomplish several key objectives which can be categorized into the following areas: deal structure, risk management, price structure and protection, quality assurance, change management, personnel management, IP protection and access, regulatory and legal issues, and governance. Let's look at each of those individually.

**Deal Structure.** One of the most important aspects in structuring an offshore supplier contract is the ability of the client to use third parties and to negotiate other contracts independently. Deal structure should also give specifics as to control, project management, dispute resolution and deliverables.

**Risk Management.** The contract should include a well thought-out plan for limiting the risk exposure of the client and assigning responsibilities for unforeseen circumstances. What happens to the contract if geopolitics get in the way? What are the supplier's contingency plans and disaster recovery plans?

**Price Structure and Protection.** How the contract is priced is very important, and being specific as possible is key. Will it be on a per-transaction basis? If so, be sure to include what defines a transaction. Also, some flexibility should be built in so that the price deliverables are not only actual but relative to changing market prices. And there are key clauses that, when included, prevent clients from being nickeled and dimed for unforeseen costs.

**Quality Assurance.** Benchmarking is key, along with meeting certain service levels. It's important to have well defined service levels and financial credits and penalties that are tied to meeting, exceeding or failing to meet them. As in pricing, the ability to add, modify or delete quality service levels is essential.

**Change Management.** No agreement lasts forever, and in the rapidly changing offshore outsourcing landscape, change is inevitable.

Every good contract should have ample language about how to manage that change—whether it's a change in the contract deliverables, a change in supplier partnerships, or an exit strategy if the client decides to cancel the contract.

**Personnel Management.** Contracts should have a well defined plan for who has the ability to hire and fire workers, and clients should retain the ability to approve or remove personnel in key positions. Also, provisions should be included whereby the client might have the option to transfer personnel to its own payroll when appropriate.

**IP Protection and Access.** The contract should be specific about who has access to what types of client documents, data and processes, and should limit as much as possible the supplier's use of client IP beyond what is essential for performing the work. In many countries, notably China, IP laws are not reliable and IP theft is abundant. Contract protections can ameliorate some of those problems.

**Regulatory and Legal Issues.** Contracts should have clearly defined criteria for who is responsible for meeting regulatory issues, and what responsibilities the supplier has in helping the client to meet its own regulatory issues such as Sarbanes-Oxley compliance.

**Governance.** Among the key aspects of a contract are the governance clauses that establish the ongoing monitoring and health audits so that the deliverables not only are met but continue to improve. Such language can be sensitive if all parties are expected to work together effectively to achieve the client's objectives and to avoid finger pointing.

## KEY POINTS

- Knowing how to sift through sales presentations and identify differences among suppliers is a key challenge to supplier selection.

- Prior to formal due diligence, supplier selection can be viewed as three processes: visiting offshore suppliers, asking the right questions, and managing service provider responses.
- A "best practices" offshore visit should give you a better understanding of supplier capabilities, offshore models, supplier reputation, the competitive landscape, and geographic factors.
- Asking the right questions is the key to a successful supplier selection process, and can not only help reduce the chance of making a poor choice but can also reduce time and money spent on later due diligence.
- Geographic, cultural and time constraints can lead to a myriad of potential problems in conducting due diligence.
- Third-party due diligence programs, which feature core expertise and performance capabilities mapping, are vital to reducing risks associated with the offshore sourcing lifecycle.
- A capabilities assessment as part of a due diligence program like neoQA, can be used to uncover data to avoid picking the wrong firm and instead choose the best firm for the contract.
- The offshore supplier contract is the most important document you will sign and should cover these key areas: deal structure, risk management, price structure and protection, quality assurance, change management, personnel management, IP protection and access, regulatory and legal issues, and governance.

*Chapter* 15

# Building the Captive Center

The natural progression of the offshore outsourcing industry is the choice to forego the use of a third-party supplier and instead build a wholly owned captive offshore center. In most cases, companies that choose this route have had numerous experiences with offshore suppliers, and now feel confident that they can do it on their own. The choice to build a captive center is made for a variety of reasons, including the belief that an even lower cost model can be accomplished, because security issues are a concern, or because the company believes that no existing third-party supplier could adequately fulfill the service requirements. Whatever the reason, building captive centers is a growing trend.

At first glance, it might seem that building a captive center is a way to capture all of the advantages of offshoring while eliminating most of the risks. However, building a captive center involves its own set of risks, and if not done properly the cost and quality advantages can suffer as well. In this chapter, we discuss how to build a captive center to maximize quality, minimize costs, and keep risks to a minimum. We also provide an overview of some of the decision factors, challenges and opportunities for the wholly owned captive center ownership model.

## BACKGROUND

During the last decade, companies such as GE, American Express, Dell and AOL have taken offshore outsourcing a step further by opening their own captive centers in places like India and the Philippines. These and many other Fortune 500 companies have lowered costs by as much as 50 percent while improving quality and overall customer satisfaction. As each one of these organizations put together an offshore strategy, one of the factors they carefully examined and evaluated was their ownership option—how best to structure an offshore services platform.

As technology has advanced in networking and enhanced bandwidth availability, using offshore locations with a lower cost base has clearly become an attractive option. Other benefits such as improved processes and service quality, as well as geographic advantages, have also driven companies to set up captive centers. More flexible work practices and the exploitation of different time zones can, for example, create 24-hour processes which were previously limited to certain parts of the day. Access to highly qualified and motivated staff in some locations also assists in the improvement of service quality.

The key drivers behind the majority of outsourcing strategies are the desire to reduce costs, transform processes and improve service quality. With these objectives in mind, the choice of ownership model depends on a number of factors. In broad terms, a traditional outsourcing arrangement will usually be the preferred option where cost savings and local supplier expertise are important and/or the customer wishes to limit risk. A joint venture or captive facility approach may be of interest where proprietary issues, operational and management control and risk ownership is important and/or there is a long-term commitment to the region and the business is looking for the function to become a profit center. Figure 15.1 illustrates how the various ownership models compare for control and value capture criteria.

## WHY CAPTIVES

The process of choosing a specific type of global ownership model depends upon an analysis of a company's strategic requirements, decision influencers and key benefits afforded. In this section, we outline a situation where the captive model is the best choice.

Figure 15.2 highlights the major requirements, decision influencers and key benefits that support the decision to select a captive ownership model.

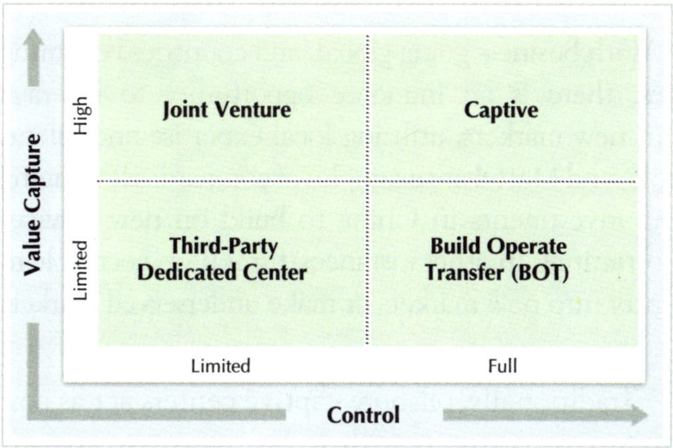


FIGURE 15.1

Examination of the benefits of global ownership models.

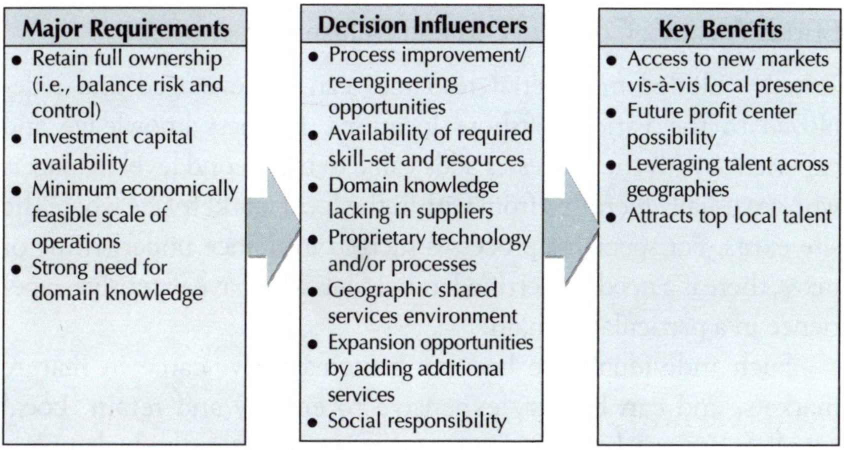


FIGURE 15.2

Major requirements, decision influencers and key benefits for choosing a captive ownership option.

## BENEFITS

The opportunities to reduce costs and improve processes are only a few of the benefits for companies looking to globalize their services. Below, we outline additional benefits that are specific to captives.

**New Markets.** With business going global, and countries becoming virtual boundaries, there is an immense opportunity to leverage old investments in new markets, utilizing local expertise and talent. GE, Intel, Motorola, and Mattel are examples of companies leveraging old manufacturing investments in China to build on new services globalization opportunities. In other instances, firms have been able to either speed up entry into new markets or make underserved markets attractive.

**Profit Centers.** Traditionally, offshore captive centers act as cost centers. The long-term opportunity with such centers is to convert them to profit centers, or strategic business units, which can help generate additional revenues. Historically, best-practices captive centers have reincarnated as best-of-breed suppliers. Successful examples of firms turning a captive into a profit center include British Airways, Conseco, Citi and Deluxe Corporation.

**Talent.** Skilled managerial resources can be leveraged and redeployed to the various offshore locations. Business knowledge and experience with the processes adds value to the second level managers who are usually recruited from within the local marketplace where the site exists. For specialist processes such as insurance underwriting or taxes, there is a need for certified individuals who have extensive experience in a particular domain.

Such individuals are becoming increasingly scarce in mature markets, and can be very expensive to employ and retain. Local suppliers are not likely to train and retain these individuals unless they are involved in client work. Captive centers have a good chance of attracting top-talent for industry-specific skills. AIG and Ernst & Young have done this successfully.

**Human Capital.** A captive center will generally attract a more educated worker than it would in the parent country. These same workers are also more likely to be committed to a multinational captive center than a local supplier. Jobs in captive centers are usually seen in the local offshore market as a career, not just a stepping stone to better things. The people are driven not only by the opportunity to work for respected organizations, but also by the fact that the company has made a long-term commitment to the local market.

## CHALLENGES

After reviewing some of the advantages of a captive center, it may seem to be an easy process. However, it is important to understand that with these opportunities, there are also challenges. In general, the captive offshore phenomenon presents significant challenges to management, including the key impacts of the organizational, processes, and finances management of an enterprise. Offshore impacts include:

**Organizational.** From the organizational point of view, offshore captives challenge the staffing, style, and formal and informal information systems of organizations that implement them. Specifically, human resource departments need to become more adept at managing disparate work forces and incorporating stylistic and cultural differences in communication and problem solving. Management needs to develop policies and practices to incorporate a more flexible approach to labor allocation. Regulatory and legal issues are important as countries deal with the political issues that offshore sourcing is rising. The management structure needs to support relationships with offshore operations and assure that objectives, contracts, delivery models, and measurements are aligned.

***Attrition Management.*** Because of higher initial costs, compensation offered by captives is typically 75 to 90 percent of the industry average. This can have a detrimental impact on employee motivation and retention. In the early days, attrition management therefore is crucial. These organizations often lack the ability to align the compensation structures with the overall industry averages because of inadequate benchmarking and a lack of understanding of the dynamics of the offshore workforce and resource management.

***Transition Management.*** Transition planning and management is critical for the success of a captive. This often requires expatriates to spend significant time at the offshore location. Also, different management styles adopted by the parent company's transition team and the local transition management team can be detrimental to the success. Such conflicts can arise out of processes such as portfolio assessment, training and knowledge transfer, recruitment and staffing, benefits calculations, etc.

**Process.** Human interactions as well as IT systems and applications will need to enable the dynamic allocation of workflow and support quality assurance. Organizations will need to gain a level of comfort in relinquishing control over previously proprietary applications and processes while implementing capabilities that allow offshore processes to be measured and improved over time. These processes must support change and avoid becoming sources of stagnation. It is one thing to have a "legacy" process or application running in a remote facility—with newer processes and applications, the risk of disconnection from other enterprise processes and resources is even greater. Finally, the disciplines of program and process management must address the advantages and challenges presented when part or all of a project "moves offshore," and managers must develop and disseminate best practices for achieving project success as well as cost savings.

***Infrastructure and Technology.*** Offshoring is greatly enabled by technology, tools and the availability of communications bandwidth. However, the same are also primary challenges. Replication of on-shore infrastructure is not the answer—and there is a great necessity to understand the needs and constraints and implement an optimized solution. Technology and bandwidth costs are a major part of the total cost of offshoring. Latency in data transmission impacts performance and should be one of the guiding principles for engineering the bandwidth and selection of technology and tools.

**Financial.** Firms need to manage cross-border cash flows, assure that cost advantages are real and are being preserved over time by the enterprise's sourcing strategy, and manage a diverse portfolio of assets and facilities. In managing captive facilities, especially in the initial stages, it is a challenge to manage and stay within original budget estimates.

***Higher Start-Up Costs.*** Typical investments in infrastructure, hardware, software, and facility service provisioning, as well as human resources related costs such as recruitment, hiring and marketing, require high initial setup costs. These costs are usually significantly higher in building a captive center when compared to outsourcing to a third party.

***Expat Costs, Retention and Management.*** Challenges exist in attracting top expat talent to relocate to offshore countries, training them to perform well in a different culture, ensuring execution and succession planning. The commitment level of local employees often faces a setback at the time of succession of an expat.

While many organizations today have experience in working internationally, an offshore captive center takes this challenge to the next level, calling on organizations to not only sell, market, and manufacture in other parts of the world but to also embed offshore delivery in the core business and IT processes of the company.

## CASE STUDY Building the Captive Center

Rather than walk you step by step over how to set up a captive center, we thought it would be more helpful to use a case study of one company's recent, highly successful experience.

*Exult* had already been outsourcing some of its IT requirements when, in late 2002, it began to consider whether similar benefits could be achieved by offshoring business processes as well.

From the start, it was clear that this would be a much more strategic decision. After all, Exult was one of the world's largest providers of BPO for the HR industry. Last year alone, the company managed over 11 million employee payments and 2.1 million transfers, promotions and pay changes; recruited over 21,000 professionals; managed 2,500 expatriate assignments, and administered 150,000 learning enrollments for its Global 2000 clients worldwide.

The business processes Exult was considering offshoring were core to the company's entire business model and much closer to the client than the IT functions it was already offshoring. Could Exult offshore some of these processes and still meet the same quality control parameters its clients were used to? If so, which processes were ripe for offshoring? What were the risks involved?

To help answer these questions, Exult's first step was to hire neoIT, which had advised Exult on setting up the IT supplier relationship and had managed that contract from the get-go. Trust was a key issue—neoIT's offshore business had grown along with that of Exult, and the management teams of both companies had developed a close working relationship.

After an initial assessment was completed of Exult's offshore requirements and its internal processes, RFPs were sent out for Exult's BPO needs. Soon after, however, neoIT and Exult quickly came to the decision that none of the BPO suppliers that had bid for the work were mature enough in their mastery of the specific HR processes to meet Exult's stringent requirements.

It was mostly a lack of domain expertise. The suppliers were fine in terms of infrastructure and overall BPO experience, but they couldn't guarantee quality delivery of back-office processes such as payroll and benefits administration, and management of the vast networks of expatriates for Exult's Global 2000 clients.

As a result, the bold decision was made that Exult would build its own captive center. neoIT quickly prepared a short list of possible cities and potential sites, and within no time Exult had selected a location in Mumbai.

neoIT provided not only offshore consulting services, but also advised Exult on a host of new "captive management" solutions—technology, building selection and management, interiors, finance, HR, recruitment, even government and regulatory relations.

Exult's priorities in setting up the captive center were the same as they were in selecting an IT supplier:

- **Savings.** They wanted to meet or exceed the 45 percent savings margin they were gaining by offshoring IT services to India.
- **Skill.** They wanted to tap into new sources of expertise while replicating the level of skill that Exult's customers had come to know from its onshore facilities.
- **Scale.** By being close to large pools of low-cost talent, they wanted to be able to provide additional capacity to accommodate Exult's growing global business.

A main difference between the IT supplier relationship and the BPO captive was the relationship proximity of the functions to Exult's clients, and the attention to quality that would be required.

After selecting a building, neoIT helped in contract negotiation, and then found an architect to redesign interior work spaces that were a blend of Exult's project-specific needs and the unique requirements of the Indian worker. Compensation ranges were calculated, taxes were taken into account, regulatory, customs and legal documents were signed. And when it came time to announce the venture and begin the hiring process, press releases were sent out to local newspapers and ads were placed.

neoIT also helped Exult set up a training program for Exult's new hires, and implemented a westernization, voice and accent coaching program.

Another key value add that neoIT provided was in negotiating procurement of hardware, software and networking equipment from global providers such as Cisco and Avaya. Exult had already budgeted the cost of that equipment according to the rates those same companies charged Exult in the U.S. But this was India, and Exult was able to get the prices down by about 45 percent.

The end result is that Exult now owns and operates a 320-person captive BPO center in Mumbai that in less than a full year of operations is already saving the company close to 40 percent, compared with the costs of running similar processes from onshore facilities. As time goes by, Exult expects those savings will increase, especially once it adds additional shifts and ramps up to its planned expansion to 1,100 employees in Mumbai.

From the time the decision was made to build the captive center in late 2003, it took only about six months before the first back-office processes went online.

Since then, neoIT has also helped Exult forge a disaster recovery center in another India-city, Chennai, which can go online almost immediately if some unseen disaster were to render the Mumbai Center inoperable.

## KEY POINTS

- There is a range of ownership options available to organizations seeking to leverage global locations for IT services and business processes, and companies should study all of them before making a decision on any one type.

- The decision to build and run a captive center should be driven by a rigorous evaluation of the firm's strategy, risk factors, control factors, cultural norms and benefits afforded. This analysis will (in most cases) focus on areas of business and/or a specific process rather than the overall organization. So, a firm may end up with a range of different ownership options for their multiple lines of business.
- In general, captive centers will best serve clients that want to migrate core business processes offshore or technology companies that want to establish IT development, support and maintenance in a multi-shore structure.

# Part 5

# The Managing of the Offshore Presence: The Governance Structure

*Chapter* 16

# The Transition Stage

In the outsourcing of IT functions and business processes, offshore outsourcing has long been advertised as the key to reducing costs and improving performance. Cost savings, process improvements, a focus on core competencies and access to the best and brightest can all be accomplished in offshore engagements. Yet, too often companies have the impression that once the contract is signed, the hard part is over. However, the level of success is highly dependant on the on-going management that occurs post-contract signing. Competent program management is essential to services globalization success.

If there is one area where having outside advice and help is key, it is in the transition stage to full offshore operations. This process normally takes about six months and aims to eliminate the road-blocks and bumps you inevitably will face as your offshore strategy is executed. If the proper structural and project management framework—along with a certain amount of process reengineering—are not instituted from the beginning, your offshore experience will be built on an inefficient base, and occurrence of savings will be pushed further into the future or eliminated.

Lately, we have seen more and more companies move quickly into the strategy and planning phase and then on to the sourcing phase, moving processes and projects to distant shores. And we have seen these same companies lose sight of the original objectives once they transition to the management phase. This loss of focus is not uncommon in the steady drudgery of day-to-day operations, and it makes a negative impact on the company's ability to manage offshore risk and execute a successful engagement. The lack of focus during this phase, combined with a distance from executive level priorities, is why many offshore programs fail.

The keys to successful offshore program management are:

- Dedication to transition execution
- Continuous monitoring of metrics, scope and issues
- Maintaining a local program office
- Knowledge of offshore outsourcing best practices
- Experience in dealing with offshore suppliers
- Attentiveness to typical pitfalls
- Understanding of long-term offshore outsourcing contracts

## TRANSITION MANAGEMENT—WHY IS IT SO CRITICAL?

When a company makes the decision to outsource, customer needs, wants, concerns and crises do not stop. Transition management takes place simultaneously with 'business as usual.' Hence, there is a critical need for an accurate and prompt transition schedule, knowledge transfer process, and regular status monitoring.

In a typical outsourcing deal, the retention of people is high. Frequently, people are asked to move from the payroll of the company that is outsourcing to the payroll of the supplier. However, in offshore outsourcing this is not the process. Often an entire function is handed over to a new team—the vendor's team of resources. Adding to the complexity of the transition is the fact that on top of an entirely new team, the vendor must adjust to the uniqueness of client business processes for individual companies, which are often in contrast. While these transition challenges may be easy for a domestic supplier to adjust to in a typical outsourcing deal, the offshore vendors have not reached a common level of maturity for standard business process delivery despite their exceptional IT capabilities and credentials. Hence, each transition is customized depending on the type of work, the workflow model, the rate of transitioning resources and the level of work and information division between onsite and offshore. In Figure 16.1, a high-level outline of the steps one organization took during transition.

Long before the contract is signed, companies need to work with the vendor (and preferably a subject matter advisor) to detail the transition plan. This is not only about setting dates and goals, but also about planning out the steps that it will take to get where you need to be. It is essential to think deeply about how many resources need to be transitioned, time frames, resources needed to manage the transition, the need for a local company representative, the process documentation procedure, training logistics and planning. Remember, in offshore outsourcing, one needs to include more and

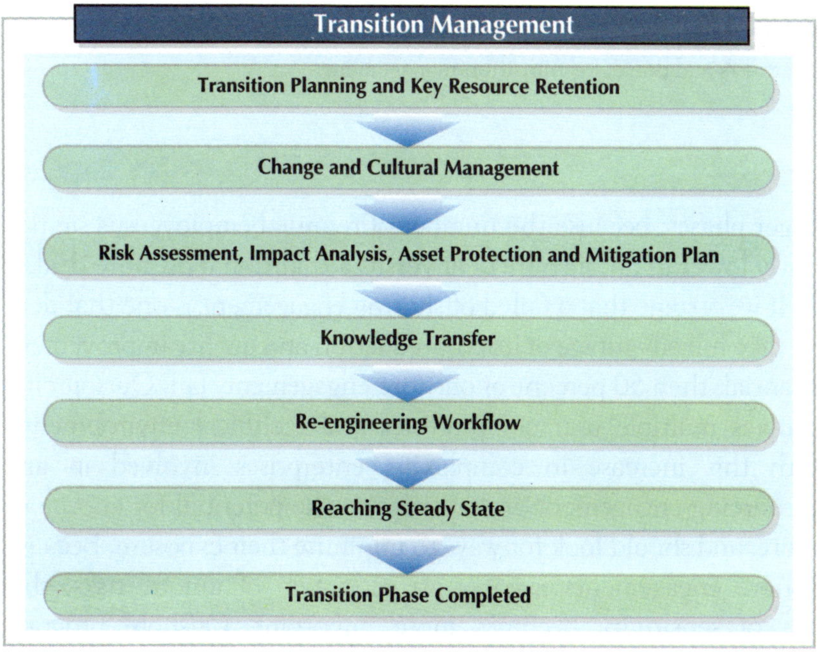


FIGURE 16.1

High-level example of transition management process.

Expert Do's:

- Do design a detailed transition map that includes several waves of phases.
- Do ensure time for sufficient process documentation.
- Do ensure proper training—it's the key to successful knowledge transfer.
- Do schedule shadowing, reverse shadowing and readiness tests in the training program.

Expert Don'ts:

- Don't assume the supplier is the expert on transition management. For offshore, because the market is relatively immature, every engagement must be considered uncharted territory.
- Don't hand over full responsibility too early. Follow the transition schedule, but don't be afraid to make adjustments if the team is not ready to face customers.

FIGURE 16.2

Expert do's and don'ts for transition management.

longer phases, because the number of retained employees is significantly lower in an offshore deal versus a traditional onshore deal.

If we assume that a failed offshoring engagement is one that does not take full advantage of its cost reduction and quality improvement potential, then 50 percent of offshore engagements fail. Outsourcing involves multiple user communities and technical environments. With this increase in complexity, enterprises involved in any outsourcing engagement are sensitive to the potential for enormous failure, and should look for ways to minimize their exposure. Because offshore engagements involve an ecosystem of unique risks, this type of sensitivity becomes more important. Offshore program management responsibilities can be mapped to five strategic competencies (M5 Methodology) that include performance, relationship, contract, resource and financial management. Table 16.1 outlines some common challenges encountered in an offshore deal under each of these five strategic competencies.

Experts who have navigated the offshore experience through other engagements can help clients mitigate offshore program risks. A good offshore program manager can ensure the success of the contract, in achieving ROI, bottom line targets and cost savings.

| Performance | Relationship |
|---|---|
| **(Client Issues)**<br>• Lack of user buy-in/ acceptance<br>• Insufficient resources<br>• Executive sponsorship dissipates as the engagement is no longer seen as part of the overall business strategy<br>• Lack of subject matter experts available to the supplier team as knowledge resources<br><br>**(Supplier Issues)**<br>• Insufficient resources<br>• Inexperienced/non-insightful planning | • Miscommunication<br>• Cultural gaps<br>• Poor planning for change management programs<br>• Deficient in coordinated team organization and execution<br>• Not having demarcated roles<br>• Unclear responsibilities between client and supplier |
| **Contract** | **Financial** |
| • Program and service level timelines and deadlines mismanaged<br>• Incomplete requirements<br>• Unrealistic expectations<br>• Changing requirements, scope and specifications<br>• Engagement is "no longer needed" by the client<br>• Contract amnesia (meaning nobody refers to the contract or remembers what was in it) | • Cost overruns<br>• Not planning for changes<br>• Unrealistic ROI analyses and expectations<br>• Unexpected costs (travel, training, turnover, infrastructure, technology) |

*continued*

| Resource |
|---|
| • Transition is too fast<br>• Bait and switch—resources pitched in the contract are not the same as those working on the deal<br>• Vacation and holiday schedules are not understood or managed<br>• Buffer staff is not properly planned<br>• Training program is mismanaged (or ignored)<br>• Transition resources are not hired or transferred from other projects according to schedule<br>• High turn-over rates |

TABLE 16.1

Common challenges encountered under the five offshore program management competencies.

However, an expert offshore program manager can turn what may have been a negative, drudging offshore relationship into a strategic opportunity for your company to expand the offshore vendor relationship into an extension of the company.

Even though each client believes that their case is unique, the majority of all questions, doubts and how-to's are mapped and have been dealt with before. Offshore program experts are able to anticipate and pay attention to risk factors and make changes before minor issues become serious problems. By assigning program management responsibilities to an expert, the resulting resource issues, missed target dates, cost overruns or other traumas can be avoided, or at least minimized.

## KEY POINTS

- Most offshore programs fail not because the engagement was improperly sourced or planned but because it was improperly managed.

- Among the keys to successful program management are: dedication to transition execution; continuous monitoring of metrics, scope and issues; maintaining a local program office, and knowledge of offshore outsourcing best practices.
- Other important steps are: designing a detailed transition map that includes several waves of phases; ensuring time for sufficient process documentation; and establishing a proper training regime.
- Don't assume the supplier is the expert on transition management. For offshoring, because the market is relatively immature, every engagement must be considered uncharted territory.
- Don't hand over full responsibility too early. Follow the transition schedule, but don't be afraid to make adjustments if the team is not ready to face customers.



Chapter 17

# The Offshore Program Management Office

Offshore program experts do more than identify risks and develop risk management plans. They also monitor risk factors throughout the engagements and are prepared to implement risk containment plans as the risk levels fluctuate. As conditions change and evolve, offshore program experts estimate and manage the potential impact in dealing with challenges within each of the offshore program competencies.

Throughout the life of the engagement, from transition to exceeding expectations, a dedicated offshore program manager can make the difference between "everyday fires" that need to be put out and a seamless delivery.

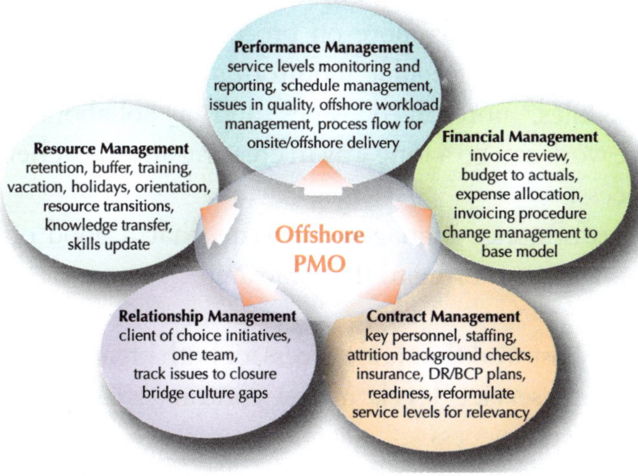


FIGURE 17.1

Best practice offshore program management framework, M5.

## PERFORMANCE MANAGEMENT

Managing performance is at the top of the list of critical success factors. If due diligence has been done well, companies can be assured that the vendor has managed service levels to client expectations in the past. However, the past does not necessarily guarantee continuing success.

One of the first steps in the transitioning phase is to map out and document internal processes, information flow and interdepartmental handoffs. Remember, this is about merging the work processes and flow of two organizations. Discipline and organization at this point will lead to an operational relationship that maximizes process efficiency and ensures repeatable over-achievement of performance parameters.

Besides peace of mind, a program expert can contribute to innovative solutions that help avoid internal/supplier politics or the supplier's innate difficulty to see the worldview. This native expertise comes from direct experience and knowledge of supplier methodologies, experience with cutting-edge industry and offshore practices, and an acute awareness of the client's business processes. A program management practitioner can act as a sounding board for both the client and the supplier to aid in managing expectations.

In the end, quality depends more on process and governance than tools and technology. Regular monitoring of the status of deliverables, schedules, unresolved issues and a collaborative planning of future work can go a long way in creating an atmosphere conducive to success.

Among the performance management items that a good offshore program manager can bring to the table are:

- Evolving a robust workflow and process for both organizations
- Agreement on service levels in the contract that have a direct bearing on success
- Agreement on gap closing processes
- Assignment of a dedicated program manager on-site and offshore that represents you, the client

- Ensuring executive sponsorship, user acceptance and buy-in throughout the engagement

## FINANCIAL MANAGEMENT

Preparation and managing financial expectations in the contracting phase will put a company in a prime position for entering the engagement, but what if preparation isn't enough? What happens when there are unexpected costs? Regardless of the terms of the contract, continual financial management is important to ensure the financial and commercial considerations that were the initial motivators are met and exceeded.

Unlike a traditional outsourcing program, a lack of awareness for unbudgeted expenses can often derail the budget in an offshoring contract. An understanding of the client's financial pressures coupled with a perceptive knowledge of supplier resource management strategies can lead to a methodical and efficient framework for unbudgeted expenses such as resource transitions, vacation and cultural holiday coverage strategies, unallocated travel costs, resource training needs, turnover costs, etc.

An inevitable challenge met by organizations is how to push the envelope on performance without exceeding budgetary constraints. An expert's knowledge can help clients formulate a strategy to push for exceptional performance and can also help financially manage other intangibles such as supplier billing practices, vendor rebates and standard freebies[1]. Outside expertise is also helpful in objectively adjudicating which party should pay for one-time expenses that invariably come up over the long-term.

Once the savings start to roll in, clients should expect the offshoring engagement to expand into other areas of partnership.

---

[1] Freebies refers to items that may be overlooked such as free training to keep resources up-to-date on technologies, free transport during client visits, etc.

Some of the financial management deliverables of a good program manager include:

- Managing financial expectations in the contracting phase
- Preparing for the offshore engagement to expand into other areas of the business
- Creating an awareness around unbudgeted expenses such as resource transitions, turnover, cultural holidays, etc.

## CONTRACT MANAGEMENT

Typically, a lot of time and effort is devoted to negotiating an offshore contract. Clients should expect that an equal or greater amount of effort should be devoted to monitoring and managing the contractual compliance. By maximizing the benefits of the time and intelligence that went into the making of the contract, clients can prepare for the conditions that may need to be enforced.

Enforcing contract compliance with periodic reviews will preempt issues relating to questions on areas of responsibility, work processes and performance and delivery. It is important to ensure that compliance reviews are scheduled monthly and client visits quarterly. Lack of contract compliance can lead to disasters such as an application that crashes, affects many end-users and leaves no clear responsibility or accountability for the client or the vendor.

Good contract governance is important to ensuring compliance. It is not feasible to suddenly apply the terms of the contract if it has not been applied consistently from the beginning. It would be like setting a curfew of 9 o'clock for your teenager after you have let them stay out all night. Just like the parent of the teenager, a client without contract guidance and governance loses respect and the ability to enforce the guidelines set in the contracting phase. When both parties have a consistent view and management of the contractual framework, a healthy partnership evolves.

Contract management deliverables of a program management office should include:

- Setting up consistent compliance meetings as a regular check-point for deliverables, unresolved issues and service level monitoring
- Applying the terms of the contract from the beginning
- Monitoring adherence to contract terms.

## RELATIONSHIP MANAGEMENT

In the beginning, as the client and supplier follow the learning curve of offshore management, the program manager facilitates people-related issues, communicates across cultures, and provides a liaison service for the teams to exchange ideas and relate to work culture differences. An outside expert can ease the difficulties of working in a developing country and serve as a reminder to the supplier of a client's very justified expectations. In essence, the program manager bridges any and all communication gaps and levels the occasional bumps in the relationship.

Above all, a program manager is responsible for developing, nurturing and evolving the client-supplier relationship. A healthy relationship is important for continued partnership and building trust. While not a substitute for well-defined contracts and service levels, trust is an important element of successful long-term relationships between buyers and suppliers.

A successful relationship can be fostered by a program manager who:

- Hand picks the user/IT staff that forms the core team from those that have a positive stake in your offshoring success
- Is patient—building trust, relationships and effective partnerships take time

- Secures and checks executive sponsorship throughout the engagement
- Manages issues pro-actively so that they do not snowball
- Employs regular communications vehicles, especially during times of transition.

## RESOURCE MANAGEMENT

Resource management—and in particular human resource management—is inherently more important in offshore deals than in traditional outsourcing engagements. It is essential that the people assigned have enough domain knowledge, prior transitioning experience and good communication skills, for unlike a traditional outsourcing arrangement where the majority of the work continues to be carried out by the same individuals, here the work is being handed over to an entirely new set of people.

In offshore outsourcing, companies must dedicate time and effort to establishing a framework for the management of the buffer resources, training and on-boarding of new personnel, allocation of travel, vacation and holiday costs, assignment of key personnel, etc. To complicate matters, all vendors do not operate in the same manner, and there can be a lot of hidden costs that do not show up on the contract or during negotiations. It is important to have a good insight into how offshore vendors manage their resources and avoid typical pitfalls.

Offshore program managers should be prepared to:

- Specify a key personnel list that cannot be reassigned without prior client approval
- Prescribe a 15–20% buffer for resources
- Allow 2–3 weeks overlap for handover to transitioning resources, not just during transition but throughout the entire deal lifecycle

- Agree on process of addition and movement of personnel on your projects
- Oversee investment in both technical/process training and management/professional training

## OPERATIONS RISK MANAGEMENT

Any offshore relationship or operation, whether it's a captive center or a supplier-direct engagement, requires constant and vigilant monitoring in order to ensure success.

An annual health audit, a strict vigilance over security matters, and the day-to-day continual improvement in processes and deliverables are essential.

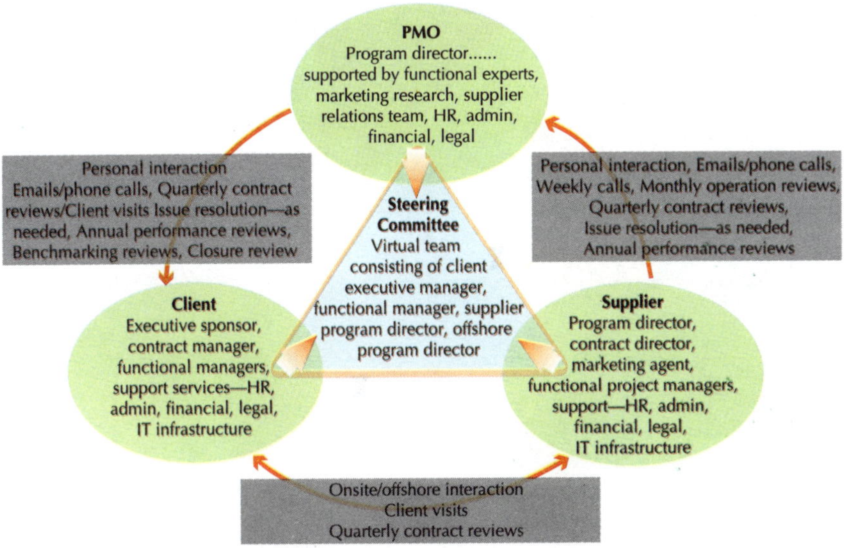


FIGURE 17.2

Offshore program management office framework and relationships to onshore, offshore, client and supplier teams.

Every offshore engagement, whether it's a supplier relationship, a captive center, or something in between, should have a system in place to perform a health audit at least once a year. A health audit is key to the maintenance and continual improvement of the offshore engagement and covers such issues as an evaluation of service levels, updated benchmarking, productivity, pricing vs. the market, adherence to best practices in the industry, etc. Your offshore program management office can help you manage this health audit.

Mitigating security risks is applicable to any outsourced engagement, especially in a post-9/11 world where hackers are everywhere and corporate theft and espionage are rampant. However, in an offshore environment, asset protection and information security strategy, and how it is executed, is much more crucial to the success of the engagement.

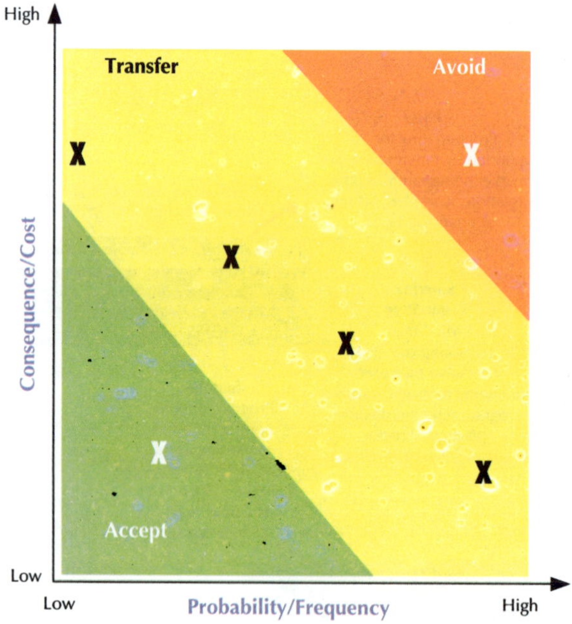


FIGURE 17.3

Risk measurement and prioritization framework used by program management experts.

Security practices cannot be taken for granted in offshore initiatives. Companies must understand how much security documentation and management is necessary, how to contractually agree to terms, and ultimately ensure compliance. Because security is often overlooked and viewed as a lesser issue of focus in negotiations, it is crucial to ensure compliance. Compliance can be achieved by actively managing the security concerns or hiring a third-party Security Organization (SO) to oversee the process.

The next chapter goes into further detail on this area.

## KEY POINTS

- After investing time and resources to plan, source and negotiate an offshore contract, clients need to continue to invest in the management phase and not rely on the vendor to carry the relationship.
- A common mistake is to try to manage the offshore program through the supplier.
- In-house expertise or a neutral third-party firm can help maximize the returns from implementation and delivery and make sure the engagement achieves full potential.
- When recruiting a third party program manager, clients should look for someone with a local presence, supplier neutrality, and experience in delivering offshore (domain specific) deals.
- The expert should have experience in transition management and approach offshore program management as ongoing monitoring of five key areas of success: financial, relationship, contractual, resource and performance.

*Chapter* 18

# Operations Risk Management

Back in Chapter Five we mentioned that one of the great myths of offshoring is that once the contract is signed the client can sit back and let things happen. Nothing could be further from the truth. Any offshore relationship or operation, whether it is a captive center or a supplier-direct engagement, requires constant and vigilant monitoring in order to ensure success.

An annual health audit, a strict vigilance over security matters, and the day-to-day continual improvement in processes and deliverables are essential.

Every offshore engagement, whether it is a supplier relationship or a captive center or something in between, should have a system in place to perform a health audit at least once a year. A health audit is key to the maintenance and continual improvement of the offshore engagement and covers such issues as an evaluation of service levels, risk profile, updated benchmarking, productivity, pricing vs. the market, adherence to best practices in the industry, etc.

Mitigating security risks is applicable to any outsourced engagement, especially in a post-9/11 world where hackers are everywhere and corporate theft and espionage are rampant. However, in an offshore environment, asset protection and information security strategy, and how it is executed, is much more crucial to the success of the engagement.

Security practices cannot be taken for granted in offshore initiatives. Companies must understand how much security documentation and management is necessary, how to contractually agree to terms, and ultimately ensure compliance. Because security is often overlooked and viewed as a lesser issue of focus in negotiations, it is crucial to ensure compliance. Compliance can be achieved by actively managing the security concerns or hiring a third-party organization to oversee the process.

Security concerns cover both the internal and external environment and can be segmented into nine broad categories.

| | |
|---|---|
| Business Continuity | Intellectual Property Rights |
| Customer Privacy | Network Security |
| Information Protection | Personnel Security |
| Disaster Recovery | Physical Security |
| Insurance Coverage | |

Best practices in each of these areas are being adopted by many of the offshore suppliers. Often these suppliers adhere to global compliance benchmarks such as BS7799, ISO 17799, Safe Harbor, US GLBA, CoBIT and others to conform to the global client's security standards. Still, companies need to be aware of the best practices and ensure that the supplier they choose has the capability and process in place that will meet the security needs of the organization.

## BUSINESS CONTINUITY AND DISASTER RECOVERY

Before building a Disaster Recovery and Business Continuity Plan, companies should perform an objective risk assessment to identify business-critical applications and/or processes. Once potential risks are defined, assigning accountability is crucial. Determine 'what is the expected degree of assurance' and 'what level of backup is required' as these points will decide the required number of resources and associated costs. Ensure implementation of the policy by a combination of preventive measures and technical controls.

The Disaster Recovery and Business Continuity Plan should cover these areas:

- **Risk Assessment.** Identify the areas of offshore risk. Keep in mind that some risks are geography-specific. The recent SARS epidemic in Singapore, Hong Kong and China is an example of this type of risk. Other examples include: civil disorders, outbreak of war, breakdown of public services (basic amenities like water, electricity, and roads/access). A key component of the assessment is to determine the maximum allowable downtime.
- **Restoration Process.** Outline, in the event of a disaster, how quickly the services can be restored. Identify the minimum and maximum time schedule for restoration of basic services versus full services.
- **Testing of Backup Systems.** Regular testing of backup arrangements should be organized to ensure they meet the requirements of the Business Continuity Plans.
- **Audits.** Develop an audit calendar to verify the accuracy of data and process restoration.
- **On-going Monitoring.** Indicate a schedule for plan reviews (quarterly, bi-annual, annually). Plan to also monitor compliance and preparedness through mock disaster recovery drills. Be sure to reform the plan as needs change.
- **Managing the Alternate Site.** Identify levels of disaster and plan for backup sites. Include one alternate site for low-level disaster and another secondary site for a higher level of contingency.
- **Key Resources.** Planning for movement of key resources/ personnel is crucial. One best practice is to have two sets of equally prepared teams located in two different geographical areas to dilute the risk.
- **Post Disaster Communication.** Outline a communication plan that includes who to contact and the plan of

action in the event of an emergency. This plan should also include details for any external communication.

## INFORMATION PROTECTION

Offshore supplier organizations generally use different information protection methods for different clients based on the business needs of the engagement. An Information Protection Agreement is a must and should cover the basic areas mentioned below in detail.

- **Vulnerability Assessment.** Analyse the information assets within an organization to determine their sensitivity to outages. This includes identifying technical and non-technical weaknesses that may impact the secure environment.
    - ***Technical Criticalities***—Use of scanner tools like SATAN, ISS etc. to identify and document the technical weakness of the IT systems.
    - ***Non-Technical Weaknesses***—Interview custodians of information assets for non-technical and process weaknesses and document the same.
- **Data Access.** In order to protect important and confidential data, information should be exchanged strictly on a need-to-know basis. Monitor and restrict access to source data. All workstations should have disabled CD and floppy drives to disallow any wrongful data transfer. All team managers and associates should have secure workspaces including secure lockers.

  **Note:** *In general, personnel/customer/sensitive data should not reside in the offshore location. However, for faster execution of work, a working copy with specific information can be made available to offshore employees. Information Protection can still be ensured through various means such as* *encrypting the data, creating 'test' data with all the sensitive fields randomized or deleted, etc.*

- **Data Audits.** Perform data security audits and report test results. Types of audits common in offshoring include: periodic audits, surveillance audits, penetration testing, etc. Clients can hire an independent local third party to audit and certify compliance.
- **Data Security.** Appropriate access control procedures must be established which include logging individual access/actions. Use of firewalls is critical for segmenting and protecting information and limiting access.
- **Data Transmission.** Electronic transmission of data should be controlled as per Safe Harbor/BS 7799/ISO 17799 or other guidelines. Data transfer only through dedicated lines, VPN, using 3DES encryption methodology and/or digital certification will ensure the integrity of information during transfer.
- **Data Storage.** All data should be stored on the server at the client onsite locations rather than the desktops. Again, the goal is to have no sensitive data reside offshore.
- **Virus Management.** Virus and worm incidents are now a routine international issue. Although attacks break out in different parts of the globe, they spread so rapidly that a proactive stance is required. The supplier at the offshore facility should, at a minimum, replicate the virus management process in place at the client location. In fact, offshore virus management should be far more vigilant and should take extra precautionary measures to prevent/contain the damage to the project data. Some common virus management controls are:
  - A robust patch management plan and schedule
  - A process for virus reporting, identifying and taking corrective actions
  - Automatic virus scanners
  - Anti-virus updates

## DATA BACKUP AND RECOVERY

Backing up data is critical in offshore outsourcing. Tape backups should be taken at pre-specified schedules and should be specified in the company security guidelines. The backups could be full backups at specific periods or daily incremental backups. Routinely, it is a combination of the two. Backup tapes should have a unique number for easy identification, and should be stored as archives in off-site locations as part of disaster recovery plans.

**Note:** *It is important to have scheduled backups not only for data residing within the organization but also for data that is being carried around. For example: data residing within laptops of various key people in the organization.*

Data Recovery—the provision of adequate tools to recover data quickly—is also key.

*All sensitive data should reside on a dedicated server at the client site.* However, all project management records, quality tracking documents, project related documents, source code, dummy development/working environment, should reside on the local server at the offshore facility and should have a backup and recovery policy. Periodic testing and verification of the test results ensures compliance.

Sensitive data should be disposed of using a shredder on a daily basis.

## INSURANCE COVERAGE

In an offshoring engagement, apart from standard liability insurance coverage for building, equipment, personnel, it is important to insure electronic information as well. Adequate insurance coverage should be in place to protect equipment and information not only within the premises but also offsite. For example: laptops.

A third-party Security Organization could add considerable value by conducting an "Information Risk Assessment" on offshore suppliers, quantifying the scope of risk, identifying risk mitigation measures and insurance coverage.

## INTELLECTUAL PROPERTY RIGHTS (IPR) PROTECTION

IPR protection is one of the most critical concerns in an offshoring scenario. Security of IP encompasses facilities, assets, services and personnel. IP protection can be achieved by using the following security controls, but companies also need to work with a local legal representative to ensure total protection.

- **Agreements.** should be structured through different levels of security confidentiality both at the organizational and individual levels.
- **Country Laws.** Different government laws pertaining to IP, piracy, and copyright must be addressed. Companies should carefully evaluate the country's track record and compare the laws on the books with the actual implementation and enforcement of those laws.
- **Data Security.** *See the Data Security section.*
- **Physical Security.** *See the Physical Security section.*
- **Legal Compliance.** Companies should structure the contract so the offshore supplier is liable for any breach of confidence.
- **Compliance to Security Standards.** Companies need to ensure compliance of the supplier organization to accepted International Security Standards like BS7799, ISO 17799, Safe Harbor, CoBIT etc.
- **Log and Auditing.** *See the Data Audit section.*
- **Employee Contract.** Companies should also specify in the contract that (supplier) employees cannot work for a competitor for a fixed duration after leaving the present

company. They cannot divulge confidential data to competitors, press, or make other non-approved disclosures.

- **Security Management Training.** The supplier should have a process in place for periodic Information Protection training for all offshore employees.

## NETWORK SECURITY

A good infrastructure is the basic requirement for successful execution of the project and addresses the responsibilities of suppliers for establishing, maintaining, implementing, administering, and interpreting organization-wide network security policies, standards, guidelines, and procedures. Aspects of a good infrastructure are:

- **Dedicated Infrastructure.** Suppliers should use customer-dedicated racks for housing servers, routers, switches and firewall products.
- **Network Security.** The supplier system administrator should be responsible for performing network security risk assessments, preparing network security action plans, evaluating network security products, and performing other activities necessary to assure a secure network environment.
- **Network Device Security.** High-level security for network devices is necessary to prevent unauthorized access.

## PERSONNEL SECURITY

Personnel security addresses the potential risk from current and past employees, and factors to mitigate that risk. Diligence in this area is as appropriate as in onshore engagements. Government rules and regulations in different geographies also play a major role.

*The level of detail allowed under U.S. law while conducting background checks is significantly different from that of Indian, Philippine or Russian laws. What could be considered a breach of personal privacy in one country could be viewed more tolerantly elsewhere.*

- **Background Checks.** Companies should conduct detailed background checks for all employees working with sensitive information based on client requests. Some best practices include:
- ***Routine Checks***—Verification of educational qualifications and reference checks of fresh candidates by HR.
- ***Reference Checks***—For all the employees with prior experience, reference checks with previous employers.
- ***Integrity Checks***—An external intelligence agency is employed to do a thorough background integrity check for those employees who would be handling sensitive data. The parameters for these types of checks could include:
  - Family Background
  - Character
  - Social Status
  - Criminal Record
- ***Special Checks.*** Specific checks like drug screening are carried out in accordance with the client's criteria and business needs.

Other important considerations for ensuring personnel security include:

- **Non-Disclosure/Confidentiality Agreements.** Mandatory for all employees to sign in a standard format.
- **Hardware Limitations.** Suppliers do not have access to the CD drives or master application.

  **Note:** *Read, write, use, and modify access can be granted according to the specific function of the employee*

- **Internet Usage.** Access to the Internet is locked to the specific applications the employee uses. Internet monitoring tools or similar mechanisms can also be used.
- **Usage of Mobile Commuting.** Restricted usage. Not allowed in the actual work area.
- **Housekeeping.** All housekeeping staff are required to work only under the supervision of the Shift Manager/ Supervisor.

## PHYSICAL SECURITY

Measures to ensure the physical security of buildings and physical assets are similar to those used at onshore sites, but in some cases should be increased. These are some typical best practices to ensure physical security:

- **Access Control.** Access control ensures only authorized personnel enter client-servicing areas.
    - Round-the-clock security presence
    - Photo ID cards
    - Swipe-card system with different levels of access. Biometric access if necessary. 24/7 operations require a higher degree of security measures
    - Entry/exit tracking system to monitor movement in each floor and each individual room. This is logged to a central computer.
    - All visitors must register at the Security Office, sign and obtain temporary ID badges. Their movement within the facility is restricted and an authorized company employee must escort them.
    - Critical facilities are secured with electronic lock devices.
    - All important/confidential information is kept secure in lockable file storage systems.

- **Limited Access.** Employee access is restricted to their area of work.
- **Restricted Access.** Access by other supplier personnel is denied to the client's floor and Isolated from the supplier LAN.
- **Dedicated Facility/Work Area.** Physical security of facilities is managed through dedicated floors. If this is not required, then logical isolation is sufficient to prevent inappropriate and unauthenticated access.
- **Camera Surveillance.** Round-the-clock surveillance to monitor any breach of security
- **Movement Restriction.** No printouts, photocopies, computer media or computing devices are allowed to enter or leave the floor. All housekeeping staff will clean the floor under the direct supervision of a supervisor for the shift.
- **Separate Meeting Rooms.** Provision for separate meeting rooms to facilitate interaction with team members, vendors and other external personnel.
- **Recreation Facilities.** Separate recreation area.
- **Fire Safety.** Fire alarms, electronic grade firefighting equipment, emergency measures.

**Note:** *Fire drills, regular upkeep of fire equipment, and fire insurance policies must not be taken for granted in offshore supplier agreements.*

## ROLE OF A SECURITY ORGANIZATION (SO)

A strong information protection policy, network security architecture, and a good disaster recovery and business continuity plan are not enough. To ensure compliance it is necessary to have an offshore presence for periodic audits and ongoing monitoring. It is often advantageous to have a third party with a local presence who can perform the role of a Security Organization. The primary objective of a Security Organization is to ensure a secure work environment.

Whether the offshore presence is with a third-party or an expatriate from the client organization, responsibilities should include:

- Conduct 'Information Risk Assessments' on prospective supplier organizations.
- Develop, monitor and review information protection and security policies.
- Ensure compliance.
- Monitor security risks and threats.
- Determine responsibilities of key individuals.
- Approve and support the implementation of Information Security Management System and information security initiatives.
- Review security incidents through reports presented by the SO covering status of security implementation, update on threats, results of security reviews, audits, etc.
- Security coordination within company and with external regulatory authorities.

## KEY POINTS

- Proper supplier evaluation and due diligence will not only award you with much higher returns, but will also make the management of the deal much easier.
- Some points to consider for a secure engagement:
  - Understand security trends and best practices in the industry.
  - Identify the risks.
  - Ensure continuous and up-to-date training programs.
  - Provide a point-of-escalation for global incident response.
  - Culture Compatibility—Understand the country where you are offshoring.

- Ask for Information Protection and network security documentation—IPR Policy, disaster recovery and business continuity plans, etc.
- Research to determine if the supplier adheres to International Security and Data Privacy Standards like Safe Harbor, ISO 17799, and BS 7799.
- Specify adherence to your information security standards.
- Ensure the security framework covers all related security threats.
- Ensure accountability/ownership is established for security framework.
- Conduct periodic vulnerability assessments and penetration studies.

# Part 6

# The Future of The Offshore Nation

*Chapter* 19

# An Economic Perspective

In Chapter One, we told you that the future belongs to those who are prepared for anything. In this chapter, we will try to give you some globalization insights from an economic perspective.

There is no reason to believe that the current rapid growth of services globalization will slow any time soon. Indeed, growth rates are just beginning to climb. Below, we highlight some forecasts, and some historical facts, from a recent study prepared by Global Insight for the Information Technology Association of America, ITAA. Keep in mind that this report was prepared exclusively for the IT software and services industry and therefore does not include business processes. Unfortunately, no such reliable report yet exists on BPO due to the immaturity of the market. Still, as BPO is only beginning to grow, we can assume that its growth rates will not only match but will likely exceed the forecasts below.

## THE MACRO IMPACT

According to Global Insight, spending for global sourcing of computer software and services is expected to grow at a compound annual rate of almost 26 percent, increasing from about $10 billion in 2003 to $31 billion in 2008. The savings this brought to U.S. companies was about $6.7 billion in 2003—or about 40 percent less than they would have spent.

The cost savings and use of offshore resources lowers inflation, increases productivity and lowers interest rates. This in turn boosts business and consumer spending and increases economic activity.

There is an incremental effect of that increased economic activity throughout the economy. By 2008, GDP is expected to be $124.2 billion higher than it would be in an environment in which offshore IT software and services outsourcing does not occur.

The impact on jobs overall will be hugely positive in the long run, although that impact will vary by sectors. For example, the IT industry will be the most directly affected by the displacement of workers. It lost an estimated 104,000 jobs due to offshore ITO from 2000 to 2003, including not only jobs that were eliminated in the U.S. but also jobs that were never created as a result of offshore IT outsourcing. Still, during that same time period another 268,000 IT jobs were lost for reasons that had nothing to do with offshore ITO, notably the economic slowdown, higher labor productivity and technological advances.

What's more, although 104,000 jobs were lost due to offshore ITO, close to 200,000 jobs were created because of the increased economic activity brought on by offshore ITO. Thus, more than 90,000 net new jobs were created, a figure which is expected to grow to 317,000 by 2008. Those sectors that will gain the most include education and health services, transportation and utilities, construction, wholesale trade, financial services, professional and business services, and manufacturing.

As the benefits compound over time, the U.S. economy operates more efficiently, achieves a higher level of output, creates more than twice the number of jobs than are displaced, and increases the average real wages. In 2008, the projected savings implied by global IT outsourcing will amount to almost $21 billion.

Another direct result will be lower prices throughout the U.S. economy. In 2003, the GDP price level was an estimated 0.6 percent lower as a result of a decade of offshore outsourcing, according to Global Insight, which forecasts that reduction in prices will amount to 2.3 percent by 2008 as a result of offshore ITO.

## THE MICRO IMPACT

On a microeconomic level, the impact of global ITO will be multilayered. On one hand, the availability of quality, lower priced IT services will allow big companies to grow faster and gain economies of scale. On the other hand, it will enable small companies to ramp up quicker and will give entrepreneurs the tools to launch companies with far less start-up capital than would have been required previously.

The productivity boost to the average enterprise will be huge.

> *The time clock of the average company will be drastically altered as companies no longer shut their doors at 5 and open again at 9 the next morning.*

It will also change the way work is planned, sourced and performed, as global project teams learn to work together to accomplish shared goals. And all of this will create demand for new, innovative technology products to allow these teams to communicate, collaborate and work together more efficiently.

The time clock of the average company will be drastically altered as companies no longer shut their doors at 5 and open again at 9 the next morning. Global ITO and BPO will allow companies to truly be 24/7 enterprises. As one shift ends in New York, another will be opening in India, and when that ends yet another will open in Eastern Europe, or China or Chile. The productivity and profitability potential of tripling the hours in the average corporate workday will be tremendous.

To the offshore firm and the offshore nation, value chains will change quickly and dramatically, forcing companies to fight to retain their competitive advantages, both against each other and against onshore outsourcing firms. India will quickly move up the value chain, and indeed already is in that process, as higher wages are already pricing India out of the market in some low-level ITO and BPO services. The Philippines will not be far behind. Jobs traditionally reserved for India and the Philippines are going to countries like China and Malaysia. However, India and the Philippines will persevere, just as the United States. Indian workers will become skilled in higher-level processes and will move up the value chain, like the U.S. before it, gaining higher wages and a higher standard of living.

The management of the global services firm—be it the onshore client or the offshore supplier—will become a greater challenge. Bringing together global sales operations was one thing. Adding global manufacturing was another. To add globalization of services on top of that will require significant adjustments in everything from IT to human resources management to financial management and accounting.

To be sure, there will be pains along the way. Those who lose their jobs will need to be retrained or moved to other positions. Some companies will have bad experiences with globalization of services. But the overall benefits on both a macroeconomic and microeconomic level cannot be denied.

## KEY POINTS

- Spending on global ITO will grow from about $10 billion in 2003 to $31 billion in 2008.
- Savings to U.S. enterprise amounting to $6.7 billion in 2003 and will grow to $20.9 billion in 2008.
- The growth rate of global BPO will not only meet but most likely will exceed that of ITO.
- Global ITO and BPO will have a positive ripple effect throughout the economy on jobs, wages, productivity, lower inflation and interest rates, and increased economic activity.
- On a micro level, both small and large companies will benefit from globalization of services, although new challenges will present themselves.

# Conclusion

If you had to pick a single technology company that has successfully prepared itself for the future time and time again, it would be hard to pick any other than Microsoft. Bill Gates has done it not just by accurately forecasting the future, but by defining the future in Microsoft's own terms. And now, Microsoft is once again transforming itself based on its newest operating platform, known throughout the industry by its original codename, Longhorn.

The very structure of Longhorn is a testament to the importance of services globalization in our future. Longhorn is all about group connectivity. "It is the dawn of a new era," says London-based consultant David Frankel. "It will allow everybody to be part of one big linked community."

"Increasingly, the issue isn't whether or not you do it, it's how you get the parts to all connect," Frankel says.

And Longhorn is just one example. Already, hundreds of other companies are building new products all with the same goal in mind—allowing remote users to better connect with one another. That will allow services globalization to be much less painful going forward.

The challenge then for the rest of us is to make sure those efforts, like Microsoft's, are not wasted. To squander the opportunities that services globalization has presented us would be to deny progress, to stymie the economy and to cripple thousands of enterprises, many of them before they even get started.

To be sure, we will have to walk carefully. Rushing too fast into anything is always risky, and services globalization is no different. That is why a long-term strategy is so important.

Indeed, too many companies look at services globalization as a quick route to lower costs and profitability. It can be, but there are two things wrong with that approach:

1. It falls far short of maximizing the potential benefits of services globalization, and
2. It is risky, subjecting the company to potential short-term and long-term risks such as shocks to cash flow, geopolitical nightmares, cultural disintegration and security threats.

The process we have outlined here where companies look at services globalization as a part of an overall corporate strategy and then ramp slowly into the engagement through a four step process: Knowledge, Planning, Sourcing/Building and Management is designed to mitigate these risks and enhance the potential benefits over the long term.

Through firsthand experience over two decades, we have seen the benefits of using this process firsthand. Services globalization will continue to be a controversial and emotional debate for some time to come, but it is important to keep in mind that the re-distribution of resources to efficient global locations results in freeing up capital, lowered costs for companies and consumers and new opportunities for investments. Protectionism hampers innovation and cripples growth, as much in services as it does in manufacturing. The failure to innovate is to cede technological leadership and, ultimately, economic strength.

As we mentioned in Chapter One, the successful companies will be not so much those that are good at defining themselves and their niche, but those that are open to new markets, new processes, new resources, new products and services. In short, the successful companies are the innovation leaders.

While true stability is impossible to achieve in this world of volatility, being prepared by futurizing your organization can both reduce risks and allow a more efficient use of resources and a more accurate prediction of revenue streams and costs.

While a blueprint for the future is not possible, insights into trends such as globalization, outsourcing and labor shifts can help you be better prepared strategically and operationally.

The Offshore Nation is here. If we embrace it, we will all reap its benefits and lessen the chance of unforeseen shocks to our economy, our enterprises, and our jobs.

Good offshoring!

*Appendix* A

# The Service Nations: Country Comparison

## ITO

| ITO | India | Philippines | China | Russia | Canada | Ireland |
|---|---|---|---|---|---|---|
| Government Support | ● | ◒ | ○ | ○ | ◒ | ● |
| Labor Pool | ● | ◒ | ◒ | ● | ◒ | ○ |
| Infrastructure | ◒ | ● | ○ | ○ | ● | ● |
| Educational System | ● | ◒ | ● | ● | ● | ● |
| Cost Advantage | ● | ● | ● | ● | ◒ | ○ |
| Quality | ● | ◒ | ○ | ◒ | ● | ◒ |
| Cultural Compatibility | ◒ | ● | ○ | ◒ | ● | ● |
| Time/Distance Advantage | ● | ● | ● | ◒ | ○ | ○ |
| English Proficiency | ● | ● | ○ | ○ | ● | ● |

○ Low ◒ Medium ● High

## BPO

| BPO | India | Philippines | China | Russia | Canada | Ireland |
|---|---|---|---|---|---|---|
| Government Support | ● | ◒ | ○ | ○ | ◒ | ● |
| Labor Pool | ● | ◒ | ○ | ○ | ◒ | ○ |
| Infrastructure | ◒ | ● | ◒ | ○ | ● | ● |
| Educational System | ● | ◒ | ● | ● | ● | ● |
| Cost Advantage | ● | ● | ● | ● | ◒ | ○ |
| Quality | ● | ● | ○ | ○ | ● | ● |
| Cultural Compatibility | ◒ | ● | ○ | ○ | ● | ● |
| Time/Distance Advantage | ● | ● | ● | ◒ | ○ | ○ |
| English Proficiency | ● | ● | ○ | ○ | ● | ● |

○ Low ◒ Medium ● High

*Appendix* B

# Useful Forms and Checklists

The following forms and checklists are a sample of some of the rigorous process companies need to follow when embarking on the services globalization journey.

- Globalization Readiness Index
- Total Cost of Ownership Analysis
- Portfolio Assessment Template
- Global Supplier Visit Checklist
- Global Operations Healthcheck Analysis

## GLOBALIZATION READINESS INDEX

Assessment of the client's readiness for services globalization is one of the first steps in the Plan Process. This is carried out with the help of the Questionnaire. It also helps in furthering the client's education regarding offshoring.

The Questionnaire is ideally administered on all members of the client's core team. However, the Project Executive who is responsible for the Program Management of client's services globalization initiative is usually able to provide the answers on behalf of the core team.

This is the last stage where client's readiness and inclination for globalization is ascertained. It is captured in the following three metrics:

- Critical Success Factors (CSF) Index
- Globalization Alignment Index
- Risk Tolerance Index

**The CSF Index** indicates the company's readiness to adopt services globalization. It is also a measure of the company's ability to implement globalization best practices.

**The Globalization Alignment Index** indicates the extent of clarity about benefits of services globalization and the factors that influence globalization decisions.

**The Risk Tolerance Index** captures the level of hesitation in outsourcing and the organization's ability to prepare for, mitigate and possibly withstand potential risk factors.

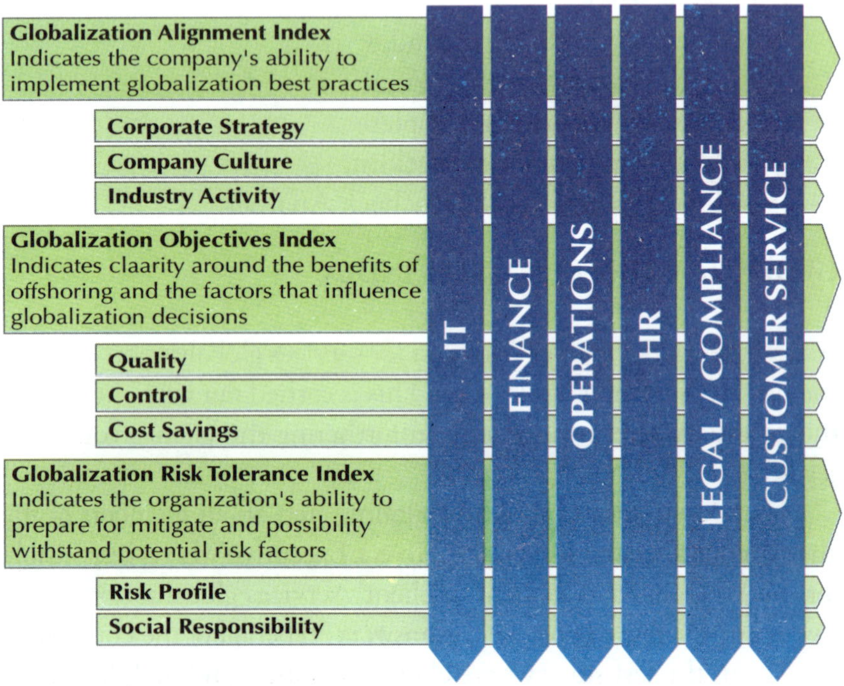


## TOTAL COST OF OWNERSHIP ANALYSIS

Any Financial Base Case Analysis of the impact of offshore outsourcing must take into account all the costs associated with an offshore initiative. The Total Cost to Offshore has the following key components:

1. Wage Rate
2. Communication Systems
3. Physical Infrastructure and Support
4. Transition
5. Governance
6. Resource Redeployment
7. HR Change Management
8. Training and Productivity
9. Disaster Recovery and Business Continuity Capabilities
10. Offshore Knowledge Development/Advisory Services
11. Travel costs
12. Exchange Rate Fluctuations

The table below shows a case study that demonstrates the relative percentage of different components of cost on the Total Cost to Offshore for an ITO or BPO engagement.

| BPO | % Cost | ITO | % Cost |
|---|---|---|---|
| Wage Rate | 42% | Wage Rate | 46% |
| Communication System | 5% | Communication System | 3% |
| Physical Infrastructure and Support | 17% | Physical Infrastructure and Support | 18% |
| Transition and Governance | 8% | Transition and Governance | 7% |
| Resource Redeployment | 3% | Resource Redeployment | 4% |
| Resource Redundancy | 2% | Resource Redundancy | 1% |
| Training and Productivity | 10% | Training and Productivity | 9% |
| Disaster Recovery & Business Continuity | 5% | Disaster Recovery & Business Continuity | 3% |
| Advisory Services | 2% | Advisory Services | 4% |
| Travel costs | 3% | Travel costs | 3% |
| Exchange Rate Changes | 2% | Exchange Rate Changes | 3% |

## PORTFOLIO ASSESSMENT TEMPLATE

The given figure is an example of a data template used to collect information to help analyze a company's portfolio of services to be considered for globalization.

## Application Portfolio

| Application Name | Technology Type | Size | Age (No. of Years) | No. of Versions | Contains Sensitive Data (Y/N)? | Contains Data Governed by Country Legal System (Y/N)? | Contains Sensitive IP Data (Y/N)? |
|---|---|---|---|---|---|---|---|
| | | | | | | | |
| | | | | | | | |
| | | | | | | | |
| | | | | | | | |
| | | | | | | | |
| | | | | | | | |
| | | | | | | | |
| | | | | | | | |
| | | | | | | | |
| | | | | | | | |
| | | | | | | | |

## GLOBAL SUPPLIER VISIT CHECKLIST

We recommend the following time allocation during the visit. This is generalized and flexible based on client needs.

1. Company information—10%
2. Growth and financials—5%
3. History, experience and capabilities—30%
4. Operations—25%
5. Client experience—10%
6. Tour of the facilities—20%

To make the process transparent and easy to understand, we've segregated the activities that a client, a third-party global advisory firm and a supplier would typically prepare prior to a supplier visit.

### Client Firm—Company Activities

#### *Prior Preparation*

1. Review and understand requirements and performance standards for scope of work.
2. Review presentations and literature from suppliers to be visited.
3. Identify the "must have" and "nice to have" qualities. Submit to expert to build into evaluation criteria.
4. Prepare other questions and submit to an independent expert for insight in advance of trip.

### Global Advisory Firm—Expert Activities

#### *Prepare the Client Company*

1. Provide briefing packets on suppliers (include local history, independent insights).

2. Provide a list of recommended questions (see below).
3. Provide a detailed schedule of and organization of supplier visits.
4. Coordination of domestic ground/air transportation, lodging and all logistics.

### *Prepare the Suppliers*

1. **Logistics**—Identify single point of contact for visit coordination and preparation.
2. **Supplier Briefing Packet**—Includes visiting company profile, key questions and agenda of visit. Also includes expected meeting format and time allocated to each topic and résumés and bios of visiting company team.
3. **Provide Capabilities Questionnaire**—this preparatory document outlines specific information that the visiting company is requesting the supplier to demonstrate. This information will be verified during the visit.

## Supplier Firm Activities

### *Prior Preparation*

1. Review and understand visit requirements.
2. Review presentations and literature to be shared internally.
3. Ensure alignment to client and advisor guidelines.
4. Identify the "best of breed" and "differentiating" qualities. Include in presentations and tour.
5. Focus on performance, process and consistency rather than marketing buzz only.

## Asking the Right Questions

Question preparation is key to understanding the capabilities and risks of each supplier. While these questions should vary depending on each client's requirements and expectations, there are some general guidelines that can help in formulating these questions. The outline below is meant to spur ideas about the types of questions that should be addressed. Keep in mind, the level of detail within each topic heading should be much greater than what is indicated here. To give companies a general idea of how much detail is in involved under each section heading, an expanded version of the human resources section is provided with specific questions. The buyer company should leave the visit with a general understanding of:

### *Company Information*

- Ownership & Control
- Locations

### *Growth & Financials*

- Growth history and future plans
- Financials

### *History, Experience & Capabilities*

- Present Clients
- Capabilities and Skills
- Pricing Models
- Quality

### *Operations*

- Infrastructure
- Technology
- HR
- Customer Orientation
- Transition & Implementation—Critical
- Business Continuity
- Program Management and Governance

## *General & Administration*

- Benchmarking
- Change Management
- Cultural Issues
- Global Standards
- Infrastructure
- Savings
- Client Satisfaction

## *Flexibility*

## *Legal, Regulatory and Tax Issues*

## *Specific Project/Process Focus*

## *Tour*

## *Selected Supplier Feedback*

## *Example: Human Resources*

### *Feedback on recruitment*

- Brand awareness in local market vs. other established employers.
- Compensation levels comparable to the industry average.
- Particular recruiting strengths and concerns or issues.

### *HR Initiatives and Policies*

- Key differentiators vis-à-vis other supplier companies.

### *Performance feedback*

- Training methodology.
- Experience with learning curve across functions.

- Ongoing quality checks on individuals.
- Feedback and re-training mechanisms.

***Staffing***

- What is the percentage of employees – onsite (US) and offsite?
- What is the average employee tenure?
- General overview of the employees' educational and experience background.
- What is the average supervisor/manager to developer/associate ratio?
- How does the present staffing profile fit with the present and future requirements? Is the supplier equipped to handle the engagement and staff as per the scope of potential work being offshored?
- What will the impact be to existing operations?
- Would they use existing resources (not pull back on-site staff)?
- Current availability of resources?
- Review actual experience versus each process in scope.

***Attrition and Retention Strategies***

- Attrition %.
- Career path for all levels.
- Initiatives particular to retention strategies?
- Are employee satisfaction surveys carried out periodically?

## GLOBAL OPERATIONS HEALTHCHECK ANALYSIS

A *Healthcheck* involves a deep analysis of the offshore operations. The Healthcheck diagram presents a framework for the areas and steps included in the process.

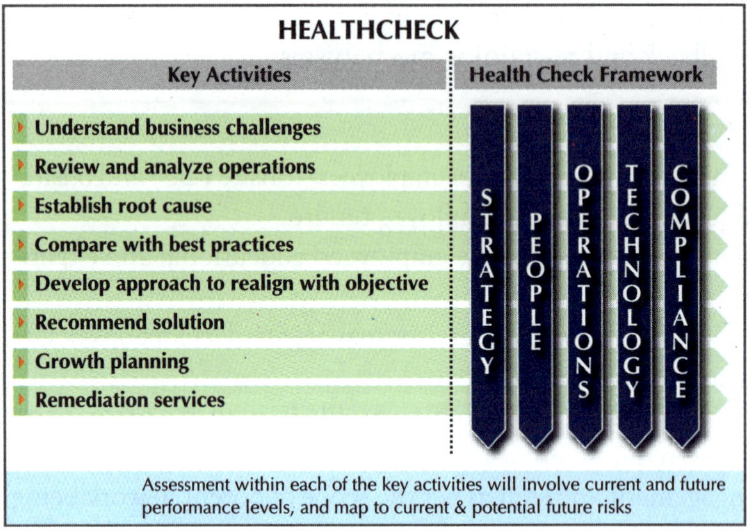


The key areas to be evaluated as part of a Healthcheck include:

- Strategy
- People
  - *Resources*
  - *Relationships*
- Operations
  - *Financials*
  - *Contracts*
  - *Performance*
  - *Risk*
- Technology
- Compliance

Each area includes a breakdown of specific topics to be evaluated. The approach for leveraging this framework includes:

- A current state review
- Comparative review to best practices
- Gap analysis
- Ideal/Future state recommendation
- Implementation

*Appendix* C

# Industry Resources

## GLOBALIZATION RESOURCES

### Firmbuilder.com (www.firmbuilder.com)

Firmbuilder.com helps corporate executives and entrepreneurs effectively use outsourcing in today's business world. The site provides an online repository of more than 300 articles, case studies, diagnostic tools, and the "Disciplines of Outsourcing". The site also provides information and links to many top outsourcing service providers and industry experts.

### neoOffshore (www.neoOffshore.com)

neoOffshore is the online resource for articles, opinions and information to help companies improve their sourcing process. The information center is moderated by neoIT sourcing professionals for sourcing professionals.

### The Sourcing Interests Group (SIG) (www.sourcinginterests.org)

The Sourcing Interests Group assists members in learning from each other's experiences in outsourcing, alliances, procurement, e-commerce and shared services. Interest areas include Information

Technology, Corporate Support Services, Business Processes and Supply Chain.

### SBPOA (www.sharedexpertise.org)

The Shared Services and Business Process Outsourcing Association (SBPOA) is a membership organization for executives, managers, consultants, administrators, and educators, with a professional interest in gaining a better understanding of what it takes to setup and lead best-in-class Shared Services or successful BPO activities.

### WITSA (www.witsa.org)

The World Information Technology and Services Alliance (WITSA) is a consortium of 46 information technology (IT) industry associations from economies around the world. WITSA members represent over 90 percent of the world IT market.

## COUNTRY-SPECIFIC RESOURCES

### CANADA: Information Technology Association of Canada (ITAC) (www.itac.com)

ITAC is the voice of the Canadian information technology industry. Together with its partner organizations across the country, the association represents 1300 companies in the computing and telecommunications hardware, software, services, and electronic content sectors. This network of companies accounts for more than 70% of the 542,000 jobs, \$132.6 billion in revenue, \$5.3 billion in R&D expenditure and \$44 billion in exports that IT contributes annually to the Canadian economy.

## CHINA: Information Service Industry Association of China (CISA) (www.cisanet.org.tw/english/)

The Information Service Industry Association of R.O.C., known as CISA, is Taiwan's sole representative body of information service industries. Founded in 1983, CISA is one of the most time-honored hi-tech associations in Taiwan. Its 650 corporate members comprise domestic, international companies and R&D institutes in software development, distribution, information and network service businesses.

## INDIA: National Association of Software and Service Companies (NASSCOM) (www.nasscom.org)

India's National Association of Software and Service Companies, Nasscom is the apex body and umbrella organization for IT Software and Services industry in India. The member companies of Nasscom are in the business of Software, IT Services, Internet, E-commerce and IT Enabled Services. Thus Nasscom is not only a Chamber of Commerce, but also a single point-reference on any information on IT and Services and Industry in India.

## ISRAEL: Israeli Association of Software Houses (IASH) (www.iash.org.il)

Founded in 1982, the Israeli Association of Software Houses (IASH) is the umbrella organization for Israeli software and IT companies, representing the common interests of its member companies. The more than 100 members of IASH are a mixture of mature and leading companies as well as young and innovative ones.

### IRELAND: Irish Software Association (ISA) (www.software.ie)

The Irish Software Association (ISA) is a dynamic association which represents an ever increasing number of Irish and multi-national software and computing services companies. From a handful of companies a decade ago, there are now over 800 software firms in Ireland and employment of over by the year 2002.

### MEXICO: Asociación Mexicana de la Industria de Tecnologías de Información (AMITI) (www.amiti.org.mx)

AMITI is the Mexican association of the leading ITO and BPO companies in Mexico.

### RUSSIA: RUSSOFT (www.russoft.org)

RUSSOFT is an association of the leading companies in the field of Software Development from Russia and Bielorus. Currently RUSSOFT consists of more than 50 companies with 6000 highly qualified software developers who are experienced across a broad range of applications and technical platforms. RUSSOFT companies have provided services to small and intermediate sized companies as well as many of the Fortune 500 companies.

### RUSSIA: National Software Development Alliance "Silicon Taiga" (www.nsda.net)

With the aim of further developing the Russian IT outsourcing and software development industry, the most experienced and prominent local players created the National Software Development Alliance "Silicon Taiga" The target goal of the alliance is to promote the

Russian IT outsourcing market and its integration into the world software development community.

## THE PHILIPPINES: Information Technology Association of the Philippines (ITAP) (www.itaphil.org)

Organized in December 1984, ITAP was established with the following objectives in mind: (1) Foster an environment which is conducive to prosperity; that is, help the members succeed in delivering the benefits of IT to consumers, in line with the competitive nature of the information technology industry. (2) Promote interest and awareness in matters affecting member organizations, particularly regarding government laws and commercial regulations. (3) Serve as a vehicle for the free exchange of ideas and information among members. (4) Address the common socio-political obligations of its member organizations. (5) Provide the means for the settlement of inter-member conflicts. ITAP has been the accepted voice of the Philippine technological industry for over sixteen years.

## USA: Information Technology Association of America (ITAA) (www.itaa.org)

The Information Technology Association of America (ITAA) provides global public policy, business networking, and national leadership to promote the continued rapid growth of the IT industry. ITAA consists of over 380 corporate members throughout the U.S. The Association plays the leading role in issues of IT industry concern including information security, taxes and finance policy, digital intellectual property protection, telecommunications competition, workforce and education, immigration, online privacy and consumer protection, government IT procurement, human resources and e-commerce policy. ITAA members range from the smallest IT start-ups to industry leaders in the Internet, software, IT services, ASP, digital content, systems integration, telecommunications, and enterprise solution fields.

## LEGAL RESOURCES

### Alston & Bird (www.alston.com)

Alston & Bird lawyers collectively possess decades of experience advising Fortune 500 companies in their strategic outsourcing relationships. They have represented clients in the full range of IT and business process transactions, including representations in a number of recent marquee transactions. Their sourcing clients have spanned almost all major industries. They have over 700 attorneys and the firm is recognized in the US as a leader in a number of specialties, including most recently by IP Worldwide in a survey of American businesses as one of the top 10 general practice firm's nationwide for protecting intellectual property.

### Brown Raysman (www.brownraysman.com)

Brown Raysman Millstein Felder & Steiner LLP practices all major areas of business law and is one of a handful of law firms internationally known for its outsourcing practice. Their attorneys structure outsourcing alliances, identify strategic objectives, evaluate the benefits of specific transactions, negotiate agreements and provide ongoing support through implementation, benchmarking, and renegotiation/renewal. The firm has extraordinary experience in all aspects of IT and Business Process outsourcing, and has an alliance with a European/Asian firm that enables us to seamlessly represent clients in global deals, whether negotiation is centered in the United States or elsewhere.

## Cooley Godward (www.cooley.com)

Cooley Godward offers clients an exceptionally experienced, client-service oriented team of lawyers who provide unparalleled legal expertise and business savvy in a wide variety of Information Technology, Telecommunications and Business Process outsourcing transactions. Their partners and associates are recognized as among the leading technology lawyers in the world. With outsourcing specialists located throughout their integrated network of offices in California, Colorado and Reston, Virginia and strategic relationships with leading technology lawyers in the U.K., Europe and Asia, they handle complex outsourcing transactions across the world.

## Goodwin Procter (www.goodwinprocter.com)

Goodwin Procter LLP is one of the leading law firms in the US. Headquartered in Boston with offices in New York, New Jersey and Washington, D.C., the firm conducts a national practice, serving clients across a broad range of industries. They concentrate on select areas of practice, allowing their 500 attorneys to collaborate efficiently and effectively.

## Hughes & Luce (www.hughesluce.com)

Hughes & Luce has almost 30 years of experience in outsourcing and has represented clients in more than $100 billion of telecommunications, information services and process re-engineering outsourcing transactions. There is an art to negotiating and drafting major outsourcing agreements. The issues, the standards to be employed, the flexibility that must be built into an outsourcing relationship to accommodate new technologies, changing needs, and different economic environments, and mechanisms to maximize incentives for the outsourcer to operate more efficiently and economically are not addressed by the "form" documents that many marketing or "contract administration" representatives of outsourcers propose. The industry is constantly changing and there are a handful of attorneys in the world who are truly on top of the issues. Our industry experience includes computer services, technology outsourcing, food service, financial services, airlines, insurance, telecommunications, health care, software and hardware and government.

## Mayer, Brown, Rowe & Maw (www.mayerbrown.com)

Mayer, Brown, Rowe & Maw's 1,300 lawyers worldwide bring value and world-renowned legal expertise to our clients' outsourcing needs. We advise clients in structuring cutting-edge outsourcing solutions and pride ourselves on forging successful and lasting relationships. Mayer, Brown, Rowe & Maw stands at the forefront of the outsourcing revolution, bringing sound advice and legal acumen to our clients in the Germany, UK, United States and the Americas. We represent clients in a wide variety of outsourcing transactions, including the outsourcing of business processes and functions, energy management, e-commerce transaction processing and support, mainframe and midrange systems, desktop and laptop computers, help desks, local and wide area networks, telecommunications, Internet/intranet, audio/video conferencing, application development and maintenance, and leasing/procurement.

## Milbank, Tweed, Hadley & McCloy (www.milbank.com)

Milbank, Tweed, Hadley & McCloy's Global Technology Transactions Department maintains a thriving practice in such specialty areas as outsourcing; technology joint ventures; computer system acquisitions and financings; domestic and foreign software licensing and distribution; information technology and privacy; etc.

## Sonnenschein Nath and Rosenthal, LLP (www.sonnenschein.com)

With 700 attorneys and other professionals in nine U.S. offices and a global reach throughout Europe, Asia, the Middle East, Latin America and Canada, Sonnenschein serves many of the world's largest and best-known businesses, nonprofits and individuals. Founded in 1906, the firm is a leader in innovative legal services, serving its clients through integrated, inter-office cooperation and teamwork among practice groups to provide efficient, effective and timely legal services and business counseling.

*Appendix* D

# Worldwide Globalization Event Resources

| | |
|---|---|
| American Conference Institute | www.americanconference.com |
| Michael F. Corbett & Associates | www.corbettassociates.com |
| Forrester | www.forrester.com |
| Gartner | www.gartner.com |
| HRO World | www.hroworld.com |
| IDC | www.idc.com |
| Marcus Evans | www.marcusevans.com |
| NASSCOM | www.nasscom.org |
| neoIT | www.neoIT.com |
| Outsource World | www.outsourceworld.org |
| SBPOA | www.sharedxpertise.org |
| Strategic Research Institute | www.srinstitute.org |
| The Sourcing Interests Group | www.sourcinginterests.org |
| The Conference Board | www.conference-board.com |

*Appendix* E

# The Offshore 100

The first annual 'Offshore 100' project was initiated in September 2004 with surveys issued to global service providers in 13 different countries to assess four primary areas: service provider company information, client data, operational capabilities and human resource policies. Over the ensuing 2 months, neoIT and *Managing Offshore* collected over 250 different data points from a wide range of service providers located in thirteen countries with strong representation from offshoring destination leaders India, The Philippines, China, Russia, Malaysia and Mexico.

In this first, and only, study created to rank offshore BPO and IT suppliers, *Managing Offshore* and neoIT sought to identify categories of competencies with a goal of setting supplier benchmarks. At the same time, the goal was to create the first-ever forum to recognize the leading and emerging offshore suppliers. The results of the study will be beneficial to corporate decision makers seeking information about the rapidly expanding, and shifting, range of offshore BPO and IT supplier options.

Growth among service providers has grown substantially in recent years, with the compounded annual aggregated revenue growth rate (CAGR) among the 'Offshore 100' at 20% between 2003 and 2005 and the median annual revenue at $32 million. Seventy percent of the 'Offshore 100' have established delivery operations in the United States, an important consideration for U.S. customers that want to hold suppliers accountable under American jurisdiction. Banking and Financial Services dominate the revenue mix for the Offshore 100, with Manufacturing, Software/High Technology, Telecommunications and Healthcare ranked at second, third, fourth and fifth places respectively.

A summary of the results is listed below and a full copy of the study can be obtained at **www.theoffshore100.com** or at **www.managingoffshore.com** (subscription required).

## THE TECH AWARDS

**Top 10 Best Performing IT Services Firms**

1. ACS
2. IBM
3. Wipro Limited
4. Perot Systems Corporation
5. HCL Technologies Limited
6. TATA Consultancy Services
7. Cognizant Technology Solutions
8. Infosys Technologies, Ltd.
9. Cap Gemini
10. HP

**Top 10 Specialty Application Development Leaders**

1. i-flex solutions limited
2. Hexaware Technologies
3. EPAM Systems, Inc.
4. Sierra Atlantic, Inc.
5. Larsen and Toubro Infotech Limited
6. Patni Computer Systems, Inc.
7. International Business Alliance
8. Neusoft Group Ltd.
9. Adea Solutions, Inc.
10. Deloitte

**Top 10 Specialty Offshore Infrastructure Service Providers**

1. HCL Technologies Limited
2. Wipro Limited
3. HP
4. TATA Consultancy Services
5. GE Capital Information Services
6. IBM
7. EDS
8. CSC
9. ACS
10. Satyam

## THE CUSTOMER & BUSINESS PROCESS AWARDS

**Top 10 Best Performing BPO Providers**

1. WNS Global Services Pvt. Ltd
2. ACS
3. Wipro Limited
4. ExlService Holdings, Inc.
5. HCL Technologies Limited
6. MphasiS Corporation
7. Secova eServices, Inc.
8. Astron BPO
9. Hewitt Associates
10. Accenture

**Top 10 Offshore Call Center Firms**

1. Wipro Limited
2. HCL Technologies Limited
3. eTelecare International, Inc.
4. 24/7 Customer, Inc.
5. ClientLogic

**Top 10 Offshore Call Center Firms**

6. Convergys
7. vCustomer Corporation
8. ICICI OneSource Limited
9. Daksh
10. EDS

**Top 10 Leaders in Human Capital Development**

1. WNS Global Services Pvt. Ltd.
2. Hinduja TMT Ltd.
3. Cognizant Technology Solutions
4. MphasiS Corporation
5. Secova eServices, Inc.
6. eTelecare International, Inc.
7. Infinite Computer Solutions Pvt. Ltd.
8. Wipro Limited
9. Hewitt Associates
10. Satyam Computer Services Ltd.

## THE REGIONAL & ROOKIE AWARDS

**Top 5 to Watch South of the Border**

1. North American Software
2. Softtek
3. ASCI S.A. de C.V.
4. Appteck, S.A. de C.V.
5. Informatica Integral Empresarial, S.A. de C.V.

**Top 10 to Watch in China**

1. Bleum, Inc
2. Neusoft Group Ltd.
3. AsiaInfo Holdings, Inc.
4. Hangzhou Handsome Electronics Co. Ltd. Global Services
5. U-soft Co., Ltd
6. Datang
7. Sichuan Yinhai Software Limited Liability Company
8. Information Technology I.T. United
9. Kingdee
10. Powerise

**Top 5 to Watch in Central and Eastern Europe**

1. EPAM Systems, Inc.
2. International Business Alliance
3. Luxoft
4. Akela, LLC
5. CT Group

**Top Rookies in Global Outsourcing**

1. GE Capital International Services
2. Outsource Partners International
3. Promantra Synergy Solutions Ltd.
4. Bleum, Inc.
5. Akela, LLC

# Index

# Authors' Profile

### Atul Vashistha

Atul Vashistha is the CEO of neoIT, a leading management consultancy focused on offshore and global sourcing and management of services. He is a leading authority on globalization and outsourcing and was recently recognized by *Consulting* Magazine as one of the 'Top 6 IT Power Brokers' and a Superstar by *HRO Today*. Wall Street analysts, Global 2000 executives and top business journalists from CNN, *Wall Street Journal*, *New York Times*, *Fortune*, *Forbes* and *Business Week* seek out his thought leadership. His personal passion is to help improve developing economies and business models around the globe.

### Avinash Vashistha

Avinash Vashistha is the Founding Managing Partner of neoIT, the leading management consultancy firm focused on offshore and global sourcing of services. Avinash, a pioneering visionary has used his strategy and delivery knowledge and expertise to guide Fortune 10 to Global 2000 firms execute global sourcing decisions. Global media like CNBC, *Fortune*, *Business Week*, *CNN*, *Times*, *La Monde*, *Financial Times*, Wall Street analysts and fund managers seek and reference his industry knowledge. A true globalization leader, Avinash has nurtured offshore IT/BPO markets like India, Philippines, Russia, China, Vietnam, Eastern Europe, Ireland and has given direction to emerging markets for over two decades including pioneering Nortel's outsourcing operations in the early nineties.

**Book Project Leader and Supporting Writer**

Allisson Butler, *Marketing Director, neoIT*